More Than a Momentary Nightmare

MORE THAN A MOMENTARY NIGHTMARE

The Yokohama Incident and Wartime Japan

Janice Matsumura

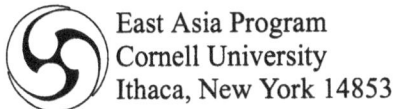

East Asia Program
Cornell University
Ithaca, New York 14853

The Cornell East Asia Series is published by the Cornell University East Asia Program and has no formal affiliation with Cornell University Press. We are a small, non-profit press, publishing reasonably-priced books on a wide variety of scholarly topics relating to East Asia as a service to the academic community and the general public. We accept standing orders which provide for automatic billing and shipping of each title in the series upon publication.

If after review by internal and external readers a manuscript is accepted for publication, it is published on the basis of camera-ready copy provided by the volume author. Each author is thus responsible for any necessary copy-editing and for manuscript formatting. Submission inquiries should be addressed to Editorial Board, East Asia Program, Cornell University, Ithaca, New York 14853-7601.

Photographs are reprinted courtesy of the University of Toronto.
Cover photograph is from Kimura Tōru, *Yokohama jiken no shinsō: tsukurareta 'Tomari kaigi'*, Tokyo: Chikuma shobō, 1982.
Photographs on pages 19 and 20 are from Ono Sada and Sumiko Kiga, *Yokohama jiken: tsuma to imotō no shuki*, Tokyo: Kōbunken, 1978.

Cover design by Karen K. Smith

Number 92 in the Cornell East Asia Series
© 1998 Janice Matsumura. All rights reserved
ISSN 1050-2955
ISBN 1-885445-92-X pb
ISBN 1-885445-52-0 hc

13 12 11 10 09 08 07 06 05 04 03 02 01 00   8 7 6 5 4 3 2 1

CAUTION: Except for brief quotations in a review, no part of this book may be reproduced or utilized in any form or by any means, electronic or mechanical, including photocopying and recording, or by any information storage or retrieval system, without permission in writing from the author. Please address inquiries to Janice Matsumura in care of East Asia Program, Cornell University, 140 Uris Hall, Ithaca, NY 14853-7601.

Contents

Introduction 1

1 The Incident 13

Illustrations 19

2 The Incident and the Journalists:
   Assessing the Conventional Explanations 25

3 The Incident and the Researchers:
   *The Wartime Purge of Former Leftist
   Thought Control Offenders* 45

4 The Incident and the Authorities:
   *The Creation of a Wartime Communist
   Threat* 75

5 The Postwar Trial of the Yokohama
   Incident Police Officers:
   The Campaign Against the Wartime State 111

Conclusion 147

Bibliography 159

Acknowledgements

I have enjoyed the cooperation and assistance of many individuals and institutions in Canada, Japan, and the United States in completing this work which is based on my doctoral dissertation. My thesis advisor, Prof. B.T. Wakabayashi of York University, was incredibly patient and unflagging in his encouragement. Prof. Kano Masanao, Prof. Yui Masaomi and Prof. Anzai Kunio of Waseda University, Prof. Eizawa Kōji of Senshū University, and Prof. Ogino Fujio of the Otaru University of Commerce were also generous in providing advice and information. Prof. Richard H. Mitchell of the University of Missouri-St. Louis saved me from making some factual errors, informed me of additional reference material and, together with Mr. Hashimoto Susumu and Ms. Kaneda Tomie, provided many useful suggestions. Both Prof. E. Patricia Tsurumi of Victoria University and Prof. Diana Wright of Western Washington University were kind enough to read and critique this manuscript. Ms. Nakamura Tomoko, whose interviews of those arrested in the Yokohama Incident was a major source of information, kindly answered questions raised by her book. Ms. Inohara Shōko of the Waseda University Microform Library helped in tracking down government documents, and she and Ms. Matsuzaka Maki provided assistance in obtaining interviews. Mr. Yamaji Yasushi of the National Diet Library of Japan was most helpful in providing information on sources for the chapter dealing with the Occupation. Finally, the Japan Foundation and the Social Sciences and Humanities Research Council of Canada provided the financial support for my graduate studies and research in Japan.

It is with great pleasure that the above persons and institutions are acknowledged for their assistance and guidance. But, most of all, I owe a special debt of gratitude to Mr. Kimura Tōru, Mr. Kobayashi Eizaburō, the late Mrs. Ono Sada, the late Mr. Takagi Kenjirō, and the late Mrs. Hiradate Toshio for agreeing to meet with me and share their experiences.

Introduction

In a January 1996 *Asahi shimbun* article Kimura Tōru discussed the potential danger of broadening the application of the Subversive Activities Prevention Law so that it could be used against religious cults, such as the Oum Shinrikyō, which was suspected of carrying out a fatal poison gas attack in central Tokyo.[1] The Subversive Activities Prevention Law, which had never been enforced, had originally been enacted in 1952 to control left-wing groups, and Kimura noted the similarities between the Subversives Activities Law and the notorious prewar Peace Preservation Law, which had been used before the Pacific War to limit freedom of speech and thought. Kimura's argument was that public safety had to be ensured by methods less open to abuse. That is, he argued that reliance on laws which could impose official limits on individual activities could very well lead the nation back into the prewar "Dark Age" when the authorities could more freely designate and punish anyone as an enemy of the state.

One could view Kimura's concerns as somewhat excessive. But few can dispute his knowledge, acquired through experience, of the hardships and continuing frustration that can be visited upon those unjustly accused of being enemies of the state. During the Pacific War he was among the more than forty journalists and researchers arrested in the Yokohama Incident on trumped-up charges of spying, spreading leftist propaganda, and conspiring to re-establish the outlawed Japan Communist Party. Some of those arrested in this affair were incarcerated for almost four years. They were completely at the mercy of the police who repeatedly resorted to physical coercion to get them to agree to the charges against them. Besides being beaten with bamboo swords and

---

1. "Oum e no habōhō ga kakudai saretara ankoku jidai ni," *Asahi shimbun*, January 11, 1996: 3. For a discussion of Oum shinrikyō case and the efforts to revise laws to deal with the cult, see Sheldon Garon, *Molding Japanese Minds: The State in Everyday Life* (Princeton: Princeton University Press, 1997), 212-14.

burned with cigarettes, those arrested were psychologically tormented and deprived of sleep and food for extensive periods of time.

Physically coerced by police interrogators into signing admissions of guilt, faced with judicial officials who were indifferent to their attempts to refute these bogus confessions, many of those arrested in the Yokohama Incident survived to seek legal redress for the wrongs they had suffered. Almost immediately upon their release from custody, at the start of the American Occupation, they launched a court case against the police officers who had tortured them. On March 28, 1951, the Tokyo District Higher Court found the police officers in question guilty of abusing their authority and handed down prison sentences of about two years. The ruling was unprecedented and marked the first time that the Japanese courts had ruled in favour of private citizens, victims of thought control, who had lodged a complaint against government officials.[2]

The event nevertheless was only a partial victory for those arrested in the affair. The police officers were found guilty, but were not compelled to serve out their prison sentences. In addition, the courts' guilty verdict on the police did not mean that those arrested had their names cleared. Although the Peace Preservation Law was rescinded in October 1945, all those sentenced under it retained their criminal records. Finally, the Trial was meant to be a citizens' repudiation of the wartime state, but hopes for attracting widespread popular interest and support went unfulfilled.

The Trial of the Yokohama Incident Police Officers would appear to have had the ingredients to attract the attention and support of a number of groups during the early years of the Occupation. Both the Japan Communist Party and the publishing industry could have embraced the Trial as their own cause. Leftist parties consisted of many individuals who had experienced government persecution, and their leadership had been very vocal in demanding the punishment of prewar officials who had abused their authority. Many in the publishing industry had been colleagues and friends of those arrested in the affair and had been themselves harassed by thought control and censorship officials for decades. However, members of the Party and the publishing industry refrained from involving themselves in the Trial. Balance of power issues in both groups as well as concerns about possibly arousing the

---

2. Lawyer Masaki Hiroshi uncovered evidence that a coal mine worker had been beaten to death by the police. Masaki brought suit in the autumn of 1944 against the policeman in charge of interrogating the worker. But at the so-called "Kubinashi jiken" Trial, the officer was acquitted. See, Richard H. Mitchell, *Janus-Faced Justice: Political Criminals in Imperial Japan* (Honolulu: University of Hawaii Press, 1992), 146.

displeasure of the Occupation authorities appear to have acted as disincentives for participating in such events. Those who launched the court case against the Police Officers had aspired to carry out a completely independent Japanese endeavour and felt little need to be concerned about the attitudes of the American Occupation authorities. The attitudes of these authorities nevertheless had an impact on their activities insofar as it affected how much domestic support they could hope to attract. The Japan Communist Party, for example, had adopted a "hands-off" position with regard to any issues related to the punishment of wartime personnel in keeping with what it believed was the wishes of the Occupation authorities.

In addition, it has been suggested that the Japan Communist Party may have wavered in pursuing the topic of war responsibility because even some of its own members, those who had undergone ideological conversion and especially those who found employment in government offices, could be criticized for having collaborated with the wartime state.[3] As for the publishing industry, many journalists and editors who had continued to work during the Pacific War were aware that they could be denounced as propagandists. Writers have noted that there were very few individuals in Japan after the War who were completely safe from accusations of having collaborated with the authorities in some fashion or at some point in their lives. The military trials of low-ranking soldiers and the purge of minor officials seems to have driven home the message that anyone, not just the leadership and social notables, could be punished as war criminals or collaborators. In the end, labour disputes involving accusations of wartime collaboration had the effect of making the Yokohama Incident a taboo subject within the industry.

An examination of the Trial of the Yokohama Incident Police Officers, the circumstances surrounding it and the reaction of various groups to it can shed light on certain conditions during the Occupation that stood in the way of domestic campaigns to rally opinion against the old order. Nakamura Masanori has observed that, in comparison with West Germany, Japan has not been as thorough in "exorcising the past" and that the reasons for this may be traced back to events during the Occupation. He agrees that "postwar" Japan, insofar as it is characterized by a conscious desire to escape from the authoritarianism,

---

3. Sodei Rinjiro and Takemae Eiji, "Nihon senryō to wa nani ka: Nihonjin ga etamono ushinatta mono," in *Sengo Nihon no genten: Senryōshi no genzai*, Vol. 1, ed. Rinjiro Sodei and Eiji Takemae (Tokyo: Yūshisha, 1992), 352. The order of surname first will be used to refer to Japanese authors whose works have been written in their native language. However, when referring to works in the English language, the order will be reversed and surnames will be preceded by given names.

militarism and poverty associated with the "prewar" period, ended sometime in the mid-1970s as the generations who had lived the Pacific War were surpassed in number by younger individuals with no such experience. But he states that the many movements which have arisen since the 1980s and which have further exposed Japan's past atrocities clearly indicate that issues of the wartime period, much less the postwar, still need to be resolved.[4]

The Trial of the Yokohama Incident Police Officers marked the beginning of what would become an interrupted, but recently resuscitated struggle on the part of those arrested in the affair to draw public attention to the dangers of official misconduct. In the 1980s, more than four decades after the Incident, survivors among those arrested and their families came together to demand a retrial. The stated purpose behind this retrial movement was not just to conclusively establish the innocence of those arrested. It was to prevent the Japanese people from forgetting the past and becoming too complacent about government policies.

Many members of the retrial movement have tried to draw attention to the continuing abuse of police suspects in Japan as well as those actions that they suspect are meant to exonerate the prewar state. The public, they argue, needs to become more outspoken in denouncing the views of the past expressed by some of their government representatives. In one of their 1994 newsletters they discussed the different domestic and foreign reactions to some remarks made by a former Justice Minister. It was reported that this Minister claimed that the Pacific War was an effort to liberate Asia, that the Nanjing Massacre of thousands of Chinese civilians was a fabrication, and that the Comfort Women forced to service Japanese troops were willing camp-followers.[5] The writers of the newsletter observed that whereas the Japanese public responded indifferently to such statements, individuals in foreign countries reacted so angrily that the Minister felt compelled to resign. It is both clear and regrettable, they concluded, that the Japanese people would have been content to allow a man with such views to remain in office.

One of the lawyers involved in the retrial movement has also observed that the information about the Yokohama Incident revealed through the courts' reexamination of the case could help clarify the public's understanding of the prewar period and provide a timely rebuttal to efforts to depict the Pacific War

---

4. Nakamura Masanori, "Sengo kaikaku to gendai," in *Senryō to sengo kaikaku*, ed. Nakamura Masanori (Tokyo: Yoshikawa kōbunkan, 1994), 8, 11, 14.

5. *Yokohama jiken o kangaeru kai no kaihō*, No. 15, 1994, June, 1.

as a crusade to liberate Asia.⁶ Such interpretations, Lawyer Okawa Takashi argues, lose all credibility in view of the fact that the Japanese authorities had arrested some of the suspects in the Yokohama Incident simply because they had helped edit an essay that had only been calling for official support of independence movements in Asia.

As a result of being unjustly accused of and punished for anti-government activities, many of those arrested in the Yokohama Incident have eventually become real or active "enemies of the prewar state" in the decades following the Pacific War. In light of the many political and social transformations that took place in Japan during and after the American Occupation, one could argue that the legal struggles of these individuals may be nothing more than a battle against a state which no longer exists or which exists only in memory. However, efforts to address the wartime past remain pertinent to many Japanese.

This is evident in the response to the *Asahi shimbun*'s publication of a series of letters from readers regarding Japan's last war.⁷ The newspaper received thousands of letters from readers belonging to various age groups. Certain readers found the idea of recalling the past too painful and argued that "raking up what happened in the past can be very destructive" to efforts to forge better relations with neighbouring countries. Many other readers nevertheless welcomed the opportunity to talk about the hardships they suffered or the cruelties they witnessed being inflicted upon others.

Those involved in the Yokohama Incident retrial movement remain a small group that must contend with considerable legal obstacles, and they have yet to attract widespread active support. Still, they remain hopeful that they can somehow persuade their countrymen to go beyond just discussing the past to actually compelling their officials to redress the abuses committed in the name of the prewar state. Whereas these legal campaigns provide a means of examining the topic of efforts to address wartime issues during and after the Occupation, the Yokohama Incident itself can reveal much about conditions in wartime Japan.

Given that the Army's takeover of Manchuria in the early 1930s created in Japan an atmosphere of potential war with China, the Anglo-American powers, or Soviet Russia and precipitated preparations to ready the nation for such possibilities, "wartime Japan" can be defined as extending from 1931 to

---

6. Ono Sada and Okawa Takashi, *Yokohama jiken mitsu no saiban: Dainiji saishin saiban saishin seikyūsho* (Tokyo: Kōbunken, 1995), 107-8.

7. *Sensō, The Japanese Remember the Pacific War, Letters to the Editor of Asahi Shimbun*, ed. Frank Gibney; trans. Beth Cary (New York: M.E. Sharpe, 1995), vii-iii.

1945. This study of the Yokohama Incident covers these years and thus places the topic in this 15-year wartime context. However, in order to avoid any confusion regarding periodization and because the study maintains, as its primary goal, an examination of the state of internal security in Japan during the Pacific War, the subsequent use of the term "wartime" in this text will be to signify the period from 1941 to 1945.

The period from 1941 to 1945, besides one of the most tragic periods in Japanese history, remains shrouded in mystery because of difficulties in conducting research on it. A lot of documents, material evidence, which could provide a means of assessing conditions during the period were probably lost during the course of the Pacific War. Diaries and correspondence, contemporary observations and later recollections of those who lived through the War are valuable, but are not the most reliable sources of information. Inaccuracies due to personal bias or simply lapses in memory are among the obvious pitfalls of the above sources.

Studies of the wartime, of course, should not be avoided simply because of problems in documentation, and examining specific events remains a viable means of exploring general conditions during the period. That is, the Yokohama Incident itself can act as a prism for viewing the wartime period and distinguishing some important features of the political and administrative situation. While the Incident has not been totally neglected, many aspects have been overlooked.

The Yokohama Incident was one of the most brutal instances of Japanese thought control, and for many individuals it remains symbolic of the oppression faced by the publishing industry during the Pacific War. Resulting in the wartime government's shut down of two very prestigious journals, *Kaizō* and *Chūōkōron*, the affair holds an important place in the history of journalism in Japan. However, the Yokohama Incident was not simply the result of the authorities' desire to control or punish the publishing industry and should not be perceived just as a case of mass media suppression. Its significance is not limited to the subject of wartime journalism, and a study of it should not be focussed exclusively on one aspect or group.

It is important to keep in mind that journalists were not the only ones arrested in the Yokohama Incident. Existing official documents on the affair reveal that wartime authorities were far more concerned about the researchers than the journalists. Many of these researchers had been arrested in the past for some minor so-called leftist activities, such as participating in study groups examining Marxist literature, and they included employees in the Foreign, East Asia and Communications Ministries, the South Manchurian Railway Company, and companies such as Furukawa Electric, Japan Steel and Japan

Copper. In examining the experience of these researchers as well as the wartime authorities' views of the Incident one can observe both changes and problems within the prewar thought control system. During the Pacific War the Japanese authorities had at their disposal a decades-old thought control system, which had been established for the purpose of enforcing the official ideology of a harmonious state centred on the Imperial Family and eliminating ideas that contradicted this orthodoxy. The system consisted of censorship bodies, a specialized police force,[8] a judicial bureaucracy to handle subversives, and laws concerning intellectual, literary and political activities. At the core of its legal structure was the aforementioned Peace Preservation Law, which forbade the existence of any organizations and movements seeking to change the fundamental character of the state, or abolish the private property system.

The prewar thought control system was elaborate and extensive in scope, and arguments for its effectiveness have pointed to the conduct of the Japanese people during the Pacific War as an example of the system's ability to control and manipulate the masses. While one cannot completely discount the influence of Japanese thought control on the individual, it should not be assumed that compliance or support for government policies was solely the result of official persuasion or coercion. Whether they possessed an extensive official thought control system or not, most nations have more often enjoyed the support of their citizens in waging a war or, at least, been free of large-scale opposition until losses began to make their effect felt on domestic conditions. Other factors, such as self-interest or the simple absence of immediate, concrete reasons to oppose official policies, should be considered in accounting for popular support or compliance, and caution should be maintained not to exaggerate the effectiveness of the thought control system or to assume that officials experienced little difficulty in administering control.

The prewar system of thought control in Japan, in fact, eventually became a victim of its expansion. That is, increases in personnel and the creation of additional organizations did nothing to improve its efficiency. On

---

8. The *Tokubetsu kōtō keisatsu* [The Special Higher Thought Control Police] or *Tokkō*. There was more than one ministry which had thought control bureaus and police, but the terms *Tokkō* or thought control police used in this work refer to the specialized police force directly responsible to the Home Ministry. For detailed studies of the *Tokkō* up to the 1940s, see Richard H. Mitchell, *Thought Control in Prewar Japan* (Ithaca: Cornell University Press, 1976) and, especially, Elise K. Tipton, *The Japanese Police State* (Honolulu: University of Hawaii Press, 1990). Tipton examines the history and traditions of the police, the system of recruitment and socialization as well as discusses the relationship between the police and their external environment.

the contrary, expansion promoted such a reckless and often misguided pursuit of subversives that the system increasingly did more to magnify rather than alleviate concerns about internal security. During the Pacific War officials actually became convinced that subversives were successfully infiltrating all sectors of society, and, ten years before the Americans, they felt compelled to carry out something akin to the communist "witch-hunts" of the early 1950s. An examination of major wartime incidents and documents reveals that the Japanese authorities were carrying out a purge of former leftist thought control offenders from government offices and positions of social influence. The Yokohama Incident, which involved the arrest of many government and industrial researchers, was part of this purge. The Incident reinforced existing official views of the state of communist activity and helped to further justify actions against former thought control offenders.

Given the anti-communist nature of the prewar Japanese state, the government's purge of former thought control offenders may not be surprising. What is surprising, or what begs to be asked is how these former offenders managed to find employment in the government and in important private institutions in the first place. The answer lies in changes in official attitudes toward former thought control offenders. The experience of many of those arrested in the Yokohama Incident reflected the changing fortunes of former offenders. These individuals had been able to rise to positions of some importance in the 1930s despite their criminal records, but during the Pacific War they found themselves once again under suspicion and persecution.

This topic of changes in the system has been overlooked in scholarly discussion of prewar Japanese thought control. The major debate has been over the degree to which the system relied on torture and physical coercion.[9] Many Japanese Marxist scholars have argued that torture was a conspicuous feature of thought control; and from this perspective, the Yokohama Incident may appear representative of the essentially brutal nature of the system. In contrast, non-Japanese scholars have long argued that the hallmark of Japanese thought control was *Tenkō*: ideological conversion through psychological rather physical coercion. According to one scholar, the Yokohama Incident was an *atypically* harsh instance of mass media suppression.[10]

The problem with this debate and with views of the Incident as "representative" or "atypical" of the thought control system is that it presumes

---

9. For example, see Matsuo Takayoshi's review of *Thought Control in Prewar Japan* by Richard H. Mitchell. Matsuo Takayoshi, *Hongura* (Tokyo: Misuzu shobō 1983), 196-8.
10. Gregory J. Kasza, *The State and the Mass Media in Japan, 1918-1945* (Berkeley: University of California Press, 1988), 231.

that the system was static and the treatment of offenders was consistently either brutal or relatively mild. Yet, there are abundant indications that the system underwent changes and that the treatment of offenders greatly varied. During an interview conducted in the 1970s, one former high-ranking thought control officer observed that "there were cases of torture, but things could be quite different depending on the individual officer, the geographical location and the *period* [italics mine]."[11]

Although directives against torturing suspects could not be completely enforced and incidents of police brutality continued to occur throughout the prewar period, the official adoption of the *Tenkō* policy in 1931 inaugurated a change in the perception and treatment of leftist thought control offenders. *Tenkō* or the ideological conversion of offenders meant that police and justice officials were encouraged to apply psychological tactics in getting offenders to renounce their "dangerous" thoughts.

Since the early 1920s an increasing number of Justice and Home Ministry officials had been debating the adoption of a method of "controlling thought by thought."[12] It was apparent to the authorities that an increasing number of leftists belonged to privileged groups in society. The March 15, 1928 wholesale arrest of communists had revealed that a large number of university students were involved in leftist movements.[13] Consequently, the *Tenkō* policy probably emerged from the authorities' belief that it was neither proper nor effective to use force in handling leftists from elite backgrounds. As one scholar has argued, "it is doubtful that the policy of *Tenkō* would have been pursued as assiduously-and so successfully-if all those arrested as communists had been lower-class workers and Meiji-style renegade intellectuals."[14]

The avowed aim of the *Tenkō* policy was to rehabilitate the thought offender, reform him ideologically, and help him return to a useful place in society. As a result, the Thought Criminals' Protection and Supervision Law established in 1936 offices which were designed to reintegrate former thought offenders back into proper society by helping them find jobs, often in private,

---

11. Miyashita Hiroshi, *Tokkō no kaisō: Aru jidai no shōgen*, ed. Itō Takashi and Nakamura Tomoko (Tokyo: Tabata shoten, 1978), 313.
12. Elise Kurashige Tipton, "The Civil Police in the Suppression of the Prewar Japanese Left," Ph.D. diss., Indiana University, 1977: 264.
13. Atsuko Hirai, *Individualism and Socialism: The Life and Thought of Kawai Eijiro (1891-1944)* (Cambridge: Harvard University Press, 1986), 130.
14. Henry Dewitt Smith II, *Japan's First Student Radicals* (Cambridge: Harvard University Press, 1972), 268.

civil and even in military-related research organizations.[15] These offices, which had handled about 13,000 people by 1938, were successful in securing employment for their charges. Their success can be largely attributed to the fact that there was a considerable need for research personnel at the time and that even government officials, who were expected to condemn Marxism as the ideology of traitors, believed that individuals trained in Marxist theory made the most skilful and scientific researchers. Opportunities for social advancement were thus open to former offenders during the 1930s.

However, the *Tenkō* policy which helped pave the way to employment, even in government offices, created considerable problems in later years for a number of former offenders. After the Pacific War, many had to face, if not outright accusations of being collaborators, insinuations that they had been cowards by "converting" and buckling under official pressures. Under these circumstances, such individuals may have felt themselves disqualified to participate in any Occupation period movements against the former regime. Moreover, whatever benefits many of them may have enjoyed as a result of the *Tenkō* policy proved to be rather temporary.

The adoption of the *Tenkō* policy and the belief that harmful, unorthodox thought could be purged out of the thought offender marked a brief high point in the confidence of the ruling elite (that is, administrative, social, political, and financial notables). Members of the elite were never complacent about the loyalty and obedience of the common people, and the increased security concerns caused by the Pacific War, combined with the discovery of so-called false converts [*gisō tenkōsha*] among thought control offenders, quickly eroded their fragile confidence. By 1941, the relatively gentle *Tenkō* policy was losing a lot of official support. Although efforts to ideologically convert thought control offenders were not completely abandoned during the War, officials became less interested in reforming offenders and more prepared to simply purge them from society and government.

The wartime purge nevertheless did not allay anxieties about hidden communists. Instead, the Yokohama Incident and similar wartime incidents only redoubled these anxieties and contributed to the demoralization of the ruling elite of high-ranking officials and social notables. Although these fears were unquestionably excessive, they were not irrational. Studies have demonstrated that concerns that subversive movements were capitalizing on wartime popular discontent, for example, were often thoughtful analyses of developments and derived from what was accepted at the time as expert opinion. In many respects the wartime elite was misled by their subordinates'

---

15. Mitchell, *Thought Control in Prewar Japan*, 135-39.

efforts to stamp out the perceived leftist threat. Leftist activists never approached the numbers and influence noted in official documents and wartime writings, but the capture of scores of so-called communists by lower-ranking police officers made it appear that subversives lurked behind every corner. The Yokohama Incident thus illustrates this ultimate irony of police efforts during the wartime period. It was essentially a frame-up by lower-ranking police officers, and these officers appear to have formulated the charges in accordance with prevailing official notions about communist activities. Yet, those higher up in the government, such as the superiors of the police officers in charge of investigating the affair, believed that it was a genuine communist conspiracy. Attempts by the police to eliminate any threats posed by communists seemed to confirm the existence of a threat and heightened concerns about the potential for a postwar, if not wartime, revolution in Japan. In the end, the wartime police unwittingly encouraged the pessimism of their superiors and possibly even the pro-peace sentiments of a growing segment of the ruling elite.

The example of World War I and the Russian Revolution loomed large in the minds of many prominent members of Japanese society. Eventually, some of these individuals, prompted by fears that the deteriorating domestic conditions caused by the Pacific War could trigger a communist revolution, rallied behind movements calling for an end to hostilities. They imagined that the country was facing two enemies, the external foe in the guise of the Allied Powers and the internal foe in the guise of hidden leftist conspirators. By the end of War, these individuals became convinced that Japan was fighting a losing battle against both foes.

This present study concentrates on the Yokohama Incident and the wartime period, especially problems in maintaining thought control and internal security, but following Tamiya Hiroshi's advice against examining the affair too narrowly,[16] it attempts to explore its other dimensions. During the postwar Trial of the Yokohama Incident Police Officers, the Tokyo Higher Court Judges declared that the case could not be dismissed as "nothing more than a momentary nightmare."[17] This declaration or description was quite perceptive. The Yokohama Incident itself was more than a "nightmare" and can reveal more than the horrible abuses inflicted upon individuals during the wartime period. Moreover, the impact of the Incident on the lives of those arrested and

---

16. Tamiya Hiroshi, "Yokohama jiken: Gōmon o yonda maboroshi no 'kyōsantō saiken,'" *Nihon seiji saiban shiroku*, ed. Wagatsuma Sakae (Tokyo: Daiichi hōki shuppan, 1970), 520-22.
17. "Tokyo kōtō saibansho hanketsu," *Yokohama jiken shiryōshū*, ed. Sasage dōshikai (Tokyo: Tokyo ruliyūlu, 1986), 102.

their families was more than "momentary." The suffering they were forced to endure as suspected enemies of the state helped transform them in the years following the Pacific War into real enemies of the prewar state, who were willing to face long and often frustrating legal campaigns to expose the crimes committed in its name. Consequently, rather than just an analysis of the Incident itself and wartime conditions, the related events of later decades will also be discussed.

    Chapter 1 of this work provides a detailed narrative of the affair, from its origins until the wartime trial of those arrested. Chapter 2 examines the main ideas about the Incident and the problems with these interpretations. Chapter 3 examines the views of the researchers, many of whom were former leftist thought control offenders, and reveals, through documents and a comparison with other major wartime incidents, that the Yokohama Incident was part of a purge of former offenders. Chapter 4 examines the views of the wartime authorities, the impact of the Incident on the ruling elite, and the factors that contributed to fears of a growing communist threat. Chapter 5 examines the postwar Trial of the Yokohama Incident Police Officers and the circumstances surrounding it, such as the imposed and self-imposed restraints, that prevented certain groups from rallying in support of a campaign to denounce the wartime state. The conclusion provides information about the latest efforts of the survivors of the affair and their families to draw public attention to existing problems dating back to and even before the wartime period.

1
The Incident

Only a handful of works in English refer to the Yokohama Incident, and most provide just a partial description of it.[1] The majority of writers on the topic have relied heavily on the memoirs of the journalists, who naturally focus on their own experiences. In recent years the disclosures made by the researchers and the discovery of a few more official documents on the affair have helped to reveal other aspects of the Incident. Care must be taken in assessing the reliability of the memoirs and police reports, and this chapter, an account of the affair from its origins to the wartime trial of so-called suspects, was constructed by cross-referencing the information contained in the recollections of those arrested with that found in existing official documents.[2]

The term "Yokohama Incident" was coined in the postwar period and refers to the city where much of the police investigation took place. The Incident has its origins in the arrest of political writer Hosokawa Karoku by the Tokyo Metropolitan Police Board on September 14, 1942, and the arrest of labour specialist Kawada Hisashi and his wife by the Kanagawa Prefectural (Yokohama) Special Higher Thought Control Police on September 9, 1942. Hosokawa was arrested because of a censorship violation. He had published an essay, "The Trends of World History and Japan" [*Sekaishi no dōkō to Nihon*], in the August and September 1942 editions of *Kaizō*, and was charged with violating the Peace Preservation Law. Kawada, on the other hand, was

---

1. Haruko Taya Cook & Theodore F. Cook, *Japan at War: An Oral History* (New York: The New Press, 1992), 221; Kasza, *The State and the Mass Media*, 229-31; Jay Rubin, *Injurious to Public Morals: Writers and the Meiji State* (Seattle: University of Washington Press, 1984), 266-70; Mitchell, *Janus-Faced Justice*, 144-45, 153; Ben-Ami Shillony, *Politics and Culture in Wartime Japan* (Oxford: Clarendon Press, 1981), 125-26.

2. In the 1970s, Nakamura Tomoko conducted extensive interviews of those involved in the Yokohama Incident, and the information contained in her book was particularly useful for constructing this section. See Nakamura Tomoko, *Yokohama jiken no hitobito* (Tokyo: Tabata shoten, 1979).

suspected of being a spy for the American Communist Party. The Kanagawa Prefectural Police were able to tie together these two separate cases when they discovered that Kawada was acquainted with some close friends of Hosokawa. The Kanagawa Police eventually constructed an argument that Kawada, Hosokawa, their colleagues and friends were involved in a conspiracy to reestablish the outlawed Japan Communist Party. Having taken over the Metropolitan Police Board's investigation of Hosokawa, they began to apprehend many of his friends. After arresting an individual the Kanagawa Police would investigate each person's network of acquaintances, and in this manner they created group after group of suspects. These groups consisted of researchers in government offices and industries who were accused of plotting a postwar revolution, ostensibly right-wing political activists and workers who were accused of infiltrating labour organizations, and journalists and editors who were accused of spreading leftist propaganda. According to the Kanagawa Police, this widespread communist network was under the leadership of Hosokawa Karoku.

Hosokawa Karoku was a well-known China specialist and scholar of colonialism. A regular writer for intellectual publications, such as *Kaizō* and *Chūōkōron*, he was also employed as a researcher in the government-affiliated South Manchurian Railway Company (Mantetsu). Hosokawa had a number of prominent friends in literary, academic, and political circles, and even became a member of Prime Minister Konoe Fumimaro's think-tank, the Shōwa Research Association [*Shōwa kenkyūkai*]. A Marxist, he was arrested in the so-called Osaka Sympa Incident of 1933 for giving funds to the Japan Communist Party. Following his 1933 arrest, however, he apparently abandoned political activity and suffered little harassment from the authorities until 1942.

It was the Army Information Division that instigated the controversy over his 1942 essay, "The Trends of World History and Japan." Army personnel participated in the monthly meetings held by censorship officials where representatives of various publications received instructions on editorial content, and at a September 1942 editorial meeting, an Army Information Division officer claimed that the Hosokawa essay was an ingeniously disguised piece of communist propaganda. It was nevertheless through an ultranationalist activist, Tadokoro Hiroyasu, that the Information Division first learned about the Hosokawa essay.[3]

Tadokoro was a colleague of Minoda Muneki, the notorious ultranationalist critic and agitator, and belonged to Minoda's Japan Spiritual

---

3. Rubin, *Injurious to Public Morals*, 257, 266; Aoyama Kenzo, *Yokohama jiken: 'Kaizō' henshūsha no shuki* (Tokyo: Kōbundō, 166), 19.

Culture Research Institute [*Nihon seishin bunka kenkyūjo*]. On August 24, 1942, representatives at the Research Institute informed one of the *Kaizō* editors that Tadokoro had produced a pamphlet attacking the Hosokawa essay. In this pamphlet, Tadokoro argued that Hosokawa's ideas were identical to those of the Soviet spy Ozaki Hotsumi and that such individuals were trying to promote support for communism and the Soviet Union among the educated class. In the hopes of encouraging more officials efforts to prevent influential magazines from publishing allegedly subversive literature, Tadokoro had about five hundred copies of the pamphlet distributed to various offices in the Army and Home Ministry.[4]

Civil censorship bodies such as the Metropolitan Police Board and the Cabinet Information Bureau had passed the Hosokawa essay. Unfortunately for Hosokawa and the editors at *Kaizō*, the Tadokoro pamphlet came to the attention of those in the Army Information Division who lost little time in criticizing civil censors for allowing the essay to be published. In response to the Army Information Division's complaints and accusations of slip-ups, the Metropolitan Police Board was forced to reverse its decision and arrested Hosokawa on the suspicion that he was using his writing to promote communism.

In the October 1943 edition of *Tokkō geppō* [Monthly Reports of the Special Higher Thought Control Police], the Metropolitan Police Board presented the results of their investigation of Hosokawa's essays.[5] The Metropolitan Police concluded that Hosokawa's writing amounted to pro-Soviet propaganda and that the author was trying to promote the argument that Japan could only win the cooperation of the various peoples of Asia by adopting Soviet foreign and domestic policies. They claimed that, in "The Present World Policy of the Soviet Union" [*Genjitsu Soren no sekai seisaku*] (1939), Hosokawa depicted Soviet foreign policy as peaceful in order to prevent a Japanese military attack. In "The Chinese People's Movement and the Great Powers" [*Shina minzoku undō to rekkyō*] (1939), he allegedly tried to draw attention to the benefits of the Soviet Union's China policy in his discussion of the Chinese drive toward national independence. Moreover, in the "East Asia Co-prosperity Sphere's Racial Problem" [*Tōa kyōeiken no*

---

4. "Yokohama jiken hikoku Aikawa Hiroshi shuki," *Zoku gendaishi shiryō 7: Tokkō to shisō kenji*, ed. Katō Keiji (Tokyo: Misuzu shobō, 1982), 712-13; Tadokoro Hiroyasu, "Rekishi hitsuzen ron to Soren raisan ron: Hosokawa Karoku shi no 'Sekaishi no dōkō to Nihon' ni tsuite," in *Yūkoku no hikari to kage: Tadokoro Hiroyasu ikōshū* (Tokyo: Kokumin bunka kenkyūkai, 1970), 435.

5. Japan, Naimushō keihokyoku [Home Ministry, Police Bureau], *Tokkō geppō*, October 1943, 74-79.

minzoku mondai] (1941), he argued for the establishment of a Co-Prosperity Sphere that recognized the democratic movements in a number of Asian countries, and, according to the Police, he had suggested that Japan itself had to undergo a democratic revolution. Finally, in "The Trends of World History and Japan" (1942), Hosokawa sought to reveal how trends in world history had indicated the emergence of colonial independence movements and had forecast a world-wide drift toward Soviet-style socialism.

During their cross-examination, the Police were able to make Hosokawa confess that he was a communist and that he wished to change the Japanese political and social structure. However, when his case came before the preliminary trial judges of the Tokyo District Higher Court, Hosokawa was able to refute these statements and the Police Board's interpretations of his essays. On May 5, 1944, he declared that

> In my various essays, I discussed the achievements of the Soviet Union. But this was by no means an attempt to promote communism. My intention was to reveal the present conditions in the Soviet Union and the impact of that country's achievements on the peoples of East Asia whose countries are presently undergoing great changes. Moreover, my frustration over the failure of the Japanese to develop a new outlook was in no sense an attempt to encourage class struggle within the country. I was only expressing a profound desire for national unity based on a new outlook.
>
> Looking back at my experiences since the Sympa Incident, I realize that intellectual conversion is not an easy task and that it is impossible to use terms and construct sentences which do not give rise to suspicion. However, what I have just stated expresses the spirit with which I wrote [my essays].[6]

The judges at the preliminary trial apparently did not consider the case a serious matter or found Hosokawa's arguments to be persuasive, and there were indications that they would recommend that he be released. However, the Kanagawa Prefectural Police took over his case before this could happen. The Kanagawa Police claimed that they had evidence that Hosokawa was the head of a widespread leftist network and that the essay, "The Trends of World History and Japan," was a call to action for all the hidden communists scattered throughout the country.

---

6. *Hosokawa Karoku gokuchū chōsho: Yokohama jiken shōgen*, ed. Morikawa Kinju (Tokyo: Fuji shuppan, 1989), 279.

While the Metropolitan Police appeared to show little enthusiasm for investigating the Hosokawa case and only did so in response to criticism from Army censors, the Kanagawa Police seems to have entertained ambitions of uncovering a case as spectacular as the notorious Sorge spy Incident. The Metropolitan Police Board had discovered the Sorge spy ring in 1941 after its officers began investigating the return to Japan of American Communist Party members.[7] Writers on the Yokohama Incident believe that the Kanagawa Police, hoping to uncover a similar conspiracy and following the example of the Metropolitan Police in conducting their investigation, may have been on the look-out for leftists returning to Japan and saw Kawada Hisashi as a very likely suspect. Although there is no mention of this in the police reports, it has become a widely accepted theory that the Kanagawa Police targeted Kawada after some books on social problems were discovered in his luggage.[8]

Kawada was a former thought control offender. While a student at Keiō University, he had been arrested for participating in Marxist study groups. He was a relative of Kazami Akira, who was both Justice Minister in the Second Konoe Cabinet and a close friend of Hosokawa Karoku, and it was Kazami who advised Kawada to leave the country after his release from custody. The government had carried out wholesale arrests of communists and suspected sympathizers on March 15, 1928, and Kazami feared that Kawada might again be arrested if he remained in Japan.

Kawada, who remained in the United States for ten years studying labour and union issues, returned to Japan in January 1941 and was arrested a year and a half later. At the time of his arrest, he was head of the Information Department of the World Economic Research Association [*Sekai keizai chōsakai*], which was affiliated with the Foreign Ministry. Individuals in the Mantetsu and the Army as well as the Foreign Ministry often came to use the Association's research material or to participate in study groups organized within the Association. The Soviet Research Group [*Soren jijō chōsakai*] was

---

7. Members of this spy ring were accused of passing highly confidential military information to the Soviet Union and included Richard Sorge, an adviser to the German Embassy in Tokyo, and Ozaki Hotsumi, a well-known China specialist and member of former Prime Minister Konoe Fumimaro's think-tank. For a detailed study of this subject, see Chalmers Johnson, *An Instance of Treason: Ozaki Hotsumi and the Sorge Spy Ring* (Stanford: Stanford University Press, 1964).

8. Nakamura, *Yokohama jiken no hitobito*, 271-72; 22-23. Kawada had brought back with him a copy of *The History of the Development of Japanese Capitalism* [*Nihon shihonshugi hattatsushi*] by Noro Eitaro, a communist theorist who had died in police custody in 1933.

one of these study groups, and its members, beginning with Takahashi Yoshio, were eventually arrested as Kawada's accomplices.

The Kanagawa Police interrogated Kawada and his wife, Sadako, about their acquaintances and obtained the names of Takahashi and others. Of the first seven people arrested in January 1943, only Takahashi was detained and prosecuted. While he was a high school student, Takahashi had been arrested as a member of the Communist Youth Union [*Kyōsan seinan dōmei*], and the Police may have focussed their attention on him because he was a former thought control offender.

Police discovered records of the meetings of the Soviet Research Group during a search of Takahashi's home and in May 1943, they arrested the other members of this group. According to the Police, Soviet Research Group members had tried to promote communism and supposedly for the purpose of protecting the Soviet Union, had attempted to convince officials of the Soviets' superior military strength. Group members included individuals working in ministries or semi-official research organizations. Masuda Naohiko, for example, was with the Soviet Research Department of the Cabinet Planning Board, and at the time of his arrest, he was preparing for a trip to the Soviet Union as a courier for the Japanese Foreign Ministry.[9] Hiradate Toshio and Nishizawa Tomio, moreover, both worked in the Tokyo Office of the Mantetsu and, like Masuda, they were close friends of Hosokawa Karoku. All three men had been invited by Hosokawa to accompany him on a trip. It was in discovering some photographs taken during this trip that the Kanagawa Police were able to devise a means of linking Hosokawa and many of his acquaintances to their investigation of Kawada Hisashi.

In July 1942 Hosokawa and his friends had visited the town of Tomari in Toyama Prefecture. Hosokawa had received a huge royalty for a book on colonial history and was going back to his home town to perform a memorial service for his parents.[10] Some friends had helped him in preparing the book and as a token of appreciation, he invited them along on his trip. Food was more plentiful in the countryside during the War, and Hosokawa was confident that he could entertain his friends more lavishly in Tomari. Those who went on the trip took a number of photographs, and the Police came across copies of these during their arrests of Soviet Research Group members Hiradate Toshio and Nishizawa Tomio. The Police thereafter made it a point to look for these photographs, and Mrs. Ono Sada, whose husband was arrested in the affair, recalled that the officers conducting a search of the premises confiscated

---

9. Nakamura, *Yokohama jiken no hitobito*, 90.
10. Nakamura, *Yokohama jiken no hitobito*, 47.

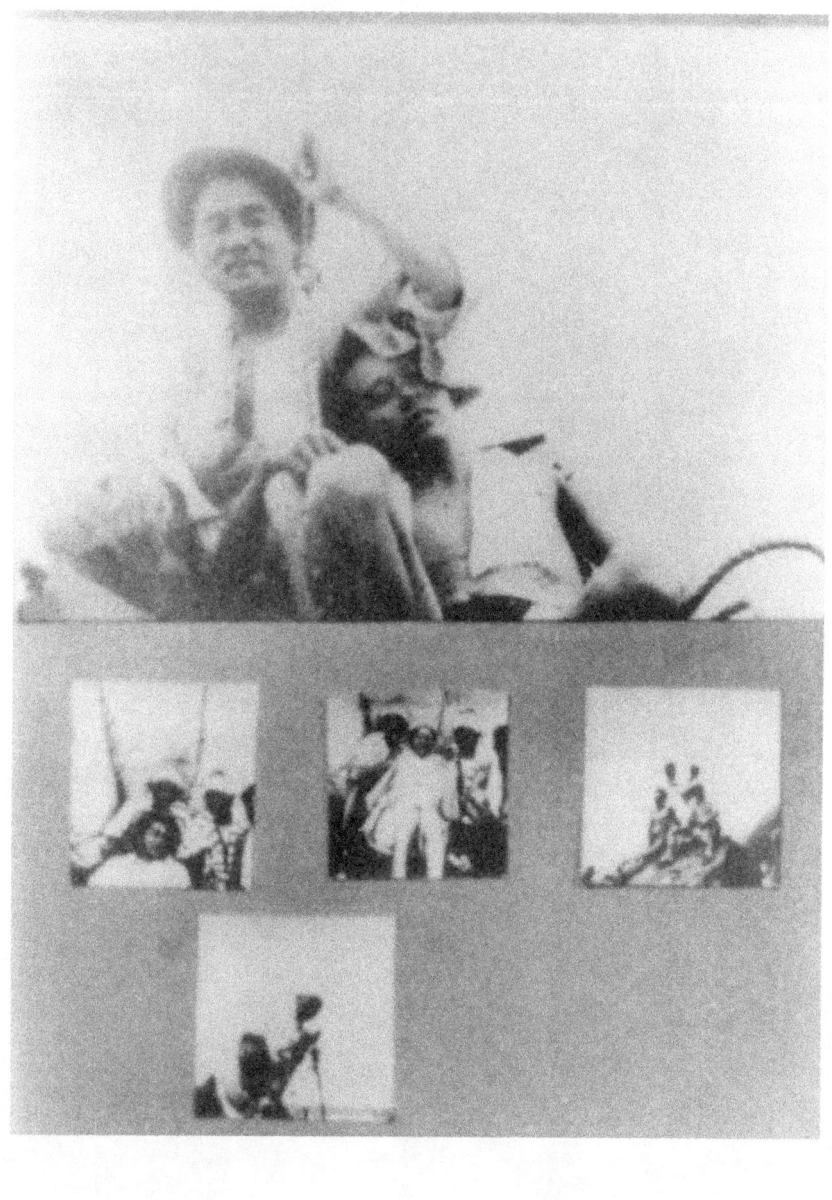

an album that contained these photographs.[11] It is thus widely believed that a single photograph of Hosokawa and his friends dressed in identical kimono and posing in the garden of an inn provided the Kanagawa Police with the sole means of linking the Hosokawa and Kawada cases. The photograph in question is extremely innocuous, especially when placed alongside the other snapshots taken at the same time (see included photographs taken at Tomari), and the Police refrained from making any mention of this dubious piece of evidence in their official reports on the Incident.

Still, in May 1943, the Kanagawa Police did arrest all of the others in the photograph as members of the so-called "Hosokawa Group" and charged them with planning to re-establish the Japan Communist Party. The Police then forced these individuals to provide the names of accomplices, and among those subsequently arrested were three Mantetsu employees who were charged with trying to help the Hosokawa Group to establish contact with the Chinese Communist Party. In addition, on July 11 and 31, 1943, the Police arrested Hosokawa's research assistant and a journalist working for the well-known publication, *Chūō kōron*. Both these individuals were members of what the Police described as the Political Economic Research Group [*Seiji keizai kenkyūkai*]. From September to October 1943, Police then concentrated on hunting down each member of this Research Group.

The Political Economic Research Group had been organized by graduates of the Shōwa Academy [*Shōwa juku*]. The Academy had been a wing of the prestigious Shōwa Research Association, which had served as an informal advisory board for the First Konoe Cabinet of 1937-39. The Shōwa Academy had been something of a refuge for students who had been expelled from school after being arrested for participating in leftist movements; consequently, members of the Political Economic Research Group included quite a few former leftist thought control offenders. Many, moreover, were employed at the time of their arrest in ministries and industries important for the war effort. According to the Kanagawa Police, these Research Group members had sought employment in these organizations in order to obtain highly confidential material. They reportedly sought to use this material to assess the war situation and prepare the way for a postwar revolution.

Although the majority of those arrested in the affair were liberal or leftist intellectuals, the Kanagawa Police did not limit their investigation to these types of individuals. They obtained, through a member of the Hosokawa Group, the name of a young factory worker associated with a labour

---

11. Ono Sada and Kiga Sumiko, *Yokohama jiken: Tsuma to imōto no shuki* (Tokyo: Kōbunken, 1978), 78-9.

organization, the Patriotic Political Comrades Association [*Aikoku seiji dōshikai*]. The Comrades Association had a rather "right-wing" following. But Police arrested its members in October 1943 on the suspicion that they were trying to establish leftist labour organizations in factories important for the war effort.

The presence of journalists in the Hosokawa Group and Political Economic Research Group also allowed the Kanagawa Police to make a case for radical elements within the publishing industry. From January 29, 1944 to May 9, 1945, they rounded up journalists and editors from *Kaizō*, *Chūō kōron*, *Nihon hyōron*, and *Iwanami shoten*, and accused them of spreading leftist propaganda. Those higher up in the police force and government, who believed that the Yokohama Incident was a bona-fide communist conspiracy, responded to the accusations put forth by the Police by demanding that these publications be closed down. As a result, the authorities forced *Kaizō* and *Chūō kōron* to shut down operations in July 1944 and made plans to do the same to *Nihon hyōron* and *Iwanami shoten*.

The Kanagawa Police constructed the Incident from the flimsiest of evidence and could only back their charges by forcing suspects to write out "confessions." Those arrested had been held under the police detention system, which prevented them from receiving legal counsel and left them completely at the mercy of the interrogating officers.[12] In his memoirs, one of the journalists arrested in the affair recalled how he and many others had entertained hopes that they would be able to refute their so-called confessions once their case came to court. However, they soon discovered that the procurators and judges of the Yokohama District Higher Court were in no mood to accept denials and expected the suspects to simply confirm what was contained in the police interrogation records. When they denied the charges against them, these judicial officials became incensed and argued that their obstinacy, their refusal to acknowledge their confessions, just seemed to substantiate their guilt.[13]

During the Trials of the suspects in the Yokohama Incident, the prosecution was nevertheless forced to drop the most serious charges because of a lack of solid evidence.[14] That is, while those arrested were accused of

---

12. *The Yokohama Case and Tortures in Japan* (n.p.: Association to Concern [sic] the Yokohama Case, n.d.), 5.
13. Hatanaka Shigeo, "Saishin saiban o seikyū shite," *Yokohama jiken: Genron dan'atsu no kōzu*, ed. Hatanaka Shigeo, Okudaira Yasuhiro and Ebihara Kogi (Tokyo: Iwanami bukkuletto, No. 78, 1987), 62; Hatanaka Shigeo, *Nihon faashizumu no genron dan'atsu shōshi* (Tokyo: Kōbunken, 1986), 278.
14. "Kōjutsusho, Kimura Toru to Kato Seiji," *Yokohama jiken shiryōshū*, 84, 87.

using their research and publications to promote support for leftist ideas and communist forces both abroad and at home, they were not accused of trying to re-establish the Japan Communist Party or pass information to enemy powers. The Trials of the suspects in the Yokohama Incident, which ran from July to September 1945, were conducted right through the Japanese surrender on August 15th. The wife of one of the journalists arrested in the affair recalled seeing mountains of papers being burned outside the courtroom where the trials were being held.[15] It is widely believed that justice officials in Yokohama were destroying government documents, including those that could have proven that the Incident was an official frame-up. At any rate, the Judges at these Trials were clearly desperate to finish up the legal proceedings before the American Occupation came into full swing.

Defense Attorney Unno Shinkichi has claimed that the Judges, in order to speed up matters, proposed to him that they would grant his clients an immediate release if they accepted the charges against them.[16] Unno, who was one of the few Japanese lawyers willing to represent individuals accused of thought control offenses, agreed to persuade his clients to accept the charges. At the time of the Trials, Unno was more concerned about getting his clients released than making sure that justice was served. He realized that some of them would not survive much longer in custody. The vast majority had often been beaten until they lost consciousness, and some, having had to endure years of torture, were in extremely poor health. Four had already died: two may have been beaten to death; one apparently froze to death in his cell; and another succumbed to tuberculosis aggravated by the harsh conditions in detention. It would take years for some of those arrested to recover their health, and three died immediately, or a few years, after their release from custody.

Unno succeeded in persuading all of his clients, except Hosokawa Karoku, to accept the charges against them. Hosokawa was the only one of the defendants who consistently maintained his innocence. He became the last to be released in September 1945, and with SCAP's October Directive abolishing the Peace Preservation Law, charges against him were dropped. Years later the others arrested in the Yokohama Incident would express deep regrets that they had not followed Hosokawa example and rejected the deal offered by the Judge at their trials.[17]

---

15. Nakamura, *Yokohama jiken no hitobito*, 262-63.
16. Unno Shinkichi, "Aru bengōshi no ayumi: IV Yokohama jiken," *Hōritsu jihō*, June 1968: 65.
17. Kimura Toru, *Yokohama jiken no shinsō: Tsukurareta 'Tomari kaigi'* (Tokyo: Chikuma shobō, 1982), 92.

The Yokohama District Higher Court sentenced the majority of those arrested in the affair to two or three years in prison, but granted them a suspended sentence.[18] Mori Kazuo, who had been working in the East Asia Ministry and was a member of the Political Economic Research Group, received the harshest sentence. The Judges sentenced Mori to four years with no suspension for taking out confidential government documents from his place of employment. In contrast, they postponed the prosecution of journalists apprehended during the last sweep of arrests and simply released them. This difference in the judicial treatment of Mori and the journalists simply reaffirms what had always been the authorities' comparatively lesser concern with the problem of subversive journalism.

---

18. Nakamura, *Yokohama jiken no hitobito*, n.p. Nakamura lists the sentences handed down in the appendices at the back of her book.

2
The Incident and the Journalists

Assessing the Conventional Explanations

Journalists have been the main interpreters of the Yokohama Incident. Their principal explanations are that the authorities concocted the affair primarily to suppress dissident elements in the publishing industry, and/or that the Incident was part of a conspiracy to undermine the political influence of former Prime Minister Konoe Fumimaro. These interpretations are either erroneous or need to be qualified.

Although the views of the journalists are important for understanding the experience of some of the individuals arrested, they cannot be accepted without reservation and the limits of their applicability must be recognized. The journalists can only describe their own experience and cannot speak for the researchers, whose experiences were different and present another dimension to the Incident. In addition, they can only provide their view of the wartime state, and, contrary to the journalists' tendency to depict the state as somewhat all-powerful, it appears that the authorities were experiencing difficulties in administering and maintaining thought control.

It is easy to sympathize and understand how awesome the authority of the state must have seemed to those arrested. In one of the earliest works on the Yokohama Incident, three journalists described themselves as weak, isolated citizens who had no means of protecting themselves against the enormous power of the state.[1] These unfortunate individuals were physically and mentally tormented by police officials who probed into the smallest details of their suspects' lives and who, as representatives of the state, boasted of their

---

1. Mimasaka Tarō, Fujita Chikamasa, Watanabe Kiyoshi, *Yokohama jiken* (Tokyo: Nihon editaasukūru shuppanbu, 1977), 237-38.

right to kill leftists at will. The Japanese state was unquestionably despotic in many respects and often tyrannized its citizens in its attempt to regulate their actions and thoughts. Yet, many individuals and groups may have cooperated with or supported the state, not just because they feared government retaliation or were duped by official arguments or appeals to nationalism but, in order to serve their own interests. One should not assume that cooperation with the state was all the result of official coercion and thought control, or overlook the possible difficulties encountered by the authorities in imposing their will over the people.

THE EFFECTIVENESS OF JAPANESE THOUGHT CONTROL

The Japanese thought control system involved propaganda, the inculcation of the national orthodoxy of a family state headed by a divine emperor, and censorship, the elimination of any ideas that seemed to conflict with this orthodoxy. The prewar authorities had at their disposal a number of institutions for promoting the values that they believed best served the interests of the state. For example, one writer has observed how the Army sought to influence the thinking of civilians through an extensive military education network of reservist associations, youth training centres and women's organizations.[2] Such Army-sponsored organizations are said to have reinforced the attitude of submitting to authority and acted as complements to the schools.

The Meiji Education Rescript of 1890, which stressed filial piety, loyalty and the transcendental emperor as the sole source of authority, provided the basis for the moral education of children. In the primary schools, teachers were expected to teach their students that the individual owed absolute obedience and loyalty to the emperor as the racial father and embodiment of the state. It has been suggested that such indoctrination at the primary school level ensured that even those trained in rational-scientific concepts at the universities remained susceptible to state-sponsored myths and dogma. Many leftists, it has been argued, fell victim to the *Tenkō* policy of eliciting ideological conversion because of their inability to abandon the social and cultural values they had learned as children.[3]

---

2. Richard J. Smethurst, "The Army, Youth, and Women," *Learning to be Japanese: Selected Readings on Japanese Society and Education*, ed. Edward R. Beauchamp (Connecticutt: Linnet Books, 1978), 140.

3. Richard H. Mitchell, *Censorship in Imperial Japan* (Princeton: Princeton University Press, 1983), 109-10; Patricia Golden Steinhoff, "Tenkō: Ideology and Societal Integration in Prewar Japan," Ph.D. diss., Harvard University, 1969: 7, 12-13.

However, it cannot be assumed that the socialization received through the primary schools was so uniform. The kind of education that children received cannot be assessed simply by the content of textbooks, and it is hard to believe that all schoolteachers taught in the same fashion and refrained from transmitting their own personal values or adding their own interpretations to the ideas they were expected to pass along to their students. More important, there are reasons to question whether the official ideas promoted by the primary schools was necessarily of so enduring a nature that they could effectively withstand the challenge of later intellectual influences. Although coming under increasing official control, the universities enjoyed some measure of intellectual autonomy even up to the mid-1930s and could provide exposure to many ideas contradictory to those taught in the primary schools. Individuals exposed to conflicting ideologies at different times in their lives could have reacted in various ways,[4] and it is not certain that the ideas learnt at an earlier age maintained a dominant influence on the thinking and values of the individual.

The present study, which focusses on the problems of administering thought control and safeguarding internal security, does not pretend to provide an in-depth analysis of susceptibility to thought control. However, it observes that works that address this subject have demonstrated that individuals may have acquiesced to official demands for a number of reasons,[5] and cautions against attributing too much of the behaviour of individuals to indoctrination or coercion.

Scholars are no longer prepared to view the apparent lack of open resistance to authority as just the product of thought control, and questions have been raised about the degree to which individuals, rather than being simply brain-washed or coerced into obedience, cooperated with the Japanese state for reasons of their own. Coercion and the manipulation of feelings of patriotism

---

4. Kazuko Tsurumi, "Six Types of Change in Personality: Case Studies of Ideological Conversion in the 1930's," *Social Change and the Individual: Japan Before and After Defeat in World War II* (Princeton: Princeton University Press, 1970), 32-34. In her study of ideological conversion, Tsurumi describes the various reactions of individuals introduced to ideologies which contradicted earlier held concepts or values. Some individuals could remain "ever-committed" to their earlier values and reject the newer ideologies; some could become "reversely-committed" to the newer ideologies and diametrically opposed to earlier values; some could become "perennial deviants" in that they would be unable to commit to either the newer ideologies or the older values; and still some could become "many-layered" or "innovators" in that they would be able to compartmentalize or create a synthesis of the conflicting concepts.

5. For a work that examines a wide range of cases of ideological conversion in both the prewar and postwar periods, see *Kyōdō kenkyū Tenkō, kaitei zōhō*, 2 vols, ed. Shisō no kagaku kenkyūkai (Tokyo: Heibonsha, 1978).

may not have been the only reasons that the Japanese people supported the Tōjō government during the Pacific War. One historian has suggested that the Tōjō government possessed for a period of time considerable popular support because of its progressive domestic policies. In order to achieve total mobilization of resources, the Tōjō government called for legal, social, economic, political, and cultural reforms which seemed to promise more opportunities for the average citizen and which appealed to popular resentment of the privileges enjoyed by the upper classes.[6]

Self-interest also appears to have played a role in pushing the publishing industry toward eventual cooperation with the authorities. It has been argued that editors and journalists were willing to assist censors by censoring themselves and that the thought control system would not have been able to function properly without the cooperation of the publishing industry. One study of the wartime mass media proposes, moreover, that mass media industries could have formed an effective common front against government controls, but that enmity born of business competition prevented them from closing ranks.[7]

Excessive competition was a problem shared by both the targets and organs of censorship. It prevented members of the publishing industry to band together to resist the authorities and, at the same time, it prevented officials belonging to different ministries from carrying out their censorship duties in a more efficient manner. According to one high-ranking wartime censor, ministerial rivalries doomed attempts to establish a more coordinated system of censoring publications.[8] Censorship and information matters were the responsibility of the Home Ministry, the Communications Ministry, and the Information Divisions of the Foreign, Army, and Navy Ministries. Concerned that the constant bickering among these ministries would give the impression that the government was divided, wartime officials formulated a plan to establish a supra-ministerial body, the Cabinet Information Board, to unite and regulate all the censorship organizations. However, various ministries disagreed with the plan, and the Home Ministry which held censorship authority through its control of the police was particularly forceful in its opposition. The Cabinet Information Board was never able to assert its authority, and censorship duties remained divided among organizations.

---

6. Amemiya Shōichi, "1940 nendai no shakai to seiji taisei: Han-Tōjō rengō o chūshin toshite," *Rekishi kenkyū*, No. 308, April 1988: 75, 70, 73.

7. Mitchell, *Censorship in Imperial Japan*, 238; Kasza, *The State and the Mass Media*, 193, 268-69.

8. Matsumura Shūichi, *Miyakezaka* (Tokyo: Sanko kobō, 1952), 226-27.

Regulatory organizations established to combat ministerial rivalries thus became nothing more than another contender in the competition. Wartime officials nevertheless continued to respond to censorship problems by recommending the creation of a more effective organization, which would be supposedly under the authority of their own ministry. On the very day that Hosokawa Karoku was arrested by the Tokyo Metropolitan Police Board, the head of the Army Information Division, Colonel Yahagi Kuniharuō, published an article calling for a more "authoritative" censorship body. The article rebuked civilian censors for "oversights," such as the Hosokawa essay, and was unabashedly partisan in its description of the meticulous care with which military censors checked suspect material:

> The censorship of magazines is conducted by the Police Board or the [Cabinet] Information Bureau, but such organizations need to be expanded. There is a need to expand their numbers and improve their quality....
> Many individuals are involved in the censorship of newspapers, but there is a regrettable defect in the censorship of magazines and other reading material. Hosokawa Karoku's "The Trends of World History and Japan," in the September issue of *Kaizō*, is communist propaganda. The publication of the essay was an oversight....
> Before the Army Ministry or the Army Information Division recommended a book, all twenty individuals with authority in the Ministry will read it. After everyone has finished, a committee will be held and opinions will be thoroughly aired. Only after he has carefully considered all the opinions will the committee chief render a decision....
> Great consideration must be given to the state's responsibility in dealing with newspapers, magazines, and books, which are the most powerful instruments in this thought war. Accordingly, what I propose is the establishment of a more authoritative organ of censorship and recommendation.[9]

This competition between rival official groups complicated the situation for publishing industry. Newspapers and journals, for example, found themselves involved in the struggle between Navy and Army, both of which were eager to find avenues for propagandizing their policies. Many journalists sided with the Navy because it had always made efforts to cultivate the good

---

9. Yahagi Kuniharuō, "Sensō to dokusho," *Dokusho shimbun*, September 14, 1942: n.p.

will and assistance of writers and intellectuals in the hopes that they would help popularize Navy policies. The upshot of the publishing industry's pro-Navy attitude was increasing attacks by Army censors.[10]

Still, such competition could occasionally mitigate some problems for the publishing industry. That is, one group of censors could be used against another, and journalists have recalled that when the Army denied them important information on government policies, they could usually turn to the Navy. Some journalists, moreover, claim that a Navy admiral helped them in having a certain Army officer who was particularly aggressive critic of the magazines removed as a censor. The publishing industry could not escape censorship, but journalists and newspapermen were probably spared more effective official control by ministerial bickering.[11]

The Japanese authorities made no effort to conceal its thought control activities until war with China and the Allies prompted a greater need to maintain an image of a united front. Censors had allowed works with objectionable phrases or words to be published as long as the phrases and words were substituted with *fuseji*. *Fuseji* were marks such as "x" or "o" which substituted for each character of an objectionable word.[12] While visually unattractive, the practice did not pose much of an inconvenience to interested readers who soon became adept at figuring out the identity of a censored word. In the late 1930s, however, censors began to instruct editors to phase out the use of *fuseji* so that readers would not notice their disappearance, and during the Pacific War, they strictly forbade their use. The authorities were clearly trying to improve, streamline, reinforce and yet make more subtle, its methods of thought control. The mark of a superior thought control system may be its subtlety. The objects of control are neither coerced into obedience nor even conscious that they are under control. By this standard, the prewar Japanese thought control system had been in many instances rather clumsy and inefficient in its control of the publishing industry.

AN ASSESSMENT OF THE CONVENTIONAL EXPLANATIONS

As noted above, journalists have been the main interpreters of the Yokohama Incident, and the Incident was first brought to the attention of the public in an article published in the *Asahi shimbun* on October 9, 1945. The

---

10. Kuroda Hidetoshi, *Yokohama jiken* (Tokyo: Gakugei shorin, 1975), 16-17.
11. Kuroda, *Yokohama jiken*, 73; "'*Kaizō*' no sanjūnen," *Kaizō*, April 1950: 136.
12. Rubin, *Injurious to Public Morals*, 30-1.

article contained what would become the conventional explanations for the affair: first, that it was a case of mass media suppression and second, that political motives were behind the arrest of certain groups. The writers of the article insisted that the authorities had used the Incident to shut down *Kaizō* and *Chūōkōron* and that the arrest of the Political Economic Research Group was part of a plot to sully the political reputation of former Prime Minister Konoe Fumimaro.

It is improbable that the affair was concocted as an attack against Konoe or for the sole purpose of suppressing certain publications. But, despite the shortcomings of these explanations, they merit examination as the most popular interpretations of the Yokohama Incident.

THE INCIDENT AS A POLITICAL CONSPIRACY

Almost all of the works in Japanese on the Yokohama Incident discuss what could be called the "political conspiracy thesis." The origins of the thesis are unknown, but it seems possible that it was inspired by a well-known explanation for the Cabinet Planning Board Incident. Common to explanations for both the Yokohama and Cabinet Planning Board Incidents is the argument that supporters and allies of arch-conservative and former prime minister Hiranuma Kiichirō tried to create a political scandal in order to discredit Hiranuma's rivals and political enemies.

The political conspiracy thesis holds that Karasawa Toshiki, the Vice-Home Minister in the Tōjō Cabinet, urged the Kanagawa Prefectural Police to expand their investigation of the Yokohama Incident in the hopes that it would result in a scandal involving Prince Konoe Fumimaro. It was rumoured at the time that Konoe was preparing to make a political comeback, and Karasawa thought that if he helped to discredit the Prince he would win the appreciation of both his boss, then Prime Minister Tōjō Hideki, and the anti-Konoe forces supposedly headed by former Prime Minister Hiranuma Kiichirō.

Supporters of the political conspiracy thesis maintain that the Kanagawa Police tried to link Konoe to their investigation when they called in for questioning Kazami Akira, the Justice Minister in the Second Konoe Cabinet, and when they arrested members of the Political Economic Research Group. The Kanagawa Police, it is argued, targeted this Research Group because many of its members were graduates of the Shōwa Academy, an intellectual society that had been sponsored by Prince Konoe. In recent years, however, more than a few Research Group members have claimed that they were in fact guilty of some of the charges against them. Consequently, there may have been reasons other than a possible desire to implicate Konoe in the Incident for the Kanagawa Police's notable interest in the Research Group.

In December 1944 the Kanagawa Police called in Kazami Akira, a longtime associate of Prince Konoe, in order to question him about his friendship with Hosokawa Karoku. Many of those arrested in the affair have argued that the Police entertained hopes that Kazami would say something incriminating during his questioning and thus implicate himself and through him, Konoe, in the investigation. It seems plausible that Kazami was suspected by a number of individuals of being a leftist sympathizer. Even prior to the Yokohama Incident, he had fallen under suspicion as a result of his patronage of certain intellectuals.[13]

Kazami had found himself involved in the Sorge Incident because it was through him that Ozaki Hotsumi, the Soviet spy, had become an informal adviser to the Konoe Cabinet. During his tenure as Justice Minister in the Second Konoe Cabinet, moreover, Kazami made quite few political enemies. He antagonized right-wing activists by refusing to provide them with cabinet funds; he got dragged into factional conflict between military factions when he sponsored Colonel Itagaki Seishirō as Army Minister; and he infuriated the bureaucracy when he supported plans to reform the civil official appointment system. Opposition from his various enemies was very likely the reason why the government refused to approve of his nomination during the Imperial Rule Assistance Election of the early 1940s.[14]

Many of Kazami's political enemies would not have been surprised and would have enjoyed learning that the Kanagawa Police had discovered his involvement in a communist conspiracy. However, there is nothing to indicate that the Police had any intention of implicating Kazami or Konoe in the Yokohama Incident. Asking a few questions about his friendship with Hosokawa was the full extent of their dealings with Kazami. It seems that the Police did not bother to investigate any further into Kazami's background or chose to ignore the fact that he was related to yet another suspect in the Yokohama Incident, the suspected American Communist Party spy Kawada Hisashi.

It is questionable whether the Kanagawa Police or their superiors would have been prepared to try to create a scandal involving individuals at the highest echelons of society. Prominent persons such as Kazami and, especially,

---

13. Suda Teiichi, *Kazami Akira to sono jidai* (Tokyo: Hatsukakai, 1965), 159; Kazami Akira, *Konoe naikaku* (Tokyo: Chūkō bunkō, 1982), 221-2. In his book, Kazami claimed that Tōjō Hideki, who was the Minister of War in the Second Konoe Cabinet, argued that one of the speeches that Justice Minister Kazami made to police officials contained phrases that implied a fondness for communist ideas.

14. Suda, *Kazami Akira*, 129; Kazami, *Konoe naikaku*, 123, 146-47, 245.

Konoe enjoyed enormous protection. Konoe and wartime Prime Minister Tōjō Hideki were political enemies, and there were many individuals who believed that Tōjō wanted to arrest Konoe. Tōjō was suspicious of Konoe's wartime activities and did place him under heavy military police surveillance. Tōjō and those around him were nevertheless aware that any scandal involving Konoe, a former prime minister and relative of the Emperor, could have a devastating effect on the people's morale. The military police eventually arrested members of Konoe's wartime entourage who were lobbying for an end to hostilities. But according to a high-ranking military police official, the investigation of Konoe's involvement in the peace movement was conducted with the utmost secrecy and there was never any intention of arresting him.[15]

The conspiracy thesis depicts the Incident as a manifestation of the wartime government's attack against Konoe and other progressive elements in society. It draws up an overly simplified scenario pitting Prime Minister Tōjō and his ally Hiranuma against the "liberal" Prince Konoe. Wartime politics, however, was not the preserve of neatly defined, hostile camps of conservatives and liberals, and alliances were forged between individuals with contrasting political reputations. In addition, it is difficult to attach political labels to an individual such as Konoe Fumimaro. Through the Shōwa Research Association and Shōwa Academy, he had been something of a patron of Marxist thinkers and former leftist thought control offenders. But in reaction to the Sorge Incident and the discovery that a member of his own brain-trust was a Soviet spy, "Konoe became suspicious of almost everyone who had any connections with the SRS [the Shōwa Research Association]."[16]

In his famous February 1945 Memorial to the Throne, Konoe openly admitted that he had been the dupe of communists and their sympathizers, and he called for greater efforts to exterminate these subversives. "There has been a notable tendency," he observed, "to regard the danger of bolshevization

---

15. Kiyozawa Kiyoshi, *Ankoku nikki* (Tokyo: Tōyō keizai shimpōsha, 1954), 155; *The Diary of Marquis Kido, 1931-45: Selected Translations into English* (Maryland: University Publications of America, 1984), 324; Ōtani Keijirō, *Shōwa kempeishi* (Tokyo: Misuzu shobō, 1966), 503. More than one contemporary mentioned rumours about Tōjō's desire to silence Konoe. According to Kiyozawa, the philosopher Rōyama Masamichi was among those who believed that Tōjō was plotting against Konoe. In addition, in a diary entry dated December 18, 1941, the Lord Keeper of the Privy Seal Kido Kōichi observed that Tōjō wanted "to muzzle Prince Konoye."

16. Robert M. Spaulding, Jr., "Japan's 'New Bureaucrats' 1932-45," *Crisis Politics in Prewar Japan: Institutional and Ideological Problems of the 1930s*, ed. George M. Wilson (Tokyo: Sophia University, 1970), 66; Suda, *Kazami Akira*, 149. Suda also discusses Konoe's reaction to the Sorge Incident and compares it with that of Kazami.

(*sekka*) lightly, but to my mind this [is] a superficial and frivolous view."[17] Konoe described in detail the domestic forces, the renovationist bureaucrats and a certain segment of the military, that were pushing the country toward a communist revolution. He argued that bureaucrats and leftists masquerading as right-wing supporters of the state had been manipulating this segment of the military which, since the Manchurian Incident of 1931, had been advocates of certain social and political reforms. Military men, Konoe pointed out, were trained to respect the *kokutai* or principle of the emperor as the highest power of the state, but leftists and their allies had succeeded in persuading these men that communism was compatible with the *kokutai*. Konoe concluded that although the goal of the military's domestic reform policy was not necessarily a communist revolution, this segment of the military had to be eliminated in order to curtail the influence of bureaucratic and civilian leftists.

One of the individuals who had helped Konoe in drafting his Memorial[18] had also thoroughly discussed the internal communist threat with Hiranuma Kiichirō on April 1942 and claims that Hiranuma seemed quite affected by their talk. In February 1943 Hiranuma also spoke of how a segment of the military was trying to use domestic unrest and war as an excuse for instituting controls and spreading "Red" ideas. The greatest concern, he observed, was not defeat or victory. It was the threat of revolution. Hiranuma did not believe that Tōjō was trying to carry out a revolution but was simply unaware that he was being manipulated in that direction. Again, in March 1943, Hiranuma talked of how leftists within the government were simply using the Pacific War as an excuse for instituting their plans and that these plans entailed making Japan even more radically communist than the Soviet Union. It is notable that in 1944 Konoe observed that Hiranuma shared his concerns about the potential transformation of Japan into a communist state.[19]

---

17. John W. Dower, *Empire and Aftermath: Yoshida Shigeru and the Japanese Experience, 1878-1954* (Cambridge: Council on East Asian Studies, Harvard University, 1988), 260. The source for information on the wartime "Red Scare" and its contribution to a movement to end the Pacific War.

18. Ueda Shunkichi, "Shōwa demokurashii no zasetsu," *Jiyu*, October and November 1960: 81-94, 89-99; Itō Takashi, "Senji taisei," *Kindai Nihon kenkyū nyūmon*, ed. Nakamura Takafusa and Itō Takashi (Tokyo: Tokyo daigaku shuppankai, 1983), 97-98; Dower, *Empire and Aftermath*, 233, 254. The idea that the Army's Control Faction was "red" owes much to Ueda Shunkichi, a former Foreign Ministry bureaucrat and private secretary to Prime Minister Tanaka Giichi.

19. Itō Takashi, "Shōwa 17-20 nen no Konoe-Mazaki Gurūpu," *Shōwaki no seiji*, by Itō Takashi (Tokyo: Yamakawa shuppansha, 1983), 200-1; *Hiranuma Kiichirō kaisōroku*, ed. Hiranuma Kiichirō kaisōroku hensan iinkai (Tokyo: Gakuyō shobō, 1955), 119-21, 127-28; *Konoe nikki*, ed. Kyōdō tsūshinsha (Tokyo: Kyōdō tsūshinsha kaihatsu kyoku, 1968), 65, 106.

Contrary to the conspiracy thesis, Konoe and Hiranuma were more allies than opponents. It was Konoe who had proposed that Hiranuma be nominated as the next prime minister in 1932. It was also Hiranuma, in turn, who had openly supported the formation of the Second Konoe Cabinet in 1940. During the July 18, 1944 and April 5, 1945 Conferences for Senior Statesmen which were convened for the selection of a new prime minister, Konoe and Hiranuma consistently backed up each other's observations and suggestions. The fact, moreover, that Hiranuma became partners with Konoe in a movement to oust Tōjō from the premiership renders implausible any argument that the former was involved during the War in plots against Konoe.[20]

The conspiracy thesis also holds that Vice-Home Minister Karasawa Toshiki tried to curry favour with Hiranuma and Tōjō by "urging" the Kanagawa Police to expand their investigation until they found something to incriminate Konoe. The Home Ministry was in charge of the civil police forces, and Karasawa may have in some fashion urged the Police to expand their investigation. However, this may have amounted to nothing more than a perfunctory remark that some official could make to subordinates, or it could have been simply a demand to increase efforts to apprehend communists inspired more by recent criticism of the Ministry and its civil police. One political observer recalled that the Tōjō Cabinet was plagued by conflict between ministerial representatives and, as an example, referred to a dispute that arose within the Cabinet when Home and Vice-Home Ministers Gotō Fumio and Karasawa Toshiki suspected that their Ministry's control of the Imperial Rule Assistant Youth Organizations [*Yokusan sōnendan*] was being called into question.[21]

Home Ministry bureaucrats may have had reasons to feel threatened. Karasawa Toshiki's biographer, referring to the semi-official *The History of the Home Ministry* [*Naimushōshi*], observes that there had been talk among government circles since the Third Konoe Cabinet of 1941 of dissolving the Home Ministry as part of plans for administrative reform.[22] These plans, which may have been supported by the military, were apparently shelved after the fall of the Konoe Cabinet. Still, the Home Ministry was forced to share its censorship duties with the Cabinet Information Board and during the Pacific War faced considerable competition from the military police in controlling

---

20. William Miles Fletcher III, *The Search for a New Order: Intellectuals and Fascism in Prewar Japan* (Chapel Hill: The University of North Carolina Press, 1982), 94-95; *Kido nikki*, Vol. II (Tokyo: Tokyo daigaku shuppansha, 1966), 766; *The Diary of Marquis Kido*, 394-95, 419-20.
21. Iwabuchi Tatsuo, *Sengō Nihon seiji e no chokugen* (Tokyo: Seiyūsha, 1967), 71-72.
22. Aritake Shuji, *Karasawa Toshiki* (Tokyo: Karasawa Toshiki denki kankōkai, 1975), 180-81.

domestic disturbances. Such developments could have very well encouraged defensive actions to preserve the Ministry's authority. One individual who was arrested during the Cabinet Planning Board Incident has suggested that certain officials in charge of peace preservation, insecure about maintaining their authority, may very well have concocted a number of incidents in order to recover their position within the administrative hierarchy.[23]

Although Vice-Home Minister Karasawa Toshiki has been described as a member of Prime Minister Tōjō Hideki's so-called "brain-trust," he may not have enjoyed Tōjō's full confidence and patronage. Tōjō was reportedly a man of strong likes and dislikes in his relationship with others. He appears to have been quite indulgent to those he trusted. However, while both Tōjō and Karasawa were close to Army Control Faction General Nagata Tetsuzan and were introduced to each other by Nagata in the mid-1930s, there is no evidence of any bonds of friendship and loyalty between the two men.[24]

In his wartime diary, the Vice-President of the East Asia Institute, Ōkura Kōmō, discussed Karasawa's participation in 1942-43 in a movement supporting General Ugaki Kazushige[25] as prime minister[26] In a May 1942 entry, Ōkura wrote that Karasawa had agreed to Ugaki's offer to be his Cabinet Secretariat Chief, and in November 1942, Ōkura observed that the Tōjō Cabinet would not last much longer because Konoe and other Senior Statesmen were throwing their support behind Ugaki. This suggests that Karasawa was not solidly in the Tōjō camp; consequently, it is possible that he was selected as Vice-Home Minister in 1943 to keep him from further involvement in the Ugaki movement. The actual Home Minister was Andō Kisaburō, a military man who owed his position to his friendship with Tōjō, but it was Karasawa who, as a long-time Home Ministry bureaucrat, functioned as head of the Ministry and who would be held responsible for its performance. As his relationship with Tōjō was professional, Karasawa could not rely on friendship with Tōjō when dealing with critics and rivals of the Home Ministry.

In addition, many individuals may have initially questioned the wisdom of appointing Karasawa to a position that placed him directly in charge of the civil police because he had been a failure as a Home Ministry police official.

---

23. Matsumura, *Miyakezaka*, 226-27; Muroga Sadanobu, *Shōwa juku: Dan'atsu no arashi no naka de mo jiyū no tō o mamoritsuzuketa hitotsu no juku ga atta* (Tokyo: Nihon keizai shimbunsha, 1979), 107.
24. Kiyozawa, *Ankoku nikki*, 160; Ōtani, *Shōwa kempeishi*, 408; Aritake, *Karasawa*, 251.
25. Ugaki had supported arms limitation during his tenure as War Minister in 1924-27 and was prevented from forming a cabinet in 1937 because of Army opposition.
26. *Ōkura Kōmō nikki dai yon maki: Shōwa 17-20 nen*, ed. Naiseishi kenkyūkai (Tokyo: Naiseishi kenkyūkai, 1975), 30-31, 84-85, 79.

Karasawa had been Police Bureau Chief during the February 26, 1936 Incident and had been absent from Tokyo during the attempted military coup. As a result, he was forced to resign amidst rumours that he had known beforehand of the plans to stage the coup and had chosen to attend a police chiefs' conference in Western Japan in order to avoid being in harm's way in the capital city. Karasawa may therefore have felt a need to prove his own competence. To vindicate his appointment as Vice-Home Minister, he may have pushed all police officials to rigorously perform their duties, especially those involving the detection of conspiracies. This may have been the full extent of the argument that Karasawa "urged" the Kanagawa Prefectural Police to expand their investigation.

There is nothing to prove that Karasawa played a more direct role in the Yokohama Incident's creation or that he had even been kept fully informed of its development. One high-ranking police official has stated that police officers usually waited until they had nearly completed their investigations before informing superiors of their findings. In a case involving individuals who might have contacts within official circles, the particulars of a case were confined to the police officers directly in charge of the investigation in order to maintain secrecy. Home Ministers and Vice-Ministers were told about arrests only after the fact because police feared that information could be leaked out if they informed their superiors beforehand.[27]

In many ways, the professional training and outlook of senior officials, including those in the civil police, catered to a rather superficial knowledge of their duties and thus, reliance on those below them for information. Unlike many of their subordinates who had to work their way up the ranks but who had little chance of occupying the highest positions, those in the police's civil service elite were university-educated and, after entering the Home Ministry, were able to begin their careers at the rank of inspector. As they were transferred, usually upward, from post to post every one or two years and tended to look upon each appointment as a mere step toward becoming prefectural police chief or even governor, elite police officials did not always bother to learn every detail of their own job, much less keep track of the activities of their underlings and the cases they were investigating.[28]

High-ranking officials were dependent on those below them for information and had little time and perhaps, even less inclination to verify what they had read or been told. Given these circumstances, where subordinates

---

27. *Abe Genki shi danwa dai nikkai sokkiroku*, ed. Naiseishi kenkyūkai (Tokyo: Naiseishi kenkyūkai, 1967), 68.
28. Tipton, *The Japanese Police State*, 98-100.

were allowed a free-hand in conducting investigations, matters of censorship and thought control may have occasionally developed beyond the control of the authorities. In the case of *Kaizō* and *Chūō kōron*, their original intention may have been to coopt, but not necessarily eliminate, these prestigious publications.

THE INCIDENT AS A CONSPIRACY TO SUPPRESS INDEPENDENT JOURNALISM

The Yokohama Incident has been described as "a conspiracy by the police and the courts to rid Tokyo of its independent journalists."[29] One journalist arrested in the affair has argued that the aim of the Incident was to silence the mass media by striking at the editorial boards of three major journals, *Kaizō, Chūō kōron*, and *Nihon hyōron*.[30]

Wartime censors made it clear that action would be taken against uncooperative publications. One *Chūō kōron* journalist recalled that at an Army-sponsored censorship meeting officials castigated the editors of the journal for publishing novelist Tanizaki Jun'ichirō's *The Makioka Sisters*. Officials felt that the novel, in concentrating on the "soft, effeminate, and grossly individualistic lives of women," glorified qualities that had to be shunned during the War. As an open threat, they told magazine representatives that they "intend to put an immediate stop to the publication of any magazine that continues shamelessly to print such novels and essays at a time like this."[31]

Kaizō and *Chūō kōron* had been under fire by one group of censors, but wartime officials did not need to fabricate the Yokohama Incident if they wanted to take action against these publications. They could have, for instance, simply used the Nakanishi Kō case, a bona fide communist incident, to demand that the magazines be suppressed as leftist propaganda organs. In June 1942, the Metropolitan Police Board arrested Nakanishi Kō, a researcher with the Investigative Department of the South Manchurian Railway Company, and uncovered a Japanese communist group in league with agents of the Chinese Communist Party. The Metropolitan Police accused Nakanishi and his comrades of using magazines, such as *Kaizō* and *Chūō kōron*, as forums for leftist debate and indoctrination. According to the October 1943 *Tokkō geppō*,

---

29. Rubin, *Injurious to Public Morals*, 266.
30. Matsumoto Masao, "Yokohama jiken: Chōōgata detchiage," *Dokyumento Shōwa gojūnenshi*, Vol. 6 (Tokyo: Shiobunsha, 1975), 100.
31. Rubin, *Injurious to Public Morals*, 264.

the suspects in the case participated in magazine debates on the China problem in order to help the CCP formulate a theoretical basis for its activities.[32] More important, after 1943, the authorities had effectively gained control over these publications. As a result of the Hosokawa essay controversy, *Kaizō* was forced to change its editorial staff in order to continue publishing and thereafter, became nothing more than another mouthpiece for the government. As for *Chūōkōron*, after being attacked by censors for publishing *The Makioka Sisters*, the magazine also changed its editorial staff and became nothing more than an "ultra-nationalistic propaganda sheet."[33]

It is important not to exaggerate the wartime authorities' concerns about the publishing industry and assume that the Yokohama Incident was, from start to finish, an official plot to eliminate certain journals. In their accounts of the Yokohama Incident, some of the journalists fail to even mention non-journalist groups arrested in the affair and thus provide too abridged an account of the case.[34] That is, they tend to simply draw a connection between the Hosokawa essay controversy, the discovery of the Tomari photograph which provided the Kanagawa Police with a means of involving magazine personnel in an alleged plot to re-establish the Japan Communist Party, the mass arrests of journalists, and the shut down of *Kaizō* and *Chūōkōron*. Yet, the controversy over *Kaizō*'s publication of the Hosokawa essay was not the first step in some elaborate plan to shut down such publications.

The Metropolitan Police Board, which realized that the Army Information Division had stirred up the essay controversy to embarrass civil police censors, was conspicuously unenthusiastic about investigating the Hosokawa case. One specialist of the history of Japanese thought control has observed that it was unusual that the Police Board had arrested Hosokawa for violating the Peace Preservation Law, which implied that he had tried to "further the aims of the Comintern and the Japan Communist Party." According to this source, the Metropolitan Police should have charged him with violating the Publication Law.[35] However, they may have been reluctant to accuse Hosokawa of breaking the latter law because it could have been interpreted as an acknowledgement of the Army's claims that the civil police had been lax in carrying out their censorship duties.

---

32. *Tokkō geppō*, October 1943, 7-74.
33. Rubin, *Injurious to Public Morals*, 267, 266.
34. Ikejima Shimpei and Mimasaka Taro, "Genron tōsei ni taeru," *Shōwa shisōshi e no shōgen* (Tokyo: Mainichi shinbunshi, 1968), 318.
35. Okudaira Yasuhiro, *Chian ijihō shōshi* (Tokyo: Chikuma shobō, 1977), 234-35.

The investigation of the Hosokawa case, which involved over a year of cross-examinations, proved to be quite frustrating for the Metropolitan Police. The Police faced the dilemma of having to establish a case against Hosokawa without leaving themselves open to criticism that they had failed to detect seditious material. Many of the essays that they accused Hosokawa of using to promote communism had been passed by police censors. The Metropolitan Police probably wished to finish up the embarrassing case as quickly as possible, and they apparently raised no objections when it appeared that the judges of the Tokyo District Higher Court might release Hosokawa.

The wartime police did not consider the elimination of leftist or critical journalism their major concern. The Kanagawa Prefectural Police, who took over the Hosokawa case from the Metropolitan Police Board, were far more interested in the activities of the researchers and concentrated on apprehending individuals in research and labour groups before moving on to the journalists. The majority of journalists were not arrested until the close of the investigation; and one journalist recalled being told by the Police that they had intended to arrest him earlier, in the summer of 1943, but that they had been simply too busy to do so.[36]

At least in the earlier years of the Pacific War, officials may have sought to impose their control over the publishing industry, not so much because they viewed members of the industry as posing a grave security threat but, because they recognized the value of the mass media in mobilizing support for the war effort and government policies. The educated middle-class had been rapidly expanding in the decades before the War. For example, the high school population doubled from 58,000 to 110,000 and the university population tripled from 22,000 to 69,000 from 1920 to 1930. Publications, such as *Kaizō* and *Chūō kōron*, exerted a great influence on the educated. In addition, they were attracting a more popular following by putting out inexpensive series of works ranging from Japanese classics to translations of Kant. Typical of these immensely popular "one yen books" was the *Kaizō* Publishing Company's *Collection of Japanese Literature*, which attracted 600,000 subscriptions and was designed to introduce the arts of the privileged class to the average person.[37]

Contemporary observers have suggested that the wartime authorities, instead of wishing to crush these publications, wanted to capitalize on their

---

36. Hatanaka, *Nihon faashizumu*, 200.
37. Masukazu Yamazaki, "The Intellectual Community of the Showa Era," *Showa: The Japan of Hirohito*, ed. Carol Gluck and Stephen R. Graubard (New York: W.W. Norton & Company, 1992), 246-48, 264.

popularity and turn them into propaganda organs. Kiyozawa Kiyoshi, a journalist whose broad network of friends included the President of *Chūō kōron*, recorded his observations of the magazine's troubles in his wartime diary. He noted that the Home Ministry had fewer auxiliary organizations than the Finance, Agriculture and Commerce Ministries and that its officials may have set out to create a problem so that their Ministry could take over *Chūō kōron* and increase the number of organizations under its control. By 1943, censorship authorities had succeeded in installing their own candidates among the senior personnel of *Kaizō* and *Chūō kōron*. Consequently, the destruction of these publications would have made futile all the efforts to gain control over them, and Kiyozawa has suggested that the shut down may have been an unexpected and unwanted development arising from the police investigation of the Yokohama Incident. "Those around the Special Higher Police of the Home Ministry," he wrote in his diary, "having started the affair, now have no means of rectifying the situation."[38]

The shut down of the publications occurred as a result of the Yokohama Incident. But the affair was not fabricated in order to eliminate these publications. Rather than being a triumph of government control over the publishing industry, the shut down of *Kaizō* and *Chūō kōron* could have been an instance of matters developing beyond the control of the authorities. The Kanagawa Prefectural Police may have been too successful in convincing their superiors of the existence of dangerous subversives within the publishing industry.

The Police provided documents, such as the so-called Confession of former *Kaizō* journalist Aikawa Hiroshi, which described how individuals in the publishing industry had devised various means of evading censorship. *Kaizō* editorial meetings, besides supposedly providing a forum for debating theory and raising leftist consciousness among personnel, were organized for the purpose of selecting the theme for the next issue and the choice of writers. Editors reportedly classified writers into four categories: those in the "A" group were leftists; those in the "B" were liberals or individuals who were only pretending to have abandoned their leftist beliefs (*gisō tenkōsha*); those in the "C" group were labelled right-wing renovationists; and those in the "D" group were viewed as reactionaries. According to the Aikawa Confession, editors learned that it was possible to pass by the censors an "A" group writer's article by having it published alongside an article by a "B," "C," or "D" group writer. The Confession also observed that members at a February 20, 1941 *Kaizō* editorial meeting decided that words that could raise the suspicions of censors

---

38. Kiyozawa, *Ankoku nikki*, 153-54.

such as revolution (*kakumei*) were to be substituted by less alarming words such as renovation (*kakushin*).[39]

The Kanagawa Police fabricated much of the activities of the journalists. However, they were able to uncover some correspondence that cast suspicion on certain journalists. Kimura Tōru, a *Chūō kōron* journalist, recalls that the Kanagawa Police showed him a letter that one journalist had sent to a colleague. Kimura knew both men and found it strange that two individuals working in the same office would have to correspond through letters. But more than this, he was aghast to see that the author of the letter was complimenting his co-worker on his recent studies of Marxism. Kimura was well aware that the Police could easily use this against the journalists. Even more incriminating material was uncovered when the Police got hold of a letter written by a newspaperman who had been drafted during the China Incident. In the June 7, 1941 letter, the newspaperman discussed acts of desertion, suicides and the anti-war sentiments of soldiers as well as his own wish to commit, at least once, some act against the government.[40]

The Kanagawa Police's reports of rampant communist activity within the publishing industry had a tremendous impact on wartime officials. In February 1944, Kiyozawa Kiyoshi wrote that the Tōjō Cabinet had discussed the police charges against *Kaizō* and *Chūō kōron* and that only one Minister disagreed with the decision to suspend the two journals. Officials considered the shut down a serious matter and tried not to draw too much public attention to it. The Kanagawa Prefectural Police sought to incriminate *Kaizō* and *Chūō kōron* Presidents, Yamamoto Sanehiko and Shimanaka Hōji. They succeeded in forcing one journalist to accuse Yamamoto of being a "closet communist," and got another to describe Shimanaka of being a "left-leaning liberal."[41] However, Yamamoto and Shimanaka were able to escape arrest, probably because they had politically influential friends whom they could call on for protection, and possibly because officials thought that the arrest of the heads of these two prestigious publications on charges of promoting communism would have created too great a scandal.

Rather than close down the magazines, the wartime authorities had *Kaizō* and *Chūō kōron* "voluntarily" suspend operations. They attempted to provide an explanation for this development through an essay written by one of their

---

39. "Yokohama jiken hikoku Aikawa Hiroshi shuki," *Zoku gendaishi shiryō 7: Tokkō to shisō kenji*, 683, 685.
40. Kimura, *Yokohama jiken no shinsō*, 66; *Tokkō geppō*, June 1944, 1.
41. "Yokohama jiken hikoku Aikawa Hiroshi shuki," 722; Hatanaka, *Nihon faashizumu*, 246.

favoured critics, Nomura Shigeomi. In a February 1944 article Nomura argued that *Kaizō* and *Chūō kōron* had to suspend operations because they could not be reformed. Such publications, he observed, had long been organs for promoting democracy as well as other ideas that could not be tolerated, and their reason for existence would have been eliminated if they had been forced to undergo *Tenkō* or convert.[42]

Nomura's argument was in keeping with the wartime authorities' view that leftists and former thought offenders were beyond redemption and bound to become recidivists. In the 1930s the authorities supported the *Tenkō* policy, sought to ideologically rehabilitate leftist thought control offenders and even allowed them to assume positions of social and political importance. However, by 1941, greater demands to enforce internal security necessitated by war and doubts about the effectiveness of the *Tenkō* policy precipitated a purge of former offenders from society and the government.

---

42. Nomura Shigeomi, "Sōgō zasshi hihan bunka shikan o tadasu," *Dokusho*, Vol. 4, No. 2, February 1944: 11.

3
The Incident and the Researchers

*The Wartime Purge of Former Leftist
Thought Control Offenders*

Official documents as well as the number of wartime incidents involving former leftist thought control offenders indicate that the Japanese authorities during the Pacific War sought to remove individuals with a record of leftist thought offenses from society and government. This chapter, which examines both these documents and incidents, proposes that the experiences of the researchers arrested in the affair reveals that the Yokohama Incident was part of this wartime purge.

The wartime authorities were far less concerned about the activities of the Yokohama Incident's journalists than about the researchers, many of whom were former leftist thought control offenders employed in ministries, state-sponsored institutions, or industries important for the war effort. Although the majority of these researchers had never been members of the Japan Communist Party and had been arrested while attending university simply because they had participated in some study group on Marxist literature, they found themselves during the Pacific War accused of working
for the Party or acting as spies for the Chinese communists or the Soviet Union. All of the researchers who have discussed their involvement in the Yokohama Incident have consistently denied the police charges that they had acted as spies or attempted to re-establish the Japan Communist Party.

However, some of them have claimed that they had not abandoned their commitment to leftist ideologies and had participated in certain anti-government and anti-war activities. If these claims are true, the discovery of their activities could have only reinforced beliefs in official circles that former offenders posed a security risk and had to be removed from all position of influence. Earlier studies have not examined the affair in terms of the researchers because of the tendency to focus exclusively or primarily on the experience of the journalists and because, until recently, little was known about the researchers.

THE VIEWS OF THE RESEARCHERS

The journalists arrested in the affair perceive themselves as the helpless victims of official conspiracies and rivalries. Many of them were critical of the War and the government. However, few have claimed that they were involved in illegal resistance activities. Ono Yasuhito of *Kaizō* declared that at the time of his arrest he was not a communist, but a naive patriot who believed that he could somehow help turn the Pacific War into a genuine movement for popular liberation by simply putting his utmost into his work as a journalist.[1]

In contrast, the researchers dislike being described as "victims," and more than one of them has argued that he had attempted, however obliquely, to resist the wartime state. Such claims are, for the most part, impossible to verify. Still, these relatively recent arguments have raised doubts as to whether *all* those arrested were innocent of *all* the charges levelled against them. Tamiya Hiroshi, in his examination of the Political Economic Research Group, has observed that

> One generally thinks that the Yokohama Incident was simply fabricated by the Special Higher Thought Police. To a degree, this is correct. But this perception is an oversimplification and must be qualified. That is, there was no truth to the police accusations that those arrested were attempting to re-establish the Communist Party. However, it is not correct to assume that the Incident was a complete fabrication and constructed out of thin air. . . .
>
> The arrest of the editors was nothing more than a hysterical, fascist attack against progressive liberals. And it is clear that the authorities had no right to charge them with violating the Peace Preservation Law.
>
> However, even if the arrest of one group amounted to unjust suppression, one cannot assume that everyone was innocent of the charges against them. That is, the research activities of the Shōwa Academy Group [the Political Economic

---

1. Ono and Kiga, *Yokohama jiken: Tsuma to imōto*, 47.

Research Group] indicate that some of those arrested were involved in illegal activities. One should not overlook the fact that communism and not liberalism provided the intellectual basis for this Group's research. . . . Leftist ideas were not wiped out during the War, but persisted. Thus, it is necessary to reevaluate the nature of prewar communist activities and their relationship to the postwar period.

Until now, the Yokohama Incident has been reviewed by the journalists and viewed only in terms of suppression of speech. This is not wrong. But it is a one-dimensional view. A reevaluation is necessary and from now on, efforts should be made to view the Incident from as many different perspectives as possible.[2]

One cannot unquestionably accept the researchers' account of their resistance activities. Japanese intellectuals who lived through the prewar period have a strong tendency to excoriate their generation's failure to resist prewar government policies. Katsube Gen, a member of the Political Economic Research Group, expressed something of his generation's sense of remorse or "war guilt" in his essay on the Yokohama Incident when he observed that the majority of Japanese must live with the fact that, unlike many Europeans and Asians, they failed to undertake any significant anti-fascist activities. One could suspect that individuals troubled by a war guilt mentality may tend to exaggerate acts of resistance.

Yet, the claims of resistance activities put forward by the researchers are rather modest or restrained. None of the researchers has tried to make himself out to be a grand-scale or full-fledged revolutionary. Like the journalists, they deny the charges that they attempted to re-establish the Japan Communist Party and contact foreign communist organizations. Their resistance largely consisted of attempting to influence official opinion and conducting, with the aid of stolen government documents, studies to determine the potential for revolution in Japan. In the final analysis, it is this element of restraint in their claims, together with the fact that statements made by individuals have been almost always corroborated by others, that lends some credibility to the researchers' account of their activities.

Researchers began to express their views in the late 1970s. It was also at this time that independent journalist Nakamura Tomoko conducted extensive interviews with those arrested in the Yokohama Incident. Among the

---

2. Tamiya, "Yokohama jiken-gōmon o yonda," 520-22.

researchers she interviewed were Kawada Hisashi and his wife, Sadako, Hiradate Toshio and Nishizawa Tomio of the Soviet Research Group, and Takagi Kenjirō, Itai Shōsaku and Yamaguchi Kenzō of the Political Economic Research Group. For many of these individuals, Nakamura's interviews marked the first time that they had publicly discussed the affair and their experiences.

The Kanagawa Prefectural Police accused Kawada Hisashi and Sadako of being spies for the American Communist Party and described their activities in a report that appeared in the August 1944 edition of the *Tokkō geppō*.[3] They claimed that Kawada Hisashi had become a member of the Japan Communist Party while attending Keiō University and had left for the United States after being arrested for participating in a Marxist student movement. They also noted that, under the alias of "Sugino" and "Nozaki," Kawada became a central figure among American-based Japanese communists and had used clubs frequented by Japanese labourers in organizing a communist movement. The Kawadas' other criminal activities included distributing anti-war and anti-military propaganda to Japanese sailors aboard an Imperial Navy ship in August 1936. In July 1940 the couple composed a pamphlet entitled "Japan's Political and Economic Power" which was widely distributed throughout the United States and which discussed Japan's military weaknesses and its inability to withstand Chinese resistance.

Police explained that the Kawadas were not listed in the American Communist Party registry because the Party had removed the names of foreign members after the U.S. Government began to crack down on communists in reaction to the German-Soviet Non-Aggression Pact of 1939. Increasing U.S. government pressure on the American Communist Party was also reportedly the reason that the Kawadas decided to return to Japan in January 1941. Kawada asked his brother in Japan to check if the couple might encounter difficulties with the Home and Justice Ministries upon their return. Moreover, prior to his departure, the Kawadas met with an American Communist Party member called Hoskins who asked for their help in investigating the military capacity of the countries surrounding the Soviet Union. According to the Police, the couple promised to send Hoskins statistical material which could reveal Japan's economic capacity to wage war.

Three months after the couple's return to Japan, Kawada Hisashi found a position at the Foreign Ministry-affiliated World Economic Research Association. Police argued that Kawada chose to work in the Association because he believed that it provided the best environment for carrying out

---

3. *Tokkō geppō*, August 1944, 3-27.

leftist activities. He would have access to information and documents which he could send to the American Communist Party. The Police, however, also observed that Kawada was unable to send pertinent information abroad because of restrictions on foreign mail.

During his interview with Nakamura Tomoko, Kawada Hisashi refuted the charges in the 1944 police report that he was a communist and involved in spy activities. He told Nakamura that although he was arrested as a student for participating in Marxist study groups, he had never been a member of the Japan Communist Party. Kawada suggested that he was targeted by the Kanagawa Police because a Japanese police spy stationed in New York had been sending back reports that Japanese involved in church and labour clubs were all communists. He explained that he returned to Japan because he was afraid of being drafted under the American Selective Service System. He had been incorrectly informed that the American Government was preparing to change the system to permit the recruitment of all men up to age 35 residing in the United States, regardless of their nationality.[4]

Kawada insisted that he had not been involved with the American Communist Party, had never met an individual called Hoskins or had any contact with Party members following his return to Japan. He told Nakamura that, because Japanese-American relations were quite strained at the time, he refrained from sending mail abroad and did not even write letters to friends in the United States informing them of his safe return home. He observed that the Police later arrested his brother, whom Kawada had allegedly contacted prior to his return to Japan, but suggested that the Police probably set their sights on him simply because, like Kawada, he had committed in the past some minor thought control violation.[5]

Kawada denied that he had entered the World Economic Research Association in order to advance his spy activities. As head of the Research and Information Department, his principal duties consisted of maintaining and expanding the Department's collection of foreign publications. Researchers from the South Manchurian Railway Company (Mantetsu) as well as those from the Army and Foreign Ministries often came to use the material Kawada had collected or to participate in the various study groups organized within the Association. Kawada observed that, unfortunately for everyone involved, the Police believed that these research activities were just a front for communist meetings.

---

4. Nakamura, *Yokohama jiken no hitobito*, 15, 20, 21.
5. Nakamura, *Yokohama jiken no hitobito*, 20-21, 36.

Kawada Hisashi and Sadako, however, did not dispute everything in the 1944 police report. They admitted that during their stay in the United States they became acquainted with a number of union activists who might have been American Communist Party members and had participated in the activities of certain politically radical labour clubs.[6] More importantly, they admitted that they had indeed distributed anti-war and anti-Army propaganda among the crew of a Japanese Imperial Navy ship. As members of one New York labour club, they escorted the sailors around the city and inside the gifts they gave to them they had inserted some handbills. The handbills declared that the invasion of China was the road to ruin for the Japanese people. During the trial of the suspects in the Yokohama Incident, the Yokohama District Court dropped the charges of spying against the Kawadas. But probably due to the couple's distribution of the above pamphlets, the Judges found the Kawadas guilty of participating in activities detrimental to the Japanese war effort during their stay in the United States.

Like the Kawadas, other researchers have maintained that the Yokohama Incident was not a complete fabrication. Nishizawa Tomio, who worked in the Tokyo offices of the Mantetsu, described the Incident as an "amalgamation" of truth and falsehood.[7] Nishizawa told Nakamura Tomoko that he could not accept the view that the Incident was just a police frame-up. He explained that although there were no plans to re-establish the Japan Communist Party or any attempts to contact foreign communists, he and his colleagues in the Mantetsu did take part in some anti-government activities.

Hiradate Toshio has supported Nishizawa's claims and lamented the fact that writers have never covered this aspect of the Yokohama Incident. He told Nakamura that he and his colleagues in the Tokyo offices of the Mantetsu were strongly anti-fascist and had committed small acts of resistance that amounted to "guerilla warfare" against the state. He also revealed that he had admitted while under interrogation that he and some of the others were communists. He had assumed that Hosokawa Karoku, a Marxist theorist, was a fellow communist and described Hosokawa as such to the Kanagawa Police. He did not know that Hosokawa viewed himself as a democrat and had been denying allegations that he was a communist. Hiradate later regretted being so indiscreet, but concluded that it did not really matter what anyone said because the Police simply twisted all statements to suit their purposes. For example, when he had firmly denied participating in any organized leftist party movement, the police response was something to the effect of "you go outside

---

6. Nakamura, *Yokohama jiken no hitobito*, 18.
7. Nakamura, *Yokohama jiken no hitobito*, 99.

for walks, right? Well, if a communist exercises, that can be considered a 'communist movement.'"⁸

In the November 1943 edition of the *Tokkō geppō*, the Kanagawa Police claimed that leftists had infiltrated government or semi-governmental bodies.⁹ They referred to the Soviet Research Group and observed that three of its members—Hiradate, Nishizawa, and Nishio Chūjirō—were Mantetsu employees whereas another, Masuda Naohiko, was a Soviet specialist connected with a number of ministries and government-affiliated organizations. The Police observed that these individuals had used their research to camouflage leftist activities and had taken advantage of their official status and their access to government documents and short-wave broadcast equipment to collect information on Japan and the Soviet Union. They also claimed that Masuda was scheduled to go to the Soviet Union as a Foreign Ministry courier and that Group members were making plans for him to receive Comintern funds and pass on information on conditions in Japan during his trip. Finally, the Police described how Group members tried to protect the Soviet Union and prevent a possible Japanese attack by convincing high-ranking officials of the Soviet Union's military superiority.

Like the Kawadas and Nishizawa, Hiradate indicated that not all of the charges were baseless. While he did not admit that he or the other members of the Soviet Research Group were involved in spying or that they attempted to contact the Comintern, Hiradate insisted that he did try to protect the Soviet Union. During his interview with Nakamura he detailed his activities in support of the Soviet Union. In the late 1930s he was assigned to the North China (Hopeh) Office of the Mantetsu. According to Hiradate, he had worked on studies of the Soviet economic and military strength commissioned by the Kwantung Army, and in his reports he emphasized the military strength of the Soviet Union in order to restrain any ambitions to wage war against that country. In 1940, moreover, he resigned his position in the North China Office and returned to Japan because, as he explained to Nakamura, he wanted to avoid assisting the military police in interrogating captured Russian spies.¹⁰

He observed that he was nevertheless able to continue his efforts to influence military planning by joining the Soviet Research Group. The Group organized weekly meetings with members of the Army and Navy General Staff in order to discuss conditions in the Soviet Union. Ever fearful that the Japanese Army might turn northward in response to difficulties in making a

---

8. Nakamura, *Yokohama jiken no hitobito*, 87, 81.
9. *Tokkō geppō*, November 1943, 11-14.
10. Nakamura, *Yokohama jiken no hitobito*, 82, 74, 76.

southward advance, Hiradate and the others once again worked to prevent a possible Soviet-Japanese conflict by trying to convince General Staff officers of the Soviets' military and economic strength.

The details of Hiradate's activities cannot, unfortunately, be completely verified. Although the Kwantung Army had conducted investigations of the military strength of the Soviet Union, there is nothing to prove that Hiradate himself had participated in these studies. One of his Mantetsu colleagues has credited him with strengthening the theoretical basis of Mantetsu Soviet Research. But it appears that the Kwantung Army asked for the participation of the Mantetsu's Soviet Research Office in studies of the resistance capacity of the Soviet Union around 1941.[11] At that time, Hiradate was working in the Tokyo offices of the Mantetsu. In the *Tokkō geppō*, moreover, there is no mention of General Staff officers attending the Soviet Research Group's meetings. Nakamura Tomoko attempts to account for this by suggesting that the Police had to cover up the matter because the Army and Navy would not have permitted any implication of their senior officers in a communist conspiracy.[12]

Still, Hiradate was associating with individuals and participating in groups that placed him in danger of being arrested. During his interview he stated that he could have been implicated in more than one leftist incident through his friends and colleagues. The Metropolitan Police Board, besides arresting Hosokawa Karoku, had already arrested another close friend in connection with the Cabinet Planning Board Incident (Kikakuin jiken) of 1941. Hiradate feared being implicated in the Planning Board Incident because he had written letters of recommendation for this particular friend. The Metropolitan Police who were investigating the Planning Board Incident claimed that leftist sympathizers among official circles were attempting to recruit communists within the government in an effort to subvert society from within. On top of this, the military police had arrested many of Hiradate's other colleagues during the so-called Mantetsu Incident (Mantetsu jiken) of 1942. When he was arrested on May 1943, Hiradate was only surprised that he was being taken in by the Kanagawa Prefectural Police and not by the Kwantung Army Military Police or the Tokyo Metropolitan Police Board because of his association with suspects in the Mantetsu and Cabinet Planning Board Incidents.[13]

---

11. Satō Takeo, "Mantetsu no Soren chōsa," *Ajia keizai*, Vol. 28, No. 9 (September), 1987: 84.
12. Nakamura, *Yokohama jiken no hitobito*, 76.
13. Nakamura, *Yokohama jiken no hitobito*, 76-78.

Hiradate was correct in assuming that if he had not been arrested in the Yokohama Incident, he could have been arrested in connection with other incidents. He was already known to the authorities, and both the civil and military police had been investigating his relationship to two communist spies, Nakanishi Kō and Ozaki Hotsumi. Ozaki Hotsumi, a respected China specialist and former adviser to Prince Konoe, was arrested as a Soviet spy in the Sorge Incident and executed in 1944 for treason. Police records reveal that, when questioned about his contacts and sources of information, Ozaki mentioned Hiradate and other members of the World Conditions Research Committee [*Sekai jijō chōsa iinkai*] (not to be confused with the World Economic Research Association).[14] Ozaki had been the Secretary-General of this Committee and Hiradate had been its manager. Ozaki found discussions with Hiradate and other Committee members helpful in improving his understanding of world trends, and he admitted to the police that he often reported the views of the members to Richard Sorge, the leader of the spy ring.

An official military police document on the activities of Japanese Communists in Manchuria, the *Zai-Man Nikkei kyōsanshugi undō*, reveals that the Kwantung Army Military Police were equally suspicious of Hiradate. The Military Police believed that he was responsible for recruiting leftists into the Mantetsu. They noted that more and more individuals with skills in leftist research began to be assigned to the Shanghai Office of the Mantetsu after Hiradate entered the Office in 1937. They also suspected that Hiradate and two other Mantetsu employees who would be arrested in the Yokohama Incident had assisted the Chinese Communist Party spy Nakanishi Kō with his research. Finally, the Military Police observed that while Hiradate was on a trip to Manchuria sometime prior to his arrest, members of the Xinjing Office of the Mantetsu asked him to give a talk on conditions in Japan. During the talk, Hiradate reportedly described the Japanese authorities as demoralized, pessimistic about the country's ability to wage war, and unable to cope with the crisis in Japanese-American relations.[15]

Almost all of the researchers arrested in the Yokohama Incident were employed in ministries and government-affiliated offices or had belonged to organizations patronized by political notables. Many members of the so-called Political Economic Research Group, for example, were alumni of the prestigious Shōwa Academy. The Academy, an offshoot of Prince Konoe

---

14. Miyanishi Yoshio, "Mantetsu chōsabu to Ozaki Hotsumi, Nakanishi Kō, Himori Torao I," *Ajia keizai*, Vol. 28, No. 7 (July), 1987: 54-55.
15. *Zai-Man Nikkei kyōsanshugi undō*, ed. Kwantung kempeitai shireibu (Tokyo: Gannandō shoten, Second Printing, 1969), 184, 223-24, 294.

Fumimaro's Showa Research Association, apparently attracted individuals from both extremes of the political spectrum. The November 1938 edition of the *Tokkō geppō* included in its section on "Nationalist (Agrarian) Movements" a report on the establishment of the Academy, and in this report the police observed that the ideological tendencies of members could not be clearly defined.[16]

Rightists nevertheless immediately condemned the Academy as "a breeding-ground for reds."[17] They recognized that the Shōwa Academy and Research Association provided something of a haven for Marxist thinkers and former thought control offenders. The Academy's founders hoped to cultivate the next generation of intellectual and political leaders and were rather sympathetic toward the plight of young people who had been expelled from school for studying Marxism or for participating in leftist activities. They argued that these youths deserved a second chance and opened up the Academy to them so that they could resume their studies.

According to the August 1944 *Tokkō geppō*, the Political Economic Research Group was organized in October 1941, following the disbanding of the Academy. Its members included individuals employed in the East Asia [*Daitōa shō*] and Communications [*Teishinshō*] Ministries as well as important industries, such as Furukawa Electric [*Furukawa denkō*], Japan Steel [*Nittetsu honsha*], Japan Copper [*Nihon akagane*], and the Japan Sugar Industry Combine [*Nihon tōgyō rengōkai*]. The Kanagawa Prefectural Police claimed that Group members had secured positions in government offices and industries important for the war effort in order to carry out their illegal activities. Members took out documents and other information from their places of work in order to assess the nation's war capacity and determine the best means of fostering a postwar revolution.

The Police observed that the documents handled by Group members were highly confidential, and they charged one member, Mori Kazuo, with violating both the Peace Preservation Law and the National Defense Security Law.[18] Mori, who was employed in the East Asia Ministry, removed a copy of the General Mobilization Plan of 1943 from the desk of his superior. During a search of Mori's house the Police discovered both the Mobilization Plan as well as a copy of JCP representative in Yenan Nosaka Sanzō's Declaration on the Suspension of the Comintern.

---

16. *Tokkō geppō*, November 1938, 54-57.
17. Muroga, *Shōwa juku*, 41.
18. "Mori Kazuo yōshin shūketsu kettei," *Yokohama jiken shiryōshū*, 60.

The Police described in detail some of the research presentations that took place during the Group's meetings. According to the Police, members got hold of a copy of "The Investigation of Productive Strength in 1942" and used it to illustrate how Japan's production of weapons was considerably lower than that of the United States. Members were also accused of stealing a copy of another highly confidential document, "The Present State of Steel and Iron Production" by Cabinet adviser Toyoda Sadao, and discussing at a March 1943 research meeting such matters as the rate of iron and steel production from 1926 to 1942, the production objective for iron and steel for 1943, and the allocation and volume of imported steel and ore. Data appeared to show that production had already reached its apex by 1938 and that Japan had to shift to lower-quality domestic raw materials because of the gradual shortage of transport ships and the consequent decrease in imports from China, Korea, and the South Seas. Police reported that Group members thus came to the conclusion that Japan had no hope of winning the War in view of its declining production level and was heading toward a domestic revolution.

Members of the Political Economic Research Group initially insisted that the Police had simply fabricated the charges against them.[19] However, decades after their release from custody in 1945, they began to admit that there was some truth to one of the police accusations: that is, they tried to assist the future Japan Communist Party by conducting research on the potential for a postwar revolution.

Katsube Gen was the first to make this disclosure or claim. Katsube observed that the researchers have refrained too long in discussing their role in the affair. In his essay, "My Yokohama Incident" [*Watakushi no "Yokohama jiken"*], he declared that the researchers should try to give a full account of their activities and help future generations arrive at a more complete understanding of the Incident.[20]

During the War Katsube had been employed as a researcher at Japan Steel and had learned about the Political Economic Research Group through his colleague, Takagi Kenjirō. Takagi told him that some former students of the Shōwa Academy had decided to meet secretly and study political history from the Meiji Restoration to the Russo-Japanese War under the guidance of Hosokawa Karoku and others. Katsube noted that many of the Group members were former thought control offenders who were well-versed in Marxist theory and that all were employed in important organizations. They thus had access

---

19. "Kōjutsusho, Katsube Gen," *Yokohama jiken shiryōshū*, 89.
20. Katsube Gen, "Watakushi no 'Yokohama jiken,'" *Undōshi kenkyū 3* (Tokyo: San'ichi shobō, 1979), 8, 6, 13.

to confidential official documents which revealed that it would become increasingly difficult for Japan to continue the War. Confident that Japan's defeat was inevitable, Group members began to collect information that could be useful to future revolutionaries. Katsube, for example, studied the labour structure within certain industries in the hopes of determining which section of the working class possessed the most developed revolutionary consciousness.

During their interviews with Nakamura Tomoko, other members of the Political Economic Research Group corroborated many of Katsube's statements. Like Katsube, they stated that the journalists' explanations of the affair cannot be applied to their Group. They denied that any of the individuals arrested in the Incident attempted to re-establish the Japan Communist Party or contact foreign communists, but admitted that the *Tokkō geppō* description of their Group's activities was more or less accurate. That is, Political Economic Research Group members had stolen government documents and conducted studies on the potential for a postwar revolution. Members also told Nakamura that they had been in contact with some of the other suspects or individuals questioned by the Kanagawa Police. Takagi Kenjirō stated that while members did not believe that Hosokawa Karoku was a true Marxist, they had once visited him to discuss their studies. Itai Shōsaku recalled that he and another person had also called upon Kazami Akira to urge him to use his political connections to help bring an end to the War.[21]

Besides Takagi and Itai, Nakamura also interviewed Yamaguchi Kenzō. Yamaguchi pointed out that he was not always in agreement with other Group members and frequently argued with Katsube Gen over the orthodox Marxist view that supported Japan's defeat. He explained that he could not help but regret Japan's defeat because it would result in tremendous suffering and hardship for the people. Yamaguchi also criticized the others for preferring to stay locked away in their research rooms rather than going out among the workers. In Yamaguchi's opinion, they could have done more to resist the state, and another Group member has expressed similar regrets that he and the others did not actually attempt to re-establish the Japan Communist Party and live up to all the charges against them.

The researchers' acts of resistance were small, clandestine and probably ineffectual. However, the discovery of these groups and their activities could have only alarmed the wartime authorities who magnified every act of resistance to gigantic proportions and who were becoming increasingly concerned about leftist sympathizers employed in government offices and important industries. The Yokohama Incident as well as other wartime leftist

---

21. Nakamura, *Yokohama jiken no hitobito*, 128, 140-43.

incidents thus confirmed official suspicions that former thought control offenders could not be trusted. A comparison of the affair with other thought control incidents of the period clearly reveals that the wartime authorities were carrying out what was effectively a purge of former offenders from government and society.

THE YOKOHAMA INCIDENT AND OTHER WARTIME INCIDENTS

There are a number of similarities between the Yokohama Incident and two other major wartime incidents, the Mantetsu and Cabinet Planning Board Incidents. They were all, in large measure, trumped-up cases involving former leftist thought control offenders and consisted of a number of separate groups that had no substantial connection to each other. All three Incidents began with the investigation of a few suspected leftist activists, some of whom have later admitted to participating in certain illegal movements, but rapidly developed into the wholesale arrests of all associates with a prior record of thought control offenses.

The Cabinet Planning Board Incident grew out of an investigation of a leftist study group in the Keihin area of Kanagawa Prefecture. The July 1939 *Tokkō geppō* described this Keihin Group as an illegal organization which sought to re-establish the Japan Communist Party and recruit members from among labourers in munitions factories.[22] Police explained that Group members hoped to make industrial workers the main force in their movement because they believed that the Japan Communist Party had erred in relying too much on the limited support of the intellectual class. The Group reportedly succeeded in gaining influence among the workers of some factories and sought to use these individuals to infiltrate labour organizations such as the Industrial Patriotic Societies [*Sangyō hōkokukai*].

The Metropolitan Police Board which was in charge of investigating the Planning Board Incident observed that the Keihin Group had been established by the brothers of Nakanishi Kō. Nakanishi Kō, who was arrested by the Police Board on suspicion of spying for the Chinese Communist Party, was not a formal member of the Keihin Group, but had recruited a young junior official in the Cabinet Planning Board, Shiba Hiroshi, to act as the Group's "tutor." In their reports the Metropolitan Police accused Shiba as assisting members in conducting studies of how the wartime system was promoting conditions favourable for a revolution.

---

22. *Tokkō geppō*, July 1939, 6-11.

Both the Yokohama and Cabinet Planning Board Incidents involved groups that were accused of using their research to promote a revolution and/or of attempting to recruit workers in industries important for the war effort. Moreover, like the Yokohama Incident's researchers, members of the Cabinet Planning Board Incident's Keihin Group have claimed that there was some basis to the charges against them. Shiba Hiroshi, for example, has admitted that the police account of his Group's activities was not completely fabricated and that members did indeed try to mobilize workers into a communist, antiwar movement.[23] Shiba has insisted that he had been a communist activist from the time he left high school and had put all his energy into organizing the Keihin Group.

In his account of the Cabinet Planning Board Incident, Shiba revealed issues not covered in the police reports and explained that some of the errors in these reports could be attributed to false statements that he made during his interrogation. The Keihin Group was in contact with two communist spies, Nakanishi Kō and Ozaki Hotsumi. Members had asked Ozaki to find them someone to guide their studies. Shiba recalled that Ozaki had considered asking fellow Shōwa Research Association member, Hosokawa Karoku, to guide the members' research, but decided that the Group needed a more youthful teacher. Police, however, never discovered anything linking Ozaki or Hosokawa to the Keihin Group.[24]

Among the materials used by the Keihin Group were Noro Eitarō's *The History of the Development of Japanese Capitalism* [*Nihon shihonshugi hattatsushi*][25] and the Comintern's Declaration on the Popular Front. According to Shiba, the Group acquired copies of the banned Comintern Declaration through the so-called Nagoya Marine Communists Group, which was in contact with the American Communist Party. It was the Aichi Prefectural Police who discovered both the Nagoya Marine Communists Group and the Keihin Group. However, it was the Metropolitan Police Board that arrested Shiba and the other members of the Keihin Group.[26]

---

23. Nakanishi Ko, *Chugoku kakumei no arashi no naka de* (Tokyo: Aoki shoten, 1974), 164-65.
24. "Kikakuin jiken," *Shōwashi no tennō 18* (Tokyo: Yomiuri shimbunsha, 1972), 11, 19, 37-38. A major source for information on this Incident.
25. Nakamura, *Yokohama jiken no hitobito*, 23. This work by Noro was the same book which Kawada Hisashi of the Yokohama Incident brought back with him from the United States and which supposedly made him the target of police suspicions.
26. "Kikakuin jiken," 30-2. It is possible that the Police Board violated the jurisdiction of the Aichi Prefectural Police in arresting the Keihin Group, and in its reports on the case, no mention is made of the Aichi Police's involvement or of the Keihin Group's connection to the Nagoya Marine Communists Group.

The Metropolitan Police arrested Shiba in October 1938, and its officers initially confined their questions to his role in the Keihin Group. But a year and a half after arresting him the Police began asking Shiba about his involvement in the "Village Home" [*Mura no ie*] Research Group which had been organized by some junior officials in the Cabinet Planning Board. The Police claimed that members of the Village Home Group had adopted the Comintern's the Popular Front strategy and were using organizations such as the Shōwa Research Association as sanctuaries for conducting research into socialist policies. Shiba admitted that he had hoped to use the Village Home Group in creating a "bureaucratic Popular Front," an anti-fascist union of junior and senior officials from various government agencies. However, he had been able to arrange only two or three research meetings because he had to spend most of his time on the activities on the Keihin Group.[27]

These junior officials in the Village Home Group had received permission from their superiors to hold their research meetings. Shiba observed that while members of the Village Home Group may have shared his opposition to the War, they did not share his ambition to establish a "bureaucratic Popular Front." One former member insists that his interest in the Village Home Group was strictly scholarly, that neither he nor the others were involved in a conspiracy, and that Shiba was the only political activist among them. Although he eventually disclosed during his interrogation the names of two members of the Village Home Group, Shiba has insisted that he did so only because he was confident that the police would not find anything suspicious about these individuals. He had apparently never imagined that the Metropolitan Police would have been able to implicate officials in the Cabinet Planning Board in their investigation of the Keihin Group.

In both the Yokohama and the Cabinet Planning Board Incidents, the police were able to expand their investigations through the discovery of some photographs. Shiba Hiroshi had cleared his apartment of books on illegal subjects and anything else that he thought could incriminate him. However, he had failed to dispose of a few photographs of himself and other Cabinet Planning Board employees taken during some parties. With these photographs the Metropolitan Police were able to link members of the Keihin Group, communists agitating among factory workers, to officials attached to one of the most important government organizations in Japan. Established in 1937 and consisting of influential bureaucrats from various ministries, the Cabinet Planning Board was meant to act as an "economic general staff" for the government.

---

27. "Kikakuin jiken," 35, 40, 18, 22-23, 56, 17, 44, 6-9.

In the March 1941 edition of *Tokkō geppō* the Metropolitan Police Board announced that it had uncovered the existence of two leftist organizations within the Cabinet Planning Board, the so-called Junior Officials Group and the Senior Officials Group.[28] Both Groups reportedly had attempted to take advantage of the present emergency situation to get officials to back certain policies which could pave the way for a communist revolution. According to the Police, both of these Junior and Senior Officials supported the establishment of a planned economic structure because they believed that the imposition of controls, without any fundamental alteration of capitalism, would further aggravate existing economic problems and promote the conditions for a revolution.

In the February 1942 edition of *Tokkō geppō*, the Police observed that the investigation of the Cabinet Planning Board Incident clearly revealed that communist activities were becoming more and more diverse, and to illustrate their point, they described the two-pronged nature of the suspects' attack on the state.[29] That is, while one group, the Keihin Group, attempted to bring about "change from below" by agitating among workers, the other groups, the Junior and Senior Officials Groups, encouraged internal collapse or "change from above."

The Senior Officials Group consisted of many high-ranking officials, some of whom had already left the Planning Board at the time of their arrests. Consequently, along with Planning Board employees, the Police arrested as suspected members of the Senior Officials Group individuals belonging to various ministries, the Imperial Rule Assistance Association, and the South Manchurian Railway Company. Among those arrested was Wada Hiroō who was singled out as the conspiracy's ringleader. Police claimed that Wada, who had been a long-time official in the Agricultural Ministry prior to his appointment to the Planning Board, enjoyed some influence over the recruitment of personnel and had helped many of the suspects obtain their positions.

Police also drew attention to the fact that the majority of the suspects in the Cabinet Planning Board Incident were former thought control offenders. They observed that these individuals, along with other communists, had been infiltrating state organs since 1935. Officials reportedly needed assistance in drawing up plans to economically prepare the country for war and so, recruited a huge number of private sector specialists simply on the basis of personal recommendation. The Metropolitan Police declared that such weaknesses in

---

28. *Tokkō geppō*, March 1941, 4-5.
29. *Tokkō geppō*, February 1942, 4-38.

security could not be tolerated, and they demanded that in the future officials conduct more thorough investigations of the ideological histories of potential state employees.

One specialist in the history of Japanese thought control states that the Cabinet Planning Board Incident, which the Police described as "unprecedented," had a great impact on wartime officials.[30] The Planning Board Incident seemed to prove that communists had successfully infiltrated the highest levels of government. Soon after, in 1942 and 1943, both the Kanagawa Prefectural Police and the Kwantung Army Military Police began investigating the activities of former thought control offenders employed as researchers in official or government-affiliated organizations.

The Kwantung Army Military Police argued that suspects in the Mantetsu Incident, believing that policies of economic modernization could be used to foster conditions for a revolution, had tried to undermine the state through their studies of ways to increase agricultural and industrial production in Japan, Manchukuo, and China.[31] The Mantetsu Incident occurred in 1942 and evolved out of an earlier case, the so-called Cooperatives Incident of 1940-41.

There was a movement for agricultural cooperatives in northern Manchuria, and some of the movement's leaders were employed in the Mantetsu's Investigative Bureau. One individual arrested in the Mantetsu Incident believes that the Kwantung Army took action against the cooperatives movement in response to pressure from its rural supporters.[32] The leaders of the cooperatives movement argued that food production could be greatly increased if a greater share of the profits was given to the peasantry instead of the landlords. The Kwantung Army, however, was dependent on landlords and capitalists for support in North Manchuria and was forced to concoct an incident to suppress the movement in order to appease these elements. From October to November 1941, about fifty individuals in the cooperatives movement, the Concordia Society [kyōwakai], the *Manshū hyōron* [Manchurian Review], and Mantetsu's Investigative Bureau were arrested and charged with trying to promote a revolution.

After interrogating suspects in the case involving the cooperatives, the Kwantung Army Military Police began to expand their investigation and

---

30. Okudaira, *Chian ijihō shōshi*, 231.
31. Yamaguchi Hiroichi, "'Mantetsu chōsabu jiken' (1942-45 nen)," *Ajia keizai*, Vol. 29, No. 11 (November), 1988: 68-69, 80.
32. Ishidō Kiyotomo, "Mantetsu chōsabu to 'Marukushugi,'" *Undōshi kenkyū 2* (Tokyo: San'ichi shobō, 1978), 13-14.

eventually arrested thirty more employees in the Mantetsu's Investigative Bureau. The first round of arrests in what would become known as the Mantetsu Incident took place in September 1942. However, the Military Police soon discovered that it would be difficult to incriminate these individuals without embarrassing the Army.[33] Those apprehended in the first round of arrests were senior Mantetsu employees who dealt directly with high-ranking Army officers. Accusations that these employees had organized a leftist conspiracy could create the impression that Kwantung Army personnel had been duped into assisting communist activities. Consequently, the Military Police had to carry out a second round of arrests in order to create a leadership for their fabricated incident.

By 1942 the Japanese authorities had grown increasingly suspicious of former thought control offenders, and for the Kwantung Military Police, who were eager to compete with their civil counterparts in the area of thought control, such individuals working in the Mantetsu were easy targets for arrests. The Military Police were rather inexperienced in investigating thought control cases. Fortunately for them, their suspects were knowledgeable about Marxism, official notions about communist conspiracies, and the procedures taken in investigating thought offenses. Former thought control offenders, in other words, had the experience to teach their captors how to construct a thought control incident. The Military Police even credited in their reports one suspect, Suzuki Kōhei, with greatly assisting them in their investigation.

Suzuki, a former thought control offender who had resigned from the Mantetsu's Investigative Bureau in 1940, presumably divulged the names of sixty individuals. He claimed that leftist elements in the Mantetsu were promoting Marxist-based studies and making preparations for a revolution in Japan. Six hundred and twenty two essays which had appeared in such publications as *Kaizō, Chūō kōron* and the *Mantetsu chōsa geppō* were collected as evidence against the suspects. The Military Police believed that many of the suspects had written these essays under aliases, and they called on Suzuki to scrutinize them for clues as to their authorship. Suzuki, moreover, supposedly provided the guidelines for cross-examining the suspects, and those arrested in the Mantetsu Incident have claimed that they were often forced to rewrite their so-called "confessions" until they conformed to Suzuki's set model.[34]

---

33. Yamada Goichi, *Mantetsu chōsabu* (Tokyo: Nihon keizai shimbunsha, 1977), 165-66.
34. John Young, *The Research Activities of the South Manchurian Railway Company, 1907-1934: A History and Bibliography* (New York: Columbia University, 159-60; Ishido, "Mantetsu chōsabu to 'Marukushugi,'" 17-18.

In his memoirs, *Life Along the South Manchurian Railway*, Itō Takeo recalled being told by high-ranking military officers on two different occasions that the Mantetsu Incident was part of Prime Minister Tōjō's plan for the preventive arrests of all suspect intellectuals. Shortly before being apprehended in the second round of arrests, Itō encountered a certain general who explained that

> Tōjō is aiming more and more toward defeat in this war, and if we are defeated, left-wing intellectuals will probably cause riots. He's arresting them all in advance as a defensive measure. It's not that they're left-wing but that they're intellectuals that makes them dangerous. About 50,000 people over as wide an area as possible will be apprehended. In short, the plan is to arrest 50,000 intellectuals from Japan and overseas. He took aim from the start at that den of left-wing intellectuals in the Research Department of the SMR.[35]

CCP spy Nakanishi Kō has presented a similar explanation for the Yokohama Incident, which he described as the culmination of the wartime campaign against leftist intellectuals:

> Ozaki [Hotsumi of the Sorge Incident] was arrested. I was arrested. About a hundred people in the Investigative Department [of the Mantetsu] were arrested. And in the so-called Yokohama Incident virtually all remaining intellectuals were arrested. . . . The Ozaki Incident was merely the tip of the iceberg of repression directed against the whole intelligentsia by the wartime system.[36]

More than one individual has observed a link between some of the wartime thought control incidents. Certain contemporary witnesses, such as the political critic Iwabuchi Tatsuo, had reportedly suggested that the Yokohama Incident came about because the police believed that not all of the members of the Sorge spy ring had been apprehended. Independent journalist Nakamura Tomoko, moreover, has observed some interesting similarities between the two Incidents and has proposed that the Kanagawa Prefectural Police had intended

---

35. Takeo Itō, *Life Along the South Manchurian Railway: The Memoirs of Itō Takeo*, trans. Joshua Fogel (New York: M.E. Sharpe, Inc., 1988), 190-91.
36. Chalmers Johnson, *An Instance of Treason: Ozaki Hotsumi and the Sorge Spy Ring*, revised edition (Stanford: Stanford University Press, 1990), 236.

to create a "second" Sorge Incident.[37] Both Incidents, she notes, involved the return to Japan of suspected American Communist Party members (Kitabayashi Tomo and Kawada Hisashi); both involved well-known China specialists who were connected with the Mantetsu as well as the Shōwa Research Association, the so-called "Konoe brain-trust" (Ozaki Hotsumi and Hosokawa Karoku); and both involved former Justice Minister Kazami Akira and, according to the postwar Japan Communist Party, suspected police collaborator Itō Ritsu.

In the prewar period, Itō Ritsu was constantly in and out of police custody for participating in leftist activities. He was arrested three times between the years 1939 and 1943. In August 1939, while out on bail, he had entered the Mantetsu and became friends with a number of the researchers who would later be arrested in the Yokohama Incident. Soviet Research Group member Hiradate Toshio, for example, helped get Itō part-time work as a translator for the Foreign Ministry after he was again released on bail in June 1942. In the immediate postwar period, Itō became an influential member of the Japan Communist Party Secretariat. However, rumours emerged that he had divulged information about fellow communists to the prewar police in exchange for being released from custody. It was argued that Itō had provided the Metropolitan Police with the tip that allowed it to uncover the entire Sorge spy ring and thus had sacrificed even his friend, the Soviet spy Ozaki Hotsumi. Consequently, in September 1953 he was expelled from the Party for having betrayed to the prewar police hundreds of individuals including, not only the suspects in the Sorge Incident but also, those arrested in the Yokohama Incident.[38]

Still, others trying to detect a connection between the wartime leftist incidents have observed that many of those arrested were members of the Shōwa Research Association. They contend that critics of the Association condemned the organization as a front for communist activities and even after the Association had disbanded, continued to accuse former members of capitalizing on the domestic crisis caused by the war to promote world revolution. The wartime incidents, the argument goes, were the result of relentless attacks on the Association and its affiliated organizations.[39]

The wartime incidents were part of a movement. But instead of being against some specific organization, it was more against a specific type of

---

37. Nakamura, *Yokohama jiken no hitobito*, 268, 272.
38. Kuroda, *Yokohama jiken*, 124. Whereas many of the researchers arrested in the Yokohama Incident who were associates of Itō believe that he was innocent of the JCP accusations, journalists such as Mimasaka Tarō support the argument that Itō was a police informant.
39. Murata Katsumi, "Shōwa kenkyūkai ni taisuru hyōka," *Tōyō kenkyū*, No. 9, October 1964: 60-61, 69.

individual. The police authorities in charge of investigating all three incidents soon set their sights on former leftist thought control offenders who occupied responsible positions in the public and private sectors. The civil and military police used any means to incriminate former offenders and, by 1942, had little trouble justifying their removal. Those arrested in the wartime incidents were in effect the victims of the authorities' desire to reverse an earlier policy of official patronage of former offenders. Whereas officials had even sponsored the employment of former offenders in the 1930s, they felt compelled to take measures against such individuals during the Pacific War.

CHANGES IN THE OFFICIAL ATTITUDE TOWARD FORMER THOUGHT CONTROL OFFENDERS

The persecution of political or ethnic groups as security risks is not uncommon during periods of national crisis, and Japan was certainly not alone in carrying out a purge of so-called undesirables. But even in periods of peace, the Japanese state maintained an elaborate system of thought control dedicated to the suppression of unorthodox ideas and revolutionary activity. Given this, one needs to ask why officials allowed themselves to be placed in a situation where they would have to purge ideologically suspect individuals from government offices. How, in other words, did former leftist thought control offenders acquire such influential positions in the first place?

The answer lies in a change in official attitudes toward thought control offenders, which was marked by the adoption in the early 1930s of the *Tenkō* policy of ideologically reforming offenders. Officials may have believed that the achievement of the nation's military and political aims necessitated the mobilization of all resources, even the intellectual skills of one-time opponents of the state. Moreover, because they themselves had been introduced to Marxism during university and maintained some respect for it as a research tool, officials may have been willing to gamble on the possibility of rehabilitating offenders.

During the Taishō and very early Shōwa periods, Marxism and liberalism were more freely debated in the universities. It would be hard to imagine that the young men who attended these schools, many of whom later occupied important positions in government, business and society, were unaffected by their introduction to the ideology and its view of conditions and development. Marxism had a tremendous impact on the intellectual class in prewar Japan, and many officials, while at the same time condemning it as the ideology of traitors, believed that Marxist analyses were the most scientific and accurate. Many of the so-called new or renovationist military officers and bureaucrats, for example, made no effort to conceal their respect for Marxism. In 1936, the magazine *Bungei shunjū* published a round-table discussion in which some young, renovationist bureaucrats candidly spoke of the benefits arising from the knowledge of such ideas.[40] These bureaucrats believed that Marxism had bestowed upon them a critical mind and thus helped them to adapt to and constructively confront social changes. They observed that the expulsion of gifted Marxist scholars from the universities had resulted in the production of graduates with inferior critical skills and little knowledge of society.

Many members of the military shared this high regard for the research skills of Marxists and were often even more willing to accept former thought control offenders into their organizations. During the 1930s, the Kwantung Army-sponsored Mantetsu was something of a "leftist paradise," where employees enjoyed a high salary and freedom to conduct their research. In the words of historian Joshua Fogel, the Mantetsu and the Army offered Marxist scholars and former leftists their patronage and protection:

> After the outbreak of the Sino-Japanese War in July 1937 ... the military was becoming desperate, as it now needed large-scale integrated research for long-term planning. To that end, the Research Department [Investigative Bureau of the Mantetsu] underwent an enormous expansion from early 1939. The scholars brought onto the staff in the late 1930s were largely left-wing, socialists and Communists. ...
>
> The SMR [South Manchurian Railway] research organs welcomed them with open arms, especially because the SMR was expanding and because these people, politics aside, were trained in research and had a "scientific" approach.[41]

The military police in Manchukuo had heard that more and more leftists were entering the Mantetsu and Concordia Society. But until the summer of 1940, they dismissed complaints about this as "malicious rumours aimed at causing discord among the Japanese in Manchukuo, slanders made by individuals envious of the advancement of converts."[42]

---

40. "Seinen kanshi shain wa nani o kangaeteiru ka zadankai," *Bungei shunjū*, No. 14, July 1936: 216-40.
41. Joshua Fogel, "Introduction: Itō Takeo and the Research Work of the South Manchurian Railway Company," *Life Along the South Manchurian Railway*, xv-xvi.
42. Yamada, *Mantetsu chōsabu*, 155.

The prewar authorities had developed a rather complex attitude toward Marxism and Marxists. The vast majority of Japanese Marxists and revolutionaries were not downtrodden peasants or industrial workers. They had attended high school or university in the 1910s and 1920s and had the same middle or upper class background as those who entered the ranks of government. Officials in the 1930s were probably more receptive to ideas of reforming communists because they believed that these individuals possessed useful skills and could easily resume a respectable place in society thanks to their family and educational background. The *Tenkō* policy emerged in response to the new respectability of subversives. "It is doubtful," one scholar has surmised, "that the policy of *Tenkō* would have been pursued as assiduously-and so successfully-if all those arrested as communists had been lower-class workers and Meiji-style renegade intellectuals."[43]

In 1931, when *Tenkō* or ideological conversion was officially accepted as the method for handling leftist thought control offenders, many individuals in the government seemed prepared to view leftists as troublesome, intellectually confused eccentrics who could be handled like juvenile delinquents. Police officers in charge of administering *Tenkō* were called upon to use psychological tricks rather than physical force in getting thought offenders to recant.[44] They would attempt to win the confidence of the offender and get him to talk about his family and friends. The aim of these discussions was to make the offender realize that his political activities had caused nothing but heartache for his loved ones. Methods of emotional manipulation included calling in family members or some respected figure to assist in persuading the offender to abandon communism.

From around 1931 until about 1941, when the Cabinet Planning Board Incident supposedly exposed a communist conspiracy at the highest levels of government, a countless number of offenders enjoyed the benefits of a policy that was aimed at helping them resume a useful place in society. Officials set up various organizations for the purpose of helping former offenders become "proper" citizens: individuals who would endeavour to express their gratitude for the Emperor's benevolence toward them. They sponsored the "Imperial Renewal Society," under the management of former leftist offender Kobayashi Morito, which was to provide ideological and social aid. Moreover, in 1936, the Thought Criminals' Protection and Supervision Law established offices to help former offenders find employment. Through these offices many individuals were able to obtain jobs in private, civil, and military research

---

43. Dewitt Smith II, *Japan's First Student Radicals*, 268.
44. Steinhoff, "Tenkō," 141-47.

organizations. By 1938 these centres had assisted about 13,000 people and the number of recidivists was a low one percent.[45]

The *Tenkō* policy embodied the confidence of officials that a "Japanese communist" would always be more "Japanese" (an adherent of the national orthodoxy) than a "communist" (a follower of Marxism, the Comintern and the Japan Communist Party). This confidence seemed to be vindicated in 1933 when imprisoned communist leaders, Sano Manabu and Nabeyama Sadachika, publicly announced their conversion and prompted a flood of recantations by other captured leftists. Still, the policy was not greeted with complete enthusiasm or strictly adhered to by all police officers.

As the beating deaths of leftist writer Kobayashi Takiji in 1933 and JCP Central Committee Chairman Noro Eitarō in 1934 reveal, the adoption of *Tenkō* did not put an end to police torture. Thought control offenders had no guarantee that they would not fall into the hands of police officers who were willing to disregard directives against the use of physical force. There are, moreover, indications that thought control officers under the Home Ministry maintained qualms about the policy and did not really commit themselves to it until the latter half of 1934. Elise Tipton, a specialist on the prewar police, notes that Justice Ministry officials complained that the *Tokkō* hindered the process of reforming thought control offenders and that the Home Ministry was eventually forced to order the police to stop badgering former offenders at their jobs and "avoid causing the suspect to be discharged from his position."[46] Thought control police officers may have never completely abandoned misgivings about the wisdom of the *Tenkō* policy and the trustworthiness of former offenders. As a consequence, many officers would have been more than enthusiastic about apprehending such individuals when their superiors resumed a less tolerant attitude toward former offenders.

Scholars have observed that increased official efforts to reintegrate former offenders back into society took place during what could be called the Konoe Era (1937-1941). Although he became the spokesman for the ruling elite's fears about hidden communist conspirators during the Pacific War, at the height of his political career in the 1930s, Konoe Fumimaro was known for his close relations with prominent Marxist intellectuals and was something of a patron for many former thought control offenders. Leftist thinkers and former offenders were free to enter the Shōwa Research Association and Academy,

---

45. Tsurumi Shunsuke, "Dai ippen no yōyaku," *Kyōdō kenkyū Tenkō*, Vol. 1, 30; Fujita Shozo, "Shōwa hachi nen o chūshin to suru tenkō no jōkyō," *Kyōdō kenkyū Tenkō*, Vol. 1, 47, 49; Mitchell, *Thought Control in Prewar Japan*, 135-36, 139.

46. Tipton, *The Japanese Police State*, 118-19.

and a conspicuous number of them participated in Konoe's New Order Movement [*shintaisei undō*].[47] However, even during the so-called Konoe Era, there were signs that officials were beginning to adopt a harder stance toward any association or group involved with leftists. Following Japan's unofficial war with China in 1937, they began to clamp down on the legal left. They targeted organizations such as the National Council of Japanese Labour Unions [*Nihon rōdō kumiai hyōgikai*] and arrested left-leaning Diet Member Katō Kanjū and Tokyo Municipal Assemblyman Suzuki Mosaburō.[48]

Less willing to make distinctions between theoretical Marxists and communist revolutionaries, the Japanese authorities were gradually becoming less complacent about the reliability of former leftist thought control offenders. From 1937 those in charge of handling ideological conversion became more exacting in analyzing the ideas of each individual offender and adopted a more demanding criteria for determining conversion. It was no longer enough that former offenders pledged themselves not to participate in leftist political activities or declared their rejection of Marxism. They were now required to somehow demonstrate their patriotism and loyalty to the imperial system. That is, former offenders were expected to show that they were imbued with the "Japanese spirit." Nevertheless, ironically, even officials involved in thought control had no set ideas about the Japanese spirit.[49]

Beginning in the late 1930s, officials became less willing to consider former offenders who could not publicly support Japan's war aims as true converts and took to viewing them as partially or "semi-converted." Figures published by the Ministry of Justice in March 1943 reveal that, under the new, more demanding criteria, there was no great difference in the number of converts to individuals who could only be termed semi-converts.

---

47. Itō Takashi, "Kyū sayokujin no 'shintaisei' undō," *Shōwaki no shakai undō*, ed. Kindai Nihon kenkyūkai (Tokyo: Yamakawa shuppansha, 1983), 260.
48. Mitchell, *Janus-Faced Justice*, 97.
49. Tsurumi, "Dai ippen no yōyaku," 30; Mitchell, *Thought Control in Prewar Japan*, 137, Okudaira, *Chian ijihō shōshi*, 222-23. Okudaira Yasuhiro quotes Justice Minister Moriyama Ichirō who observed in 1936 that while the essential purpose of thought guidance was to lead individuals back to the Japanese spirit, it was difficult to provide an exact definition of this spirit.

IDEOLOGICAL CONVERTS AMONG THE PROSECUTED

	Communists	Anarchists	Others
Converts	1,246	26	78
Semiconverts	1,157	29	75
Nonconverts	37	1	1
Total	2,440	56	154

Source: Kazuko Tsurumi, 42, footnote 22.

Officials could have interpreted such figures as indicating that among leftist thought control offenders there were many who could, at best, only be partially rehabilitated.

Efforts were made even in 1943 to ideologically convert thought control offenders. But one could argue that by the Pacific War period the relatively gentle *Tenkō* policy of helping former offenders to reintegrate themselves back into society had been effectively, if not officially, abandoned. It is apparent that the authorities in Japan had become less concerned with purging harmful ideas from the thinking of leftist thought control offenders and were more prepared to simply purge former offenders from society and especially, from the government.

Enforcing unity and preventing domestic sabotage or security leaks becomes a top priority during war, and concerns about national security can easily mutate into hysterical outbursts against certain groups. In Japan former leftist thought control offenders whose research skills had earned them positions in important institutions lost the trust of their official patrons and were once against persecuted as security risks. Those arrested in the Cabinet Planning Board and Mantetsu Incidents believe that they were suppressed because they knew too much about serious limitations in Japan's capacity to wage war and were suspected of spreading this information to others in the intellectual community. As Joshua Fogel observes, the authorities took to "killing the messengers" of bad tidings and arrested those Mantetsu researchers who warned them of future military setbacks.[50]

A number of the researchers arrested in the Cabinet Planning Board Incident had worked in Section Four of the Board, the so-called "efficiency section" in charge of material mobilization. They have claimed that their studies clearly revealed that Japan lacked the means to successfully wage a war

---

50. Fogel, "Introduction," *Life Along the South Manchurian Railway*, xxi.

against the Anglo-American powers. One of these individuals, for example, recalled that when they presented their findings at a meeting, someone connected with the Army General Staff angrily declared that such predictions reflected a lack of responsibility and faith in the nation's strength. Another who had helped in preparing the Emperor's address on materiel mobilization asserts that he was accused of being a traitor when he opposed his superiors' orders to omit data revealing that civilian oil reserves would soon be depleted during a war from the information to be passed along to the Emperor.[51]

Doubts about hidden communist conspirators were also heightened in the early 1940s by the incidents involving Kamiyama Shigeo,[52] Nakanishi Kō, and Ozaki Hotsumi. The discovery of "false converts" and communist spies seemed to further justify the need to carry out a purge of former offenders. Historian Awaya Kentarō observes that the Sorge Incident and the Comintern adoption of the Popular Front policy increased fears about communists infiltrating the state and that officials believed that former offenders were at the centre of this infiltration movement.[53]

Wartime documents and large scale arrests of former offenders support the claim of a reversal or backlash against the *Tenkō* policy. At a December 1941 Budget Meeting, one Diet member complained that many former leftists within the Imperial Rule Assistance Association were nothing more than opportunists and false converts.[54] Moreover, at a December 1941 House of Peers Meeting to debate the "Emergency Bill for the Control of Speech, Publication and Assembly," committee member Akaike Atsushi argued that communists, who had long been inactive, had suddenly begun to mobilize their forces to infiltrate official organizations. Akaike observed that there were thought control offenders who simply could not be ideologically rehabilitated and that, given this, it was completely absurd for officials to permit the employment of such individuals. In an attempt to reassure Akaike, government representative Nagano Wakamatsu replied that officials had at their disposal a number of laws that would allow them to promptly take care of any public

---

51. "Kikakuin jiken," 125-26, 128, 73; Hidezo Inaba, *Gekidō 30 nen no Nihon keizai* (Tokyo: Jitsugyō no Nihonsha, 1965), 61, 67.
52. *Nihon shakai undō jinmei jiten* (Tokyo: Aoki shoten, 1979), 180. Kamiyama was arrested in July 1935, but faked his conversion and was released in November 1936. In May 1941, the authorities discovered that he was trying to organize a movement among labourers in munitions factories and arrested him again.
53. Awaya Kentaro, "Chian ijihō jidai no ichi danmen," *Nihonshi kenkyū*, No. 166, June 1976: 70.
54. Murata, "Shōwa kenkyūkai ni taisuru hyōka," 61.

peace violation committed by leftists or former offenders employed in government offices.⁵⁵

With the outbreak of the Pacific War, the authorities were indeed ready to take drastic measures against suspected communists. The Peace Preservation Law forbade the existence of organizations and movements wishing to change the national polity or abolish the private property system. In 1941 the government expanded its provisions to include preventive arrests. Specifically with regard to former leftist thought control offenders, in July 1942 the Tōjō Cabinet passed a decision against the further employment of former offenders in public offices and even supported a measure to physically exile such individuals.

Awaya Kentarō states that on July 7, 1942, a month after the decisive defeat of Japanese forces at Midway, the Tōjō Cabinet secretly passed a "Measure against Former Thought Offenders." The Measure, Awaya points out, amounted to a wartime red purge and involved the arrest and relocation of former offenders to remote areas in the southern islands. The Tōjō Cabinet never acted on the idea of creating a former thought control offenders' purgatory. The military opposed the Measure on the grounds that there was no suitable location to hold the former offenders. Still, the Measure reveals the lengths that the authorities were prepared to go to in removing former offenders from Japanese society.⁵⁶

Moreover, earlier in March 1942, the Home Ministry had sent a document to the Tōjō Cabinet, "A Counterplan for Strengthening the Thought War," which called for the mass arrest of suspected leftists in nationalist movements, government offices, schools, public organizations, newspapers and magazines, and movie societies.⁵⁷ Members of a Cabinet Council held in the same year agreed to these proposals, and it appears that the Home Ministry began drawing up an extensive list of targeted individuals working in regional offices, public schools, newspapers and magazines. The authorities were apparently ready to remove former offenders from newspapers and magazines. Consequently, one might ask the following about the arrest of the journalists in

---

55. "Genron, shūkai, kessha nado rinji torishimari hōan," House of Peers Special Committee Record, December 1941. *Gendai shiryō 41: Masu media tōsei 2* (Tokyo: Misuzu shobō, 1975), 419-20, 422.

56. "Saikin no sayoku jiken ni kangami chūi o yōsuru jikō," *Tokkō keisatsu kankei shiryō shūsei*, Vol. 5, ed. Ogino Fujio (Tokyo: Fuji shuppan, 1991), 373-4; *Tokkō keisatsu kokushō*, ed. Tokkō keisatsu kokushō iinkai (Tokyo: Shin Nihon shuppansha, 1977), 102; Awaya, "Chian ijihō jidai," 70-71.

57. Ogino Fujio, *Tokkō keisatsu taiseishi: Shakai undō yokuatsu torishimari no kōzō to jittai* (Tokyo: Sekita shobō, 1984), 366-67.

the Yokohama Incident: Were they arrested, as the dominant interpretation of the Incident goes, because the authorities wanted to shut down *Kaizō* and *Chūō kōron*? Or were they just caught up in a wholesale government crackdown against former offenders? There is evidence to support the latter.

The Yokohama Incident has been considered a mass-media suppression incident because many of those arrested were journalists. However, even some of the journalists have commented on the large number of former offenders among the arrested. *Kaizō* journalist Aoyama Kenzō observed that the Kanagawa Prefectural Police seemed to target individuals with a past thought offense record.[58] To illustrate his point, Aoyama discussed how the Police decided to arrest one journalist, rather than his immediate superior who was a more likely candidate for arrest because of his greater responsibility for the controversial Hosokawa essay, simply because the former had been convicted of thought offenses while attending university.

One of the few existing official documents on the Yokohama Incident, "The Recent Leftist Incident, Facts that Require Attention" [*Saikin no sayoku jiken in kangami chūi o yōsuru jikō*], was among the materials confiscated by the Occupation Army and stored in the United States Library of Congress, Washington, D.C. In contrast to the *Tokkō geppō* or regular police reports, this 1943 document was written in a highly polite style, resembling a formal speech and may have been used by the Home Minister during a Cabinet Council address on the state of public peace. The authors of "The Recent Leftist Incident" drew attention to the fact that members of the Soviet Research Group and the Political Economic Research Group belonged to ministries, government-affiliated research organizations and important industries. In observing that many of these individuals were former thought control offenders, they complained that the whole affair could have been prevented if intellectual investigations of personnel had been more thorough. Moreover, it appears that in July 1942 the Tōjō Cabinet decided against the employment of former thought control offenders in public offices, and, in a hypothetical discussion on the activities of the Political Economic Research Group, the authors of "The Recent Leftist Incident" recommended that this decision be extended to cover industries important for the war effort.[59]

---

58. Aoyama, *Yokohama jiken*, 3, 4, 47.
59. Tomoko Nakamura, "Yokohama jiken: Mitsu no episōdo," *Shisō no kagaku*, June, 1992: 114-45; Fujio Ogino, "[Note on document] 'Saikin no sayoku jiken ni kangami chūi o yōsuru jikō,'" *Tokkō keisatsu kankei shiryō shūsei*, 18; "Saikin no sayoku jiken ni kangami chūi o yōsuru jikō," 373-4.

The Yokohama Incident seemed to vindicate measures against former offenders. As the war and domestic situation became more desperate, workers became more open in expressing their discontent, with some even resorting to strikes. The authorities attributed the rise in labour conflict to leftist agitators. In January 1943 a document entitled an "Outline for a Peace Preservation Policy" called for greater efforts to track down former offenders and other suspects in munitions companies and related industries.[60] Notably in the case of the Yokohama Incident, the Kanagawa Prefectural Police supposedly uncovered two groups with members employed in factories and industries. Besides the researchers in the Political Economic Research Group, the Kanagawa Police arrested members of an ostensibly right-wing labour group, the Patriotic Political Comrades Group. Officials reading the police reports on leftist incidents could only come away with the impression that communists and former offenders had successfully infiltrated not only government-related offices, research institutions, magazines and newspapers, but important factories and industries as well. In actuality, however, they grossly exaggerated the influence and power of hidden communist agents.

There was no serious communist threat to the state. What was growing was simply the belief in a wartime communist threat. An increasing number of officials and influential political figures were coming to the conclusion that the War was promoting communist movements in Japan and that the country was riddled with hidden leftists waiting for the right opportunity to come forward.

---

60. Ogino, *Tokkō keisatsu taiseishi*, 382-83, 375-76.

4
The Incident and the Authorities
The Creation of a Wartime Communist Threat

During the Pacific War Japanese authorities had become trapped in a vicious, self-perpetuating cycle of anxieties: concerns about communist activities spurred on police efforts to uncover hidden leftists and resulted in the purported discovery of widespread communist conspiracies which, in turn, only seemed to substantiate beliefs in a growing threat to internal security. The Yokohama Incident illustrates this ultimate irony of official attempts to deal with perceived threats to internal security, and the following chapter examines official views on the Incident, the affairs's impact on the ruling elite, and other factors that contributed to the wartime belief in a growing communist presence.

Wartime organizations and personnel in charge of peace preservation were caught up in a competition to apprehend the greatest number of communists. However, the vast majority of genuine communist activists had already been imprisoned and anyone even remotely associated with leftist thought was under heavy surveillance during the Pacific War. Consequently, through bogus cases such as the Yokohama Incident which involved the indiscriminate arrests of individuals attached to noteworthy organizations, thought control officials succeeded in only magnifying the image of a wartime communist threat.

Police reports on the Yokohama Incident possessed all the ingredients to intensify such fears. The Kanagawa Prefectural Police officers had simply tortured those in their custody into agreeing to charges conforming to prevailing official ideas about communist activity.[1] In doing so, these officers

---

1. *Tokkō geppō*, January 1942, 39-40. This early 1942 report clearly reveals that police believed that the Comintern had ordered Japanese communists in various parts of the world to return to Japan in order to gather information and infiltrate important political organizations.

were able to claim that they had uncovered a massive conspiracy involving individuals employed in ministries and affiliated research institutions, major industries, labour organizations, and prestigious journals. The seriousness with which superior officials viewed the Yokohama Incident is indicated by the fact that it was discussed at a Cabinet Council meeting (1943) and at a conference for high-ranking police officials (1944). In the immediate postwar period, moreover, Kanagawa Prefectural officials sent reports written by three of the suspects in the affair to the Home Minister in order to help him assess the present security situation.

OFFICIAL VIEWS ON THE YOKOHAMA INCIDENT

Shortly before the arrival of the Allied Occupation forces, Japanese officials tried to destroy any material that could reflect negatively on their conduct. The bulk of documents on the Yokohama Incident may have been lost in this wholesale destruction of government papers. However, some official records were preserved: a September 27, 1945 letter and reports from Kanagawa Prefectural Governor Fujiwara Takao to Home Minister Yamazaki Iwao; the 1944 "Summary of the Explanation by the Head of the Security Department about the State of Public Peace at the Conference of Police Chief," which will hereafter be referred to as the "Explanation on the State of Public Peace" [*Chian jōkyō ni tsuite keisatsu buchō kaigi ni okeru hoan kachō setsumei yōshi*]; the 1943 document, "The Recent Leftist Incident, Facts that Require Attention" [*Saikin no sayoku jiken ni kangami chūi o yōsuru jikō*], which appears to have been drawn up for use by the Home Minister during a Cabinet Council address; sections on the Incident in the *Tokkō geppō*, 1942-44 interrogation records of Hosokawa Karoku; and the so-called Confession of *Kaizō* journalist Aikawa Hiroshi.

Both the Hosokawa interrogation records and Aikawa Confession were found among the legal papers of Defense Attorney Unno Shinkichi. In the Confession, "The Memoranda of Yokohama Incident Defendant Aikawa Hiroshi" [*Yokohama jiken hikoku Aikawa Hiroshi shuki*], Aikawa emerges as the real force behind the conspirators' propaganda efforts and attempt to re-establish the Japan Communist Party. The Kanagawa Prefectural Police probably cast Aikawa in a leadership role because he was Hosokawa's self-appointed secretary.[2]

---

2. Kimura, *Yokohama jiken no shinsō*, 46-47.

Through the Aikawa Confession the Police constructed a scenario in which hidden communists, encouraged by the deteriorating domestic conditions brought about by the War, were beginning to make preparations for a revolution. Aikawa, who reportedly visited Hosokawa on January 10, 1942, is quoted as saying:

> I believe that the conditions for a communist revolution have been developing since the outbreak of the Pacific War last winter and that the time for revolution is quickly approaching. It is essential that we re-establish the Party as soon as possible and unite the communists scattered throughout the country in preparation for the coming revolution. Consequently, I would like you to write an essay which contains these directives, and I would like to have it published in *Kaizō*.[3]

The contents of the Aikawa Confession were later incorporated in the August 1944 *Tokkō geppō* analysis of the affair.[4] In that report the Police claimed that the investigation of the Yokohama Incident revealed that Japanese communists were carrying out a number of different activities. They were persistently attempting to re-establish the Japan Communist Party, join forces with foreign communist movements, and steal top secret documents in order to conduct a leftist analysis of conditions within the country. They were using legal, private organizations to promote communism among the people. These organizations supposedly included, not only publishing companies but, labour associations in key industries.

The discovery of the Yokohama Incident's Patriotic Political Comrades Group, in seeming to prove that leftist agitators had infiltrated the factories, no doubt aroused the authorities' fears that communists were encouraging strike action among workers. The Kanagawa Police appear to have discovered the existence of the Comrades Group while investigating the activities of labour activist Kondō Eizō. Kondō, who had abandoned communism around the time of the Manchurian Incident, had been active in both right-wing or national socialist movements for years.[5] However, in 1942 Kondō had been arrested on the suspicion that he was using rightist organizations as a front for carrying out his leftist activities. According to the Kanagawa Police, Kondō argued that the proper course of action for Japanese communists was to exploit the conservative nationalism of the masses and form ostensibly rightist labour

---

3. "Yokohama jiken hikoku Aikawa Hiroshi shuki," 697-98.
4. Katō Keiji, "Kaisetsu," *Zoku gendaishi shiryō 7: Tokkō to shisō kenji*, xxxvii.
5. "Tenkō shisōshi jō no hitobito," *Kyōdō kenkyū Tenkō*, Vol. 2, 478.

unions which, in actuality, would be under their control. Although it is not known exactly what Kondō's relationship was to the Patriotic Political Comrades Association, he probably met members of the Comrades Group at some labour functions. Consequently, the Police became suspicious of this organization and began to look into the background of its members.

They were eventually able to construct a link between the Patriotic Political Comrades Association and the suspects in the affair through one Association member, Tanaka Masao. Tanaka, a young industrial worker who had been previously arrested in 1938 for leftist activities, continued to participate in various labour groups even after the Patriotic Political Comrades Association was forced to disband in 1940. He established a study group among workers at the Tokyo Train Manufacturers [*Tokyo kisha seizō kabushiki kaisha*] and tried to attract recruits from other companies. He also formed the Japan Labour Youth Association [*Nihon seinen kinrō seinenkai*], with himself as president, and sought to establish similar associations in companies such as Hitachi. Tanaka had been acquainted with one of the journalists who had accompanied Hosokawa Karoku on the trip to Tomari, and Police contended that this journalist had invited Tanaka to join the conspiracy's central organization, the so-called Hosokawa Group.

By 1943 members of the Tōjō Cabinet were discussing the possibility that communists had established groups throughout the country and were on the verge of combining their groups into one radical, illegal organization. The Kanagawa Prefectural Police's description of the Hosokawa Group would have confirmed such official assessments. The Police described how the Hosokawa Group was planning to gain control over all leftist groups in Japan and how it acted as the pivot linking all of the other groups in the conspiracy: the Soviet Research Group, the Political Economic Research Group, the Patriotic Political Comrades Group, and the *Kaizō* and *Chūō kōron* Radical Editors Group.[6]

The alleged primary objective of the Hosokawa Group was the re-establishment of the Japan Communist Party, and the Police insisted that members had gathered together in June 1942 in order to make plans for the resurrection of the Party. They reported that the Hosokawa Group met at some hot springs resort [*onsen*]. But, as journalist Nakamura Tomoko points out, there were no hot springs at Tomari. Nakamura believes that the Kanagawa Police had in mind the Goshiki Hot Springs Incident of 1926 and that they were

---

6. "Chian jōkyō ni tsuite keisatsu buchō kaigi ni okeru hoan kachō setsumei yōshi," Security Section, Police Bureau, Home Ministry, January 14, 1944, *Nihon rikukaigun monjo* (Tokyo: Waseda University Microform Library, MF 1-229, 163 reels, Reel No. 218 F88663), 309-10, 307.

trying to draw parallels between the Yokohama Incident and this earlier well-known leftist case. Goshiki hot springs was the site of an actual attempt by leftists to re-establish the Japan Communist Party and even police in remote areas, Nakamura argues, would have known about the Hot Springs Incident.[7] The Kanagawa Police argued that second objective of the Hosokawa Group was to contact the Comintern and the Chinese Communist Party. One of the suspects was attached to the Japanese Foreign Ministry and had received an assignment to go to the Soviet Union. According to the Police, Hosokawa Group members planned to take advantage of this situation to pass information to and receive funds from the Comintern. Consequently, members tried to collect data on Japanese industries, agricultural production as well as information on the current political situation.

The Police reported that similar plans had been made to establish links with Chinese communists. They claimed that one suspect who had once been employed as Hosokawa's research assistant had found employment in Beijing and had been entrusted by the Group with contacting the CCP. This suspect reportedly told Police that although he had not succeeded in meeting CCP agents, he felt confident that he could make contact by the summer of 1943. In addition, Group members supposedly also recruited Japanese living in China such as Uchida Masao, an employee of the Dairen Main Branch of the Mantetsu, to act as a liaison with the Chinese communists. The Police suspected Uchida Masao for two reasons. For one thing, like so many of the others arrested in the Yokohama Incident, he was a former leftist thought control offender. He had been arrested in the past for helping the Marxist scholar Kawakami Hajime to hide from the police. For another, during a brief trip back to Japan in April 1943, he had met and had dinner with friends working in the Tokyo Office of the Mantetsu who just happened to be suspects in the affair. Police argued that this get-together was actually a meeting to discuss ways to contact the CCP.[8]

Another individual implicated in the affair simply because of social or professional ties to some of the suspects was Nawa Tsunekazu, an Osaka Commercial University professor. Before he became a professor Nawa had worked in the Mantetsu and occasionally had dinner during his trips to the capital with former colleagues presently working in the Tokyo Branch Office. He was also a contributor to a dictionary on China that was being edited by one of the journalists arrested in the affair. It was through such business and social meetings that the Kanagawa Prefectural Police were able to drag Nawa, who

---

7. Nakamura, *Yokohama jiken no hitobito*, 46.
8. Nakamura, *Yokohama jiken no hitobito*, 123, 61.

had already been arrested in February 1943 as the alleged leader of some Osaka-based communists, into their own investigation. The Police asserted that following the 1942 arrest of Hosokawa Karoku, the other conspirators had selected Nawa as their new leader because they believed he could link them with similar organizations both within and outside of Japan.

The 1944 Police Chiefs' Conference document, "Explanation on the State of Public Peace," described Nawa as the leader of a number of illegal leftist groups throughout the country. Moreover, both the "Explanation" and another document observed that Nawa was in contact with the Chinese communists and could have helped tie the Hosokawa Group to the CCP.[9] Consequently, by involving Nawa Tsunekazu in their investigation, the Kanagawa Police tried to establish the argument that the suspects in the Yokohama Incident were trying to create a nation-wide and international network.

Those who drafted the January 1944 "Explanation on the State of Public Peace" recommended that greater surveillance be applied to suspicious individuals travelling to and from the Asian Continent. They deduced that there was presently no party or centralized leftist organization in Japan. But they observed that Japanese communists sought the guidance of representatives in China, such as Nosaka Sanzō, and were increasing efforts to secure their contact with the Chinese Communist Party. The authorities believed that the suspension of the Comintern had boosted the international influence of the Chinese Communist Party and that the CCP was using its bulletin to try to guide the action of Japanese communists and encourage their anti-war activities. Included in the "Explanation on the State of Public Peace" delivered at the Police Chiefs' Conference was the following quotation from an article in the CCP bulletin entitled, "To the Japanese People": "The present war is a war of invasion carried out by the Army and Capitalists. Because it causes hardship for the people, the people should undertake strike action to eliminate the military and establish a democratic government."[10]

There was, of course, no connection between the CCP and those arrested in the Yokohama Incident, and the Kanagawa Prefectural Police probably came up with the idea of CCP involvement because some of their suspects were China specialists or had been stationed in China for a number of years. However, the attention placed on the CCP in the "Explanation on the State of Public Peace" mirrored the wartime authorities' appreciation of the CCP's potential for guiding foreign communist movements. The Japanese authorities

---

9. "Chian jōkyō ni tsuite," 309, 312, 315-16; "Saikin no sayoku jiken," 306-7.
10. "Chian jōkyō ni tsuite," 317.

believed that the CCP was sending agents abroad. In 1939-40, in the so-called CCP Tokyo Branch Incident, they accused some Chinese, Mongolian, and Korean students residing in Japan of working with the CCP to undermine the Japanese state. According to the authorities, the CCP had called upon these students to collect sensitive military information, sabotage military installations, blow up water and electrical facilities, and even assassinate some important politicians and military officers.[11] Experience had taught the wartime authorities not to underestimate the capabilities of the CCP. One scholar has written that the August 1940 Hundred Regiment Offensive in North China made it apparent that the "Communist bogey which the Japanese had so long used as an excuse for expansion in North China had become a reality."[12] At the end of the Pacific War, moreover, recognition of the potential power of the CCP contributed to the Japanese government's willingness to comply with the Kuomintang's request that Japanese forces refrain from surrendering to any government or force under Chinese communist influence.

The most serious charges against those arrested in the Yokohama Incident were attempting to reestablish the Japan Communist Party and pass along sensitive information to foreign enemy organizations. However, an examination of the official documents reveals that these were nothing more than police speculations about what could have taken place rather than crimes that had been actually committed. Those who composed the August 1944 *Tokkō geppō* report declared that if the arrests had been delayed the information obtained and analyzed by the Political Economic Research Group could have been transmitted to American, Soviet, and Chinese communists. In the 1944 "Explanation on the State of Public Peace," it was simply observed that the Kanagawa Prefectural Police had been able to suppress these activities at their initial stage.[13] In arresting individuals for what they could have done, the Police did not have to bother with obtaining evidence.

Still, the Kanagawa Police had no real need to be overly concerned about convincing to their superiors that the Yokohama Incident was an authentic case of communist intrigue. Growing fears of a communist threat, which propelled the search for hidden leftists and created an atmosphere conducive to tragedies such as the Incident, bestowed instant credibility upon

---

11. "Chūgoku kyōsantō Tokyo shibu jiken," "Kominterun no senryaku senjutsu no hensenshu toshite Nihon no kyōsanshugi undō to no kanren," 1940, Special Research Council on Thought. *Shakai mondai shiryō sōsho*, Vol. 1 (Tokyo: Shakai mondai shiryō kenkyūkai, 1975), 566-69.
12. Lincoln Li, *The Japanese Army in North China, 1937-1941: Problems of Political and Economic Control* (Oxford: Oxford University Press, 1975), 13.
13. "Chian jōkyō ni tsuite," 314.

police reports. Many of the high-ranking police officials and Cabinet Council members who had access to reports about the affair were all too prepared to believe that communists were becoming more influential and were preparing for a revolution; they simply used such reports to verify their fears. Suspects in the Yokohama Incident were forced to affix their seals to "confessions" that were written by the Kanagawa Police, or simply set down what Justice and Police officials had directed them to write. Such confessions and reports were thus more the handiwork of Police or Justice officials and provide a means of examining the views and concerns of officials during and even immediately after the Pacific War.

On September 27, 1945, Kanagawa Prefectural Governor Fujiwara Takao sent to Home Minister Yamazaki Iwao reports supposedly composed by three journalists arrested in the affair, Mimasaka Tarō, Hikosaka Takeo, and Fujikawa Kaku.[14] Kanagawa Prefectural officials presented the reports of these three journalists to the Home Minister in order to help him discern future trends in subversive activity. The reports discussed the ways in which the American Occupation could promote socialism as well as the prospect of future conflict between the United States and Soviet Union over control of Japan. The United States had quickly rejected an August 16, 1945 Soviet request for a zonal occupation of Hokkaidō. The Japanese authorities were probably aware of American efforts to seal off the country from Soviet influence, and those who composed the Mimasaka Tarō report drew attention to these diplomatic problems as an omen of future conflict between the Soviets and the Americans.

According to the Mimasaka report, the democratic movement promoted by the American Occupation would provide the groundwork for the growth of Soviet socialism in Japan. That is, the American Occupation would result in changes in the emperor system and would put the country on the path toward a bourgeoisie democratic revolution. The report insisted, however, that communists would not be content with just the establishment of party politics and discussed the means by which they could gain control of the country. Japanese communists had to try to establish a united front with liberal bourgeois parties and eliminate the fascist remnants within these groups. More importantly, they had to assume the leadership of labour and agrarian organizations, promote support for foreign communist powers and raise the revolutionary consciousness of the working classes and the intelligentsia.

---

14. "Sensō shūketsu ni kansuru byōgi kettei zengo ni okeru chian jōkyō," Security Section, Police Bureau, Home Ministry, September 1, 1945. *Nihon rikukaigun monjo*. Tokyo: Waseda University Microform University, MF 3, 1-229, 163 reels, Reel No. 221 F92388, 36-77.

The Hikosaka Takeo report also explained how Japan would undergo a two-stage revolution in becoming a communist state. The first stage which would result in a bourgeois democratic revolution would be fostered by the Japan's surrender and the American Occupation. The Americans would change the emperor system, overhaul the bureaucracy, eliminate the military factions, dissolve the giant economic monopolies, and confiscate huge land holdings. A socialist party would emerge, but would be plagued by internal splits and as a consequence a type of Kerensky government would come into being and govern for a number of years. Like the Mimasaka report, the Hikosaka report predicted a future U.S.-Soviet struggle, discussed the conditions favouring the influence of the Soviets, and hinted at the inability of the Japanese authorities to maintain internal security. In addition, the Hikosaka report observed that while the first stage of Japan's drift toward communism would be a bloodless revolution carried out by the American Occupation forces, the second stage would be presumably carried out by the Japanese people and could be somewhat violent.
   It is not known if Mimasaka, Hikosaka and Fujiwara Kaku were forced to write out these reports as a final condition for their release. But it is interesting to note that the reports were dated September 27, 1945: the very same day that their alleged authors were released from custody. A comparison of these reports, moreover, with police documents written shortly after Japan's surrender to the Allied Powers suggest that Mimasaka and the others were made to compose their reports in accordance with prevailing official ideas about communist activities. In an earlier September 1, 1945 document on internal security matters following the declaration of peace, the police announced that there were about 7,000 persons known to have been involved in leftist movements.[15] They observed that these individuals believed that Japan would become the site of a major power struggle between the Soviet Union and the United States. In preparation for what they believed would be the inevitable victory of the Soviet Union, these Japanese communists intended to re-establish the Japan Communist Party and mobilize leftist elements within factories and other important sectors of society. To combat this threat to internal security, the police recommended the prompt arrest of known leftists and greater surveillance of suspected subversives.
   Such reports written by the police and supposedly by suspected communists no doubt contributed to Home Minister Yamazaki Iwao's hardstand against the expansion of civil liberties at the start of the Occupation. In opposing the abolition of the thought control police and the rescindment of the

---

15. "Sensō shūketsu ni kansuru byōgi kettei zengo ni okeru chian jōkyō," 52.

Peace Preservation Law, Yamazaki precipitated the fall of the Higashikuni Cabinet. Yamazaki had been a police official before his cabinet appointment, and, like the other members of the Higashikuni Government, he lacked a clear understanding of the objectives of the American Occupation.[16] He and the Justice Minister nevertheless enjoyed considerable influence in the Cabinet and were able to persuade the other Ministers to ignore the Occupation authorities' orders for lifting restrictions on freedom of explanation. Yamazaki argued that the present conditions were too revolutionary and that the police had to be increased to take up any slack caused by the abolition of the military. The Occupation authorities responded to the Higashikuni Cabinet's recalcitrance by issuing on October 4, 1945, a sweeping civil liberties directive which demanded that the Japanese government release all political prisoners, eliminate all organs and laws restraining freedom of speech, press, assembly, religion, and remove from office all high-ranking police officials including the Home Minister. The very next day, on October 5, the Higashikuni Cabinet submitted its resignation. Members were unwilling to just sacrifice Yamazaki because, as one former Minister observed, they shared his concerns and believed that his efforts to maintain what he believed was the fragile state of public peace were fully justified.

THE IMAGE OF A WARTIME LEFTIST THREAT (I): THE RULING ELITE'S INTERPRETATION OF DOMESTIC AND FOREIGN DEVELOPMENTS

An examination of wartime diaries and personal correspondence reveals that concerns about international communism, the leftist infiltration of the state apparatus, and a potential postwar revolution were shared by many members of the Japanese ruling elite. Ideas about the nature and exact sources of the growing threat were various, and some even accused the police and policies for promoting the war effort of encouraging leftist sympathies. Viscount Kanō Hisaakira, the Director of the London (England) Branch of the Yokohama Specie Bank, for example, tried to warn influential friends of the dangers inherent in the legislation supported by police officials. In a December 1942 letter to Lord Keeper of the Privy Seal Kido Kōichi, Kanō discussed how everyone he met in Osaka and Kobe believed that widespread communist

---

16. James William Morley, "The First Seven Weeks," *The Japan Interpreter*, Vol. VI, No. 2, Summer, 1970: 154, 155, 159-60, 162; *Yamazaki naimu daijin jidai o kataru zadankai*, ed. Chihō zaimu kyōkai (Tokyo: Chihō zaimu kyōkai, 1960), 10.

propaganda was the greatest concern of the day.¹⁷ Kanō furthermore observed that the social legislation advocated by the police to promote "loyalty," "patriotism" and the "successful completion of the War" was, in actuality, assisting communist propaganda efforts. Police officials, Kanō wrote, were indifferent to the issue of winning or losing the War and were only concerned with "socializing" the country.

In a diary entry dated February 1940, moreover, party politician and postwar prime minister Hatoyama Ichirō wrote that communist influences were a notable feature of all the government organizations that had been established during the Konoe Era. The time was fast approaching, Hatoyama observed, when he might have to sacrifice himself in the service of the state.¹⁸ Entries in the diary of Hosokawa Morisada, who was Prince Konoe Fumimaro's son-in-law and private secretary, indicate that philosopher Nishida Kitarō, former ambassador to the United States Nomura Kichisaburō, Imperial Prince Takamatsu, and Lord Keeper of the Privy Seal Kido Kōichi also believed that Japanese leftists constituted a considerable force.¹⁹ In June 1944 Konoe told Hosokawa that Kido was worried about "Reds" and their infiltration of the Railways and Finance Ministries. Kido held tremendous political power because of his control over access to the Emperor. He never displayed anything approaching Konoe's anxieties about a communist revolution. However, in October 1940, Kido recorded in his diary that he had advised Konoe to look into the rumour that communists were involved in the New Order Movement.²⁰

Historian Itō Takashi has suggested that one of the causes behind the magnification of the communist presence may be found in the participation of former Japan Communist Party members and sympathizers in broad political movements following the eclipse of the Party in 1933.²¹ A conspicuous number of former leftists and Party members had participated in and may have

---

17. *Kido Kōichi kankei monjo* (Tokyo: Tokyo daigaku shuppankai, 1966), 591.
18. Itō Takashi, *Konoe shintaisei: Taiseiyokusankai e no michi* (Tokyo: Chūkō shinsho, 1983), 190. It is not known what Hatoyama meant by sacrificing himself.
19. Hosokawa Morisada, *Hosokawa nikki* (Tokyo: Chūō kōronsha, 1979), 223, 230, 315, 351.
20. *The Diary of Marquis Kido*, 257.
21. Itō, "Senji taisei," 94. Tsurumi Shunsuke, "Goki shinjinkai: Hayashi Fusao/Ōya Sōichi," *Kyōdō kenkyū Tenkō*, Vol. 1, 110-12. Tsurumi Shunsuke also observes that many members of the *Shinjinkai*, a leftist university students' association, eventually abandoned socialism and communism, became *Tenkōsha*, and entered the so-called *"yokusan"* movement. Such individuals included Kadoya Hiroshi, Asano Akira, Mizuno Shigeo, Ōmachi Tokuzō, Koreeda Kyōji, Murao Satsuo, Kinoshita Hanji, Murayama Tōshirō, Kamei Katsuichirō, Orimoto Tsuyoshi, Ōyama Iwao, Henmi Shigeo, Yodonori Yūzo, Koiwai Jyo, Ogawa Shin'ichi, and Utsunomiya Tokuma.

influenced the New Order Movement. The Movement attracted individuals spanning the political spectrum and its aims were extremely vague. But Itō has observed a strong anti-capitalist, reformist streak in the Movement that may have made it particularly attractive to former leftists. Itō states that those around Konoe saw the Movement as a sort of "bloodless revolution," which would bring about a complete change in economic, political, and social structures. Anti-capitalist New Order advocates claimed that the plutocracy and conservative elite were resisting the historical inevitability of capitalism's decline and clinging to an outdated liberalism-based capitalist system which was undermining Japan's industrialization. Japan, they argued, could only fulfil its destiny to liberate Asia by abandoning liberal-capitalism and transforming itself into a "National Defense State" characterized by a controlled economy and high-tech industrial base. The New Order Movement was immensely popular, and its anti-capitalist thrust could have easily led individuals to magnify the number and organized influence of potential communists and their sympathizers. According to John Dower, it was the New Order Movement that helped convince many individuals that Japan was drifting toward the Soviet model.[22]

Japanese officials had been obsessed with international communism since the Bolshevik Revolution, and by the end of the Pacific War, they were convinced that the Soviet Union planned to transform Japan into one of its satellites. Among the documents related to the Yokohama Incident, the September 1945 reports sent to Home Minister Yamazaki Iwao reflect the fears among officials that Japan might become the site of a U.S.-Soviet power struggle. Besides relying on the statements made by suspected communist agents, Japanese officials sought the opinion of Soviet specialists in the Foreign Ministry to assess the nature of subversive activities. One such expert, Ogata Shōji, whose views were used by Prince Konoe in the preparation of his famous 1945 Memorial to the Throne, observed that those in government circles were most fearful of a potential worldwide union of communist forces. "Japanese officials," according to Ogata, "showed greater concern over Soviet relations with the Chinese Communist Party than they did over the military crisis in the Philippines and Okinawa."[23] As a 1944 document on the affair reveals, officials were aware of presence of Japanese communists in Yenan and believed that communists within the country were trying to secure links to both the Soviet Union and the Chinese Communist Party.[24] In the eyes of such

---

22. Itō, *Konoe shintaisei*, 214-18; Dower, *Empire and Aftermath*, 286.
23. Dower, *Empire and Aftermath*, 281-83.
24. "Chian jōkyō ni tsuite," 315-16.

officials, Japanese communists had more than a few powerful allies, especially in enemy states, who could assist them in overthrowing the country. This concern that Japanese communist activities were gaining foreign support or that leftists in exile could gain the patronage of enemy powers was not wholly unwarranted. In 1944, for example, American officials began to consider plans to enlist the aid of foreign-based leftists, such as Nosaka Sanzō and Oyama Ikuo, in encouraging anti-government movements within Japan. In September 1944 John K. Emmerson, a member of the Ambassador Patrick J. Hurley's Dixie Mission to China, met with Nosaka Sanzō in Yenan. Emmerson believed that measures had to be taken to undermine Japanese resistance and proposed that "an organized *Japanese* force, known to the Japanese, working on our side and prepared to offer an attractive, alternative to a disillusioned, disorganized, demoralized populace, is the best means to achieve that end." In his memoirs Emmerson recalled that Nosaka Sanzō's library in Yenan was filled with Japanese books and newspapers, some of which were less than two months old, and that this indicated to him that Japanese communists abroad maintained some links to their homeland.[25]

Emmerson was clearly impressed with Nosaka and proposed including him in an internationally-sponsored, Japanese anti-war association whose other members would include Oyama Ikuo, the former leader of the Labour-Farmer Party who was in exile in the United States, and Kaji Wataru, the anti-war propagandist working with Chiang Kai-shek in Chungking. According to one scholar, "this initial program to bring Oyama, Nosaka, and Kaji together later (March 1945) developed into a plan for supporting the Japanese Communists, strengthening the antiwar underground in Japan, and sending operatives in Japan from abroad."[26] Although the State-War-Navy Coordinating Committee approved Emmerson's "Plan to Permit Overseas Japanese to Organize for Political Warfare Against Japanese Militarism" so that it became U.S. policy in June 1945, the plan was never implemented. Still, the existence of the Emmerson plan indicates that fears among Japanese officials about foreign support for Japanese leftist activities and communists abroad were not completely far-fetched.

---

25. John K. Emmerson, *The Japanese Thread: A Life in the U.S. Foreign Service* (New York: Holt, Rinehart and Winston, 1978), 192-93, 223, 225-26. Emmerson observes that during a conversation years later Nosaka also told him that he had been able to sneak in and out of Japan many times during the 1930s and had communist materials printed in the United States secretly smuggled from Los Angeles to Japan through comrades working as seamen.
26. Eiji Takemae, "Early Postwar Reformist Parties," *Democratizing Japan: The Allied Occupation*, ed. Robert E. Ward and Sakamoto Yoshikazu (Honolulu: University of Hawaii Press, 1987), 342-43.

In his analysis of Prince Konoe Fumimaro's Memorial to the Throne, moreover, John Dower reveals that beliefs in a growing communist presence and potential revolution were not the result of "abstract, hysterical rationalization," but were logically derived from observations of both external and internal developments.[27] Dower points out that Konoe could defend his views by referring to a number of domestic factors which could turn the people against the state and lead to a revolution. Among these factors was the "impoverishment of daily life."

Following the outbreak of the Pacific War agricultural productivity was increasingly hindered by the shortage of fertilizer and farming equipment as well as the depletion of labour resulting from conscription into the military or military factories. Coupled with this were transportation problems and an increasing difficulty in importing rice into the home islands. As early as the spring of 1940, government offices were receiving reports of food and cooking fuel shortages in certain areas. In April 1941 the government began rationing rice, the staple food product, and eventually a system of rationing was imposed on all foodstuffs. By 1944 an individual only received a three-day allotment of three green onion stalks and a five-day allotment of a side of fish.[28]

The Department of Welfare stated in 1941 that a male adult engaged in normal work needed 2,400 calories per day, and the government promised to guarantee this amount. However, after 1942, the government lowered the minimum standard to 2,000 calories, and in 1945 further lowered it to 1,793 calories. Increasing health problems naturally accompanied the drop in the minimum standard. In 1938 deaths from tuberculosis, already high, numbered about 140,000. This number increased to 160,000 in 1942, exceeded 170,000 in 1943, and after 1944 the government no longer announced the figures.[29] Yet another clear indication of the War's adverse effect on Japanese standards of living was the physical decline of infants born during the 1940s:

---

27. Dower, *Empire and Aftermath*, 279.
28. Suda, *Kazami Akira*, 134; Tōyama Shigeki, Imai Seiichi, Fujiwara Akira, *Shōwashi* (Tokyo: Iwanami shoten, new edition, 1992) 223-24.
29. Shunsuke Tsurumi, *An Intellectual History of Wartime Japan 1931-1945* (London: KPI Limited, 1986), 85-86.

PHYSICAL DECLINE OF INFANTS				
		1940	1942	Difference
HEIGHT	Male	51.788	49.930	-1.858
(cm.)	Female	51.680	49.320	-2.360
WEIGHT	Male	3,130.300	2,920.890	-209.410
(gm.)	Female	3,103.860	2,868.600	-235.260

Source: Tōyama, *Shōwashi*, 224.

The food supply problem and its negative impact on public morale loomed large in the minds of the Japanese ruling elite. In a diary entry dated March 1944, Prince Higashikuni Naruhiko recorded his discussion with Narita Tsutomu, the Director of the Korean Foodstuff Corporation. Narita pointed to the inability to transport food to the home country and said that there was a good possibility that a major incident would break out if conditions remained unchanged.[30]

Even before the outbreak of the Pacific War individuals such as Konoe were hearing rumours of rising popular discontent. In the spring of 1940 Konoe learned that Hosokawa Karoku had just returned to Tokyo from a trip through various parts of Japan, and he asked his former Justice Minister Kazami Akira to arrange a meeting with Hosokawa to discuss conditions within the country.[31] Hosokawa, besides insisting on an end to Japan's undeclared war with China, spoke of the demoralization of the people and the complaints against the war made by passengers in the trains. After the meeting with Hosokawa, Konoe told Kazami in private that he agreed that war-weariness caused by the China Incident could result in violence and actions against the Imperial Family.

Kazami Akira's observations during a week-long trip to Kyoto in October 1941 were in keeping with those of Hosokawa Karoku and redoubled Konoe's fears that the people were becoming hostile toward the Throne. Kazami told Konoe that he had heard reports of female students cursing the Imperial Family and that in May of the same year the Governor of Kyoto had received an anonymous letter insulting the Empress who had been visiting the

---

30. Hosokawa, *Hosokawa nikki*, 54, 214; *Hiranuma kaisōroku*, 128; Naruhiko Higashikuni, *Ichikōzoku no sensō nikki* (Tokyo: Nihon shūhōsha, 1958), 126-27.
31. Kazami, *Konoe naikaku*, 246-47.

area at the time. According to Kazami, Konoe reacted by crying out, "We're standing atop a volcano that is about to erupt. Although war-weariness has reached such levels, the military takes no notice."[32] Kazami's observations also tallied with investigations by the Home Ministry's Police Bureau for the year 1940. The Police Bureau investigations indicated that incidents of lèse-majesté as well as anti-war, anti-military movements were increasing in number.[33]

Scholars have argued that war is often "a profound catalyst of structural transformation, accelerated social change, and alteration of popular consciousness." Amemiya Shōichi, for example, has suggested that the total war system may have contributed to social equalization through its impact on both the material lives and attitudes of the Japanese people. The Tōjō Cabinet, in order to facilitate mobilization, carried out a wide array of legal, social, economic, political, and cultural reforms which promoted social mobility and political expression among the lower classes. The general mobilization system, Amemiya observes, not only encouraged the growth of an urban proletariat through the transference of labour from the agricultural to the industrial sector, but also broke down, to some degree, the previous social hierarchy. One manifestation of the War's levelling effect on society, which Konoe's son-in-law Hosokawa Morisada described as "negative equality," was greater uniformity in clothing, food, and shelter.[34]

Total mobilization invoked and reinforced notions that all individuals, regardless of their status in society, were expected to contribute to the general welfare by making sacrifices. Political leaders thus had to be wary of displaying what could appear to be excessive privileges. One high-ranking police official recalled how the police had to act promptly to suppress an incident involving pamphlets criticizing Prime Minister Tōjō for building a new house and failing to share the sufferings of the people.[35]

Feelings of resentment against the undeserved benefits of the wealthy existed among the general population long before the wartime. The atmosphere created by the War and the demand for self-sacrifice simply provided the framework within which a greater number of people could articulate and justify their complaints about social inequality. Popular discontent may not have been intertwined with politically revolutionary ideas. However, members of the

---

32. Kazami, *Konoe naikaku*, 247-48.
33. Kitagawa Kenzo, *Kokumin sōdōn no jidai* (Tokyo: Iwanami bukkuletto, Shōwashi, No. 6, 1989), 23.
34. Dower, *Empire and Aftermath*, 279-80; Amemiya, "*1940 nendai no shakai to seiji taisei*," *Rekishi kenkyū*, 308 (1988): 65-68, 70, 73; Hosokawa, *Hosokawa nikki*, 185-86.
35. *Murata Gorō shi danwa sokkiroku 4*, ed. Naiseishi kenkyūkai (Tokyo: Naiseishi kenkyūkai, 1973), 213-14.

political and social elite, conscious of their privileges, could easily imagine why an increasingly impoverished and war-weary populace might wish to overthrow them. Moreover, having had opportunities to study Marxism in the universities and convinced of the mass appeal of communism, especially in times of extreme hardship, quite a few elite members saw signs and agents of revolution in every development.

For many years the Comintern had been instructing communists to try to enter and coopt legal mass organizations and, if possible, the government itself. On May 1943 the Comintern announced that the fundamental task was to defeat the "Hitlerite bloc" by sabotaging the "Hitlerite military machine from within."[36] Such directives naturally aroused suspicions that communists were trying to infiltrate the Japanese government and even the military. The adoption of Marxist terms and phrases or the support of peers for policies that seemed to be akin to communism aroused further concern among individuals that subversive ideas had infected even the highest strata of society. In this fashion, the impact of Marxist ideas on the elite also contributed to the magnification of a communist presence.

THE IMAGE OF A WARTIME LEFTIST THREAT (II): THE IMPACT OF MARXIST THOUGHT ON THE JAPANESE RULING ELITE

One cannot deny Marxism's tremendous influence during the first half of the twentieth century on the thinking of the higher educated and influential members of Japanese society. As John Dower points out, Marxism's growing impact on Japanese thought can be measured by the fact that even its political and ideological opponents, from Konoe Fumimaro to Kita Ikki, had assimilated Marxist concepts. Since the 1930s the authorities had been concerned about similarities between rightists and leftists. At a Justice Ministry conference in April 1941, a Tokyo District Court procurator observed that the investigation of thought control violations by supposedly right-wing individuals was like opening a package of candy: the wrapper was rightist, but the contents were leftist.[37]

---

36. "Resolution of the ECCI Presidium Recommending the Dissolution of the Communist International," 15 May 1943, *The Communist International, 1919-1943: Documents*, Volume III, ed. Jan Degras (London: Frank Cass & Co. Ltd., 1971), 477-78.

37. Dower, *Empire and Aftermath*, 288; Mitchell, *Thought Control in Prewar Japan*, 178-79.

In his Memorial to the Throne, Prince Konoe did not confine his discussion to underground left-wing revolutionaries and actually singled out the Army's Control Faction and the new and renovationist bureaucrats as being primarily responsible for the country's drift toward communism. The so-called new bureaucrats [*shin kanryō*] first became conspicuous during the Saitō and Okada Cabinets (1932-36).[38] Part of a bureaucratic resurgence created by the decline in the influence of the political parties, they were forceful advocates of greater state intervention. For example, Karasawa Toshiki, who figures in one popular explanation for the Yokohama Incident and who was appointed Police Bureau Chief under the Okada Cabinet, insisted that the police be allowed to assume a more active role in political events and in projects to promote social harmony.[39] The new bureaucrats encouraged the police to consider landlord-tenant and labour mediation as part of their duties.[40] Enemies of the new bureaucrats, however, suspected that some sympathy for state socialism lay beneath the call for more official involvement in the daily lives of the people.

Although contemporary journalists called them "new," these bureaucrats were little different from their colleagues and predecessors in terms of age, education, and training. What set them apart were certain common characteristics: "a pragmatic nationalism emphasizing the economic role of the state, a willingness to collaborate with like-minded men in other ministries and in the military services, and a desire to change the existing order from within by non-revolutionary means."[41] They became allied with the military's Control Faction, whose members included Nagata Tetsuzan and Tōjō Hideki. As a result, they came under attack from members of the rival Imperial Way Faction, who accused these bureaucrats of using the Army to increase their own political power. The assassination of General Nagata in 1935 and the February 26, 1936 Incident by Imperial Way adherents resulted in temporary reversals for the new bureaucrats.

The eclipse of the new bureaucrats, however, was offset by the appearance of the "renovationist bureaucrats" [*kakushin kanryō*], who

---

38. Spaulding, "Japan's 'New Bureaucrats,'" 52-53; Aritake, *Karasawa*, 123-24, 109.

39. *Abe Genki shi danwa dai ikkai sokkiroku*, 36-37. An important prewar police official whose name has been consistently linked with the new bureaucrats, Abe Genki recalls this trend for greater police involvement in social and political movements. However, he insists that he was opposed to it because it was too open to abuse. As an example, he notes that members of the Tōjō Government used the thought control police, who were only supposed to supervise voting procedures, to interfere in the Imperial Rule Assistance elections.

40. Miwa Yasushi, "Nihon faashizumu kiseiki ni okeru shinkanryō to keisatsu," *Nihonshi kenkyū*, No. 252, August, 1983: 12, 17, 26.

41. Spaulding, "Japan's 'New Bureaucrats,'" 52, 56-57.

maintained even more radical ideas about expanding state authority and "renovating" society.⁴² In 1936 one young renovationist bureaucrat attempted to make a distinction between his peers and the older group of new bureaucrats by asserting that "the original *shin kanryō* were unable to solve Japan's problems because their 'liberalism' (riberarizumu) committed them to laissez-faire capitalism."⁴³

Suspicions about the ideological loyalty of the renovationist bureaucrats were quickly aroused and were, no doubt, intensified by the openness with which certain members sang the praises of Marxism. These bureaucrats attended university during the early 1920s when Marxism and liberalism was more freely debated. One notable renovationist even claimed that the opportunity to attend lectures on socialism and communism had helped his generation understand more clearly the great changes that were taking place throughout the world.⁴⁴

More than one scholar has noted the influence of Marxism on the new and renovationist bureaucrats and the policies that they advocated. Hashikawa Bunsō has argued that although they also adopted ideas from Nazi theories, these bureaucrats maintained a Marxist view of history and the social structure. In addition, Itō Takashi states that elements of Marxist thinking were notable in all the plans formulated by renovationists in both the bureaucracy and the Army.⁴⁵ To further illustrate his point, Itō has examined Control Faction member Ikeda Sumihisa's "Army Pamphlet."

Ikeda had written the "Army Pamphlet" or the "Basic Principles of National Defense and Proposals to Strengthen It" [*Kokubō no hongi to sono kyōka no teisho*] in October 1934 for the Army Ministry's Newspaper Unit.⁴⁶ In the pamphlet, Ikeda called for the establishment of a national defense state; that is, a centrally-controlled economy geared to military needs, which in themselves would foster the economic development of the country. He argued that both "an idea of moral economics" and "proper rewards for labour as well as a stabilization of the people's standards of living" were needed. He denounced liberalism for encouraging class conflict, a "maldistribution of

---

42. Furukawa Takahisa, *Shōwa senchūki no sōgō kokusaku kikan* (Tokyo: Kōbunkan, 1992), 18-19.
43. Spaulding, "Japan's 'New Bureaucrats,'" 60.
44. Hoshino Naoki, *Jidai to jibun* (Tokyo: Daiyamondosha, 1968), 45, 47.
45. Hashikawa Bunso, "Kakushin kanryō," *Gendai Nihon shisō taikei 10: Kenryoku no shisō*, ed. Kamishima Jirō (Tokyo: Chikuma shobō, 1965), 269; Itō, "Senji taisei," 95.
46. Nakamura Takahide and Hara Akira, "Keizai shintaisei," "'Konoe shintaisei' no kenkyū," *Senji gaku nenpyō* (Tokyo: Iwanami shoten, 1972), 74.

wealth," and the unemployment and impoverishment of workers, villagers, and small businessmen.

The "Army Pamphlet" stirred up considerable debate, eliciting fierce attacks from Diet representatives and the mainstream political parties. Under the spotlight of controversy, the Social Masses Party's endorsement of the pamphlet could not have been overlooked or easily dismissed. Asō Hisashi, leader of Japan's largest proletarian party, believed that the Pamphlet "called for the reform of the capitalist structure and the establishment of something similar to a socialist state." Furthermore, Asō argued that "it was essential, given Japan's domestic situation, that the property-less classes and the military unite in overthrowing capitalism and carrying out social reforms."[47]

Ikeda's activities and ideas eventually led Konoe Fumimaro to write a letter to Lord Keeper of the Privy Seal Kido Kōichi in January 1943 accusing Ikeda of being the leader of a clique of "renovationist" military officers plotting to transform Japan into a Soviet-style regime. There is no evidence that leftists succeeded in, or even tried, infiltrating the military. But it is interesting to note that Ikeda Sumihisa himself, while arguing that there was no truth to Konoe's accusations, has observed how his activities could have been easily misinterpreted. Ikeda claimed that certain military men such as himself recognized that the government's attempts to control communism through simple suppression were futile and that the only way to fight ideas was with other ideas. Consequently, after he graduated from Military College, Ikeda spent three years at Tokyo Imperial University studying economics and Marxist theory. These activities led some individuals to suspect him of being a leftist sympathizer. However, the purpose behind his study of Marxism, he insisted, was to gain a better understanding of the "enemy" and protect the military from "Reds."[48]

John Dower has observed that a certain irony often surrounded those who sought to combat communism in prewar Japan. "In attempting to thwart the threat from the left," he writes, "they implicitly accepted the logic and correctness of central concepts and auguries in the Marxist analysis."[49] In 1932 the Comintern made the following assessment of the impact of war on conditions in Japan:

---

47. Itō Takashi, "Rikugun panfuretto," *Shōwa keizaishi*, ed. Hiromi Arisawa (Tokyo: Nihon keizai shimbunsha, 1976), 116-17.
48. *Kido Kōichi kankei monjo*, 591-92; Ikeda Sumihisa, *Nihon no magari kado* (Tokyo: Senjō shuppan, 1968), 60.
49. Dower, *Empire and Aftermath*, 288-89.

The war intensifies all class contradictions within the country to the most extreme pitch. It confronts the Japanese proletariat and its communist party with the task of combining the fight against the war with the fight for the most vital daily interests of the workers, peasants, and all working people against their economic and political enslavement, and so to turn the imperialist war into civil war and bring about the revolutionary overthrow of the bourgeois-landlord monarchy. Japanese imperialism's robber war does not push the revolution in Japan into the remote distance but, on the contrary, into the immediate forefront.[50]

Members of Japan's wartime ruling elite readily agreed with this assessment. They feared communism so intensely because, like leftist revolutionaries, they believed in its potential triumph.

The thinking of this elite conforms to that of the practitioner of "the paranoid style."[51] American history specialist Richard Hofstadter has described the paranoid style as a mode of thinking in which feelings of persecution are systematized into theories of large-scale conspiracies against the nation or culture. This phenomenon, Hostadter points out, is neither limited to modern history nor to the American experience. It seems to come in episodic waves, is stimulated by catastrophe or the fear of catastrophe, and is often mobilized by those who feel dispossessed. It is this feeling of dispossession that accounts for the inward thrust of the perceived danger-the belief in an inner enemy. The practitioner of the paranoid style believes that his country has been taken away from him and that the old virtues and system which served his interests are being gradually undermined by outsiders/foreigners as well as by insiders/countrymen in positions of national authority.[52]

---

50. "Extracts from the Theses of the West European Bureau of the ECCI on the Situation in Japan and the Tasks of the Japanese Communist Party," May 1932, *The Communist International*, 195-96.
51. Tipton, *The Japanese Police State*, 129-30. Historians of the prewar Japanese police, such as Elise Tipton, have utilized the "paranoid style" to explain the attitude of the police toward subversives and have noted the similarities between Japanese police views of Communists and American nativist notions about Masonic or religious enemies. Tipton argues that the police were willing to try to ideologically reform Communists because they, like the Nativists, recognized that their enemies were neither racially nor ethnically different from themselves and thus could be made socially acceptable.
52. Richard Hofstadter, "The Paranoid Style in American Politics," *The Paranoid Style in American Politics and Other Essays* (New York: Alfred A. Knopf, 1965), 3-4, 6, 38-40, 23-24, 32.

Hofstadter discusses the American example, but one could imagine that he was speaking of a large segment of the ruling elite in wartime Japan. During the War Konoe and many other members of the old political parties, financial conglomerates, and aristocracy felt that they had been pushed away from the centre of power and influence by new social and political forces calling for a "renovation" of society. Hofstadter observes that the practitioner of the paranoid style perceives his enemy as being almost superhuman. Konoe respected, if not exaggerated, the powers of the leftists. He believed that they possessed great foresight and reacted quite strongly to the predictions of Soviet spy Ozaki Hotsumi. In his February 1942 interrogation record Ozaki argued that the Chinese Communist Party would join forces with the Soviet Union in promoting a Japanese revolution, which could possibly occur within a year. In his November 1944 interrogation record, moreover, Ozaki declared that a postwar revolution was imminent. It is said that Konoe "shuddered" when he heard these statements.[53]

"A fundamental paradox of the paranoid style," Hofstadter points out, "is the imitation of the enemy."[54] In the manner of the nineteenth-century American nativist, the twentieth century practitioner of the paranoid style unconsciously patterns himself after his own enemy:

> By condemning the subversive's fanatical allegiance to an ideology, he affirmed a similarly uncritical acceptance of a different ideology; by attacking the subversive's intolerance of dissent, he worked to eliminate dissent and diversity of opinion; by censuring the subversive for alleged licentiousness, he engaged in sensual fantasies; by criticizing the subversive's loyalty to an organization, he sought to prove his unconditional loyalty to the established order. The nativist moved even farther in the direction of his enemies when he formed tightly-knit societies and parties which were often secret and which subordinated the individual to the single purpose of the group.[55]

The Japanese police charged communists with carrying out anti-war, anti-military activities and encouraging defeatism. As early as 1932 the Comintern declared that the main task of Japanese communists was to agitate against their nation's war efforts and to spread word of the triumphs of socialist nations and

---

53. Muroga, *Shōwa juku*, 118; Dower, *Empire and Aftermath*, 280.
54. Hofstadter, "The Paranoid Style," 32.
55. Hofstadter, "The Paranoid Style," 33. Hofstadter quoting David Brion Davis.

foreign leftist movements.[56] However, it could be argued that it was officials and individuals such as former prime ministers Konoe and Hiranuma Kiichirō who, unwittingly, did more to encourage alarm and anti-war sentiments among the wartime ruling elite. Konoe and Hiranuma, in fact, actually attempted to rally forces against the Tōjō Government as a step toward terminating the conflict with the Allied Powers and averting a revolution.

From late 1942 onward the Tōjō Government began to come under attack for military defeats and the deteriorating domestic situation. On top of this, there was an increasingly loud whispering campaign among influential business and political circles that the Government was harbouring civil and military officials who were advocating communistic policies. Only by miraculously shifting the tide of war in Japan's favour could the Government have silenced complaints about military and domestic matters. Critics and opponents among the ruling elite such as Konoe and Hiranuma could not be easily suppressed; they could only be placated.

However, something could be done to stem the accusations that the Government was protecting leftists or quasi-leftists. The Government may have assumed that once word of its determined efforts to hunt down leftists got around in financial and political circles, charges of being soft on communism would lose credibility. Opponents and critics would thus have lost one means of attack. In this respect, the search by civil and military police for leftists hiding in the government or other important organizations may have been an act of political appeasement, a defensive move against anti-Tōjō critics within the Japanese ruling elite.

A campaign against potential subversives is hardly a surprising development during a war. But it is important to note how the political situation facing the Tōjō Government, combined with problems within and among the various peace preservation organizations in wartime Japan, may have further propelled this campaign against suspected leftists.

THE IMAGE OF A WARTIME LEFTIST THREAT (III): PROBLEMS OF THE WARTIME POLICE FORCE

Studies of the wartime "Red Scare" have pointed to a number of foreign and domestic developments that could have helped to create the impression of a growing leftist threat. However, it appears that one contributing factor has

---

56. "Extracts from the Theses of the West European Bureau of the ECCI on the Situation in Japan and the Tasks of the Japanese Communist Party," *The Communist International*, 200.

not been fully explored: the extent to which the thought control and internal security system itself heightened insecurities about the state of public peace. That is, as a result of their unbridled drive to capture subversives which resulted in the unjust incarceration of scores of individuals, the civil and military police actually magnified the communist presence and thus intensified anxieties among the social, political, financial and administrative elite.

Many individuals, especially influential political and government figures, were sincerely concerned about the spread of communism. But this does not mean that they were incapable of trying to capitalize on prevailing fears, fears that they themselves harboured, to advance their own interests. Successive Japanese governments had used the argument of a communist threat in East Asia, particularly in Northern China, to justify military expansion and occupation. The military's Imperial Way officers, hoping to undermine their rivals in the dominant Control Faction, insisted that there were "Reds" within the Tōjō administration. The business community, in an attempt to maintain control over industries and defend their right to pursue profits, argued that the New Economic Order with its proposals for a planned economy would transform the country into a Soviet state. Diet representatives, fearful that the Imperial Rule Assistance Association would threaten their political interests, claimed that the IRAA was nothing more than a haven for leftists.

The spectre of domestic communist intrigue was frequently used in the pursuit or defense of partisan interests, and the Japanese civil police were no exception and were unquestionably the major beneficiaries of the widespread fears of leftist intrigue. The discovery of communist conspiracies meant commendations and promotions. The civil police had something to gain in intensifying the sense of threat and public danger, and one contemporary has accused them of fanning the flames of class conflict. In his wartime diary, political journalist Kiyozawa Kiyoshi discussed in 1943 an incident in which the tires of over twenty cars parked on a street lined with expensive restaurants were slashed. He concluded that a revolution was imminent and hinted at the culpability of the police by observing that even young patrolmen were not immune to the growing animosity to the rich. In March 1944, moreover, Kiyozawa wrote down that the Metropolitan Police Board had ordered that high-class restaurants be closed down in order to prevent any public disturbance by resentful labourers and conscripted workers. In Kiyozawa's opinion, it was actually the police detectives, agitating among the working class, who were more responsible for fuelling resentment against the wealthy.[57]

---

57. Kiyozawa, *Ankoku nikki*, 75, 114.

Leftists provided the Home Ministry's thought control police with their raison d'être. However, during the 1930s, they began running out of targets. Figures for the number of individuals arrested for leftist thought offenses between 1930 and 1935 were 6,125 in 1930, 10,422 in 1931, 13,938 in 1932, 14,622 in 1933, 3,994 in 1934, and 1,718 in 1935. According to the source for these figures, the dramatic drop in the totals for the last two years indicates a shortage of viable suspects.[58] These officers needed an alternative supply of subversives, and this may account for their investigation of seditious activities among religious groups. In the words of one scholar, the police, fearing retrenchment, concluded that *"their salvation lay in convincing the government and the public of the need for a specialized 'religious police' (shūkyō keisatsu) to control the other social movement-the new religions."*[59] The campaign against liberals which became conspicuous after the scandal involving Minobe Tatsukichi's Organ Theory in the mid-1930s also provided officers with another group of potential suspects. However, religious groups and liberals, even if some seemed to similar to the leftists in advocating a change in the national polity, did not inspire in the public mind the same dread as communists and thus, did not provide the police with as easy a means of bolstering their position.

Japan's wars with China and the Allied Powers worked to the advantage of the thought control police. The wartime suspicions about former thought control offenders provided them with a much-needed supply of suspects, and the increased demands for internal security prompted an expansion in the number of police assigned to investigating thought control issues. In the city of Osaka alone the number of special higher thought control officers had increased from 595 at the end of 1941 to 733 in 1945.[60] Such efforts to strengthen internal security nevertheless had some adverse affects on the system's overall effectiveness, and it has been argued that during the Pacific War "the traditional mechanism of indoctrination and control became strained in the very process of being tightened."[61]

---

58. Mitchell, *Janus-Faced Justice*, 81.
59. Sheldon M. Garon, "State and Religion in Imperial Japan, 1912-1945," *Journal of Japanese Studies*, Vol. 12, No. 2, 1986: 293; Garon, *Molding Japanese Minds*, 78-79. In the latter work, Garon observes that campaign for a specialized religious police proved quite successful and that in 1935 the cabinet allowed for the establishment of such police units in each prefecture.
60. Ogino, *Tokkō keisatsu taiseishi*, 370.
61. John Dower, "Reform and Reconsolidation," *Japan Examined: Perspectives on Modern Japanese History*, ed. Harry Wray and Hilary Conroy (Honolulu: University of Hawaii Press, 1983), 344.

The main responsibility of the thought control police, according to a May 15, 1935 Home Ministry publication, was to eliminate any social movement which undermined social stability or threatened the fundamental nature of the state. Appointment as a *Tokkō* was considered a necessary step for advancement into the upper ranks of the police, and thought control police were supposedly chosen from among the most capable officers. An examination of prewar civil police textbooks reveals the high demands placed on these officers.[62] They were, in effect, required to develop some preternatural ability to detect crimes before they occurred and capture all those involved. The training required of a thought control officer could not be obtained overnight. However, the wartime demands of maintaining internal security necessitated an increase in the number of officers and appears to have led to the induction of individuals less competent or skilful in conducting investigations.

There are indications that the quality of the *Tokkō* declined, and it has been reported that during the War few stations were staffed with officers well-versed in Marxist theory. It is believed, for example, that the Kanagawa Prefectural Police relied on the opinion of a thought control offender in their custody to evaluate the seditious nature of the Hosokawa essay.[63] One individual who was arrested in the Cabinet Planning Board Incident of 1941, Okakura Koshirō, also observed that the police seemed incapable of judging what constituted a violation of the Peace Preservation Law and were arresting more and more individuals with no knowledge of socialist thought.[64] Okakura recalled that while he was in custody the police carried out a mass arrest of some innocent students who were members of a movie society. These students could not be tried and released until they had written out credible confessions. But because they were completely ignorant of Marxism, the police had Okakura tutor them or write out their confessions. Thought control officers, Okakura points out, were forced to provide introductory lectures on Marxism for their so-called leftist suspects. Although they were entrusted with the duty of preventing the spread of unorthodox thought, the police in their effort to establish their cases found themselves transmitting communist ideas to individuals in their custody.

It is evident that during the War some senior police officers maintained doubts about the competence of their subordinates. Since 1942 research and

---

62. *Nihon no keisatsu*, Vol. 8, ed. Koike Yoshimi (Tokyo: Nihon keisatsu hensankai, 1968), 113; Mitchell, *Janus-Faced Justice*, 89.
63. Kimura, *Yokohama jiken no shinsō*, 34-36.
64. "Kikakuin jiken," 60-61.

discussion groups held for the *Tokkō* provided higher-ranking officers with an opportunity to express their professional concerns. At an Osaka meeting one thought control section chief lamented that of all the thought control officers in the sixty-three stations in his jurisdiction only three could competently investigate Peace Preservation Law violations. Moreover, both a Kōchi Prefectural and Tokyo Metropolitan Police Board representative attributed slip-ups in investigations and arrests to the "recent decline in the quality of thought control officers."[65]

Besides some senior police officials, there were other individuals higher up in the state structure who also questioned the abilities and reliability of lower-level police officers. During a 1941 debate in the House of Peers over a bill to control speech, publication, and assembly, one individual proposed that permission to assemble and conduct research not be entrusted to police officers because they lacked the skills and knowledge to make judgments about research.[66] However, by the 1940s, it is improbable that even high-ranking officials could have effectively limited the activities of the police.

Civil police leaders, in order to bolster group morale, had long spoke of the ultimate mission to protect society, and this may have encouraged notions among the police that rules, proper procedures and directives could be sacrificed in order fulfil this mission. Moreover, they believed that the special tasks required of the *Tokkō* had to be performed by independent, decisive individuals who could remain indifferent to criticism. This "combination of moral righteousness and explicit rejection of criticisms from outsiders," Elise Tipton has written, "would have contributed to the insulation of the Tokkō from external control."[67] Such observations are supported by Richard Mitchell who has also commented on the excessive independence of the police force:

> The state, in promoting the severe 'Red scare,' bears responsibility for illegal treatment of communist suspects, but the root cause of parts of the *Tokkō* apparatus running amuck lay in the fact that even though the highly centralized police structure was created as a watchdog for the state, it did not always obey its master. The police, like the army, was often disobedient, marching off to the beat of its own drum. . . . Not even orders from the top of the Home Ministry could stop illegal police practices.[68]

---

65. Ogino, *Tokkō keisatsu taiseishi*, 370.
66. "Genron, shūkai," 421-22.
67. Tipton, *The Japanese Police State*, 95.
68. Mitchell, *Janus-Faced Justice*, 161.

Despite the suspicions and complaints of some officials, little was done to remedy problems and prevent abuses in the handling of thought control cases. Consequently, those individuals who were less familiar with the problems within the police force and more prone to rely on police reports could easily arrive at a rather alarmist picture of leftist intrigue. The large-scale arrests of communists during the Pacific War would have simply confirmed their beliefs that the nation was infested with hidden communists.

The induction of less qualified personnel into the force caused by rapid wartime expansion was nevertheless just one of the problems experienced by the civil police. Another important problem was rivalries: conflict between the civil police and other organizations responsible for safeguarding the public peace as well as well as competition within the civil police force itself. Elise Tipton states that Non-*Tokkō* branches of the civil police resented the rather elite status of the thought control officers and that a lack of cooperation and assistance was notable even between the *Tokkō* of different regions. There was a "tendency of the large Tokyo Tokkō to look down on the Tokkō of rural areas,"[69] and a sense of this can be noted even in the recollections of former police officials. In a late-1970s interview Miyashita Hiroshi, who belonged to the Special Higher Police section of Tokyo's Metropolitan Police Board, discussed conditions among the wartime police. Miyashita admitted that certain police officers were overly preoccupied with uncovering sensational cases, and when asked about the Yokohama Incident, he said officers in the Metropolitan Police Board had doubts about the authenticity of some claims put forth by the Kanagawa Police.[70]

It is possible that regional peace preservation officers, such as those who were investigating the Yokohama Incident, could have aspired to equal some of the accomplishments achieved by their counterparts in the nation's capital. The Metropolitan Police Board's discovery of a Soviet spy ring in the Sorge Incident was a major coup, and one of the official documents about the Yokohama Incident, in fact, claimed that the affair was as dangerous as the Sorge Incident.[71] There exists, moreover, an argument that the authorities in Kanagawa Prefecture actually sought to establish some link between the Yokohama and Sorge Incidents.

In 1981 independent journalist Nakamura Tomoko was able to interview Itō Ritsu, who had been accused of betraying members of the Sorge Incident

---

69. Tipton, *The Japanese Police State*, 97.
70. Miyashita, *Tokkō no kaisō*, 240-42.
71. "Saikin no sayoku jiken," 373.

to the prewar police and who had recently returned to Japan after many years of imprisonment in China. Itō told Nakamura that around March or April 1945 he received a visit from the Yokohama District Procurator who questioned him at length about his relationship with Hosokawa Karoku and others arrested in the Yokohama Incident. Itō informed the Procurator that he knew nothing of Hosokawa's involvement with any group conspiring to re-establish the Japan Communist Party. He also insisted that while Hosokawa and he talked about how the Pacific War was a mistake and would end in defeat, neither of them had undertaken any organized act of protest.[1] Nakamura suggests that, if one accepts Itō's disclosure, the authorities in Kanagawa Prefecture may have been trying even in the last months of the War to tie their investigation to the notorious Sorge Incident and thus share some of the Metropolitan Police Board's glory in discovering an international spy network.

Many of those arrested in the Yokohama Incident have commented on the competitive spirit of the Kanagawa Prefectural Police. When one of the journalists insisted that he was not a communist, the officer in charge of his cross-examination shouted at him, "What? You're a hopeless fellow. This is not Tokyo, you know!" In his postwar testimony against the police officers who tortured him, another journalist testified that he was terrorized by an officer who stated, "It's alright if we kill you. The Kanagawa *Tokkō* are different from the Metropolitan Police Board, you know." Still another individual who was arrested in connection with the Patriotic Political Comrades Group claimed that one officer made the following boast, "Don't underestimate the Kanagawa *Tokkō*. . . . I'm Morikawa, and I'm a true-born Kanagawa *Tokkō*." Even the wife of an arrested *Kaizō* journalist recalled hearing that the Kanagawa Prefectural Police were all in an uproar over having out-manoeuvred the Tokyo Metropolitan Police Board in discovering a significant incident. When she visited the offices of the Kanagawa Police, she noted that the atmosphere was very excited and the officers seemed to walk about with a pronounced swagger.[2]

Rivalries, however, were not just an internal issue for the civil police. Home Ministry personnel such as the *Tokkō* had long prided themselves on being the main force in internal security and jealously guarded their prerogatives in the control of thought, circulation of information and mass movements. Throughout the 1920s and 1930s thought control police and their

---

72. Nakamura, "Yokohama jiken: Mitsu no episōdo," 106, 110.
73. Kimura, *Yokohama jiken no shinsō*, 24, 31; "Kōjutsusho Hirose Ken'ichi," *Yokohama jiken shiryōshū*, 94; Ono and Kiga, *Yokohama jiken: Tsuma to imōto*, 42.

colleagues in the Home Ministry revealed themselves to be ill-disposed to cooperate with Justice Ministry officials. Justice Ministry prosecutors responsible for violations of the Peace Preservation Law often complained that Home Ministry officials repeatedly ignored their requests for copies of police publications dealing with thought crimes.[74]

Still, the principal threat to the *Tokkō*'s monopoly on thought control and internal security matters actually came from the Army's *Kempeitai* or military police. Friction between the civil and military police was notable even in the early 1930s. In fact, in an effort to counterbalance the elevated status of the Army, and thus the military police, as directly responsible to the Emperor as commander-in-chief, the civil police tried to reinforce their identification with the throne by promoting a view of themselves as the "emperor's police." This contest for institutional prestige became quite public and could erupt into scandals, such as the Go-Stop Incident of 1933 which mushroomed out of a confrontation between an Osaka traffic patrolman and an off-duty soldier. The military police officers who wrote up the reports on this Incident described the patrolman's actions as an affront to the Army. The minor scuffle quickly became a much-publicized dispute that was only resolved after the prefectural governor forced both civil and military personnel to submit apologies to each other.[75]

With the outbreak of war with China in 1937 disputes between the civil and military police became more clearly jurisdictional struggles. The semi-official History of the Home Ministry observes that in the late 1930s the military police began to increasingly interfere in labour disputes and the control of speech and assembly. The Army argued that issues of national defence and internal security were inseparable, and thus, according to this History, it planned to assume the rights and functions of the civil police in carrying out censorship and suppressing subversive movements.[76]

By the early 1940s the civil police were feeling the full force of the Army's challenge to their authority, and interference from military personnel became part of the experience of thought control officers during the Pacific War. One former officer in Shizuoka prefecture recalled that, in mid-1943, when he was unable to immediately discover the source of some letters to the Prime Minister demanding an end to the War, he was not only plagued by daily complaints from superiors. He was confronted by the regional military police

---

74. Mitchell, *Thought Control in Prewar Japan*, 126.
75. Tipton, *The Japanese Police State*, 119-20, 121.
76. *Naimushōshi*, Vol. 2, 772.

who declared that "if the local police can't make an arrest, we will."⁷⁷ This thought control officer noted that he and his colleagues resented the involvement and high-handed manner of the military police, but felt that the only action they could take was to redouble their own efforts to find the writer of the letters.

The result of this conflict between the civil and military police was an often ridiculously petty contest to apprehend subversives. Nakanishi Kō, the famous CCP spy, recalled how his arrest by the civil police in 1942 led to a dispute with the military police.⁷⁸ Both civil and military police wanted to take Nakanishi into custody and claim credit for apprehending a dangerous spy. The dispute was only resolved after both the civil and military police decided to let Nakanishi himself decide who would arrest him.

The Home Ministry's civil police were clearly under pressure during the War to outperform their military counterparts who, according to contemporary accounts, enjoyed the open support of Prime Minister Tōjō Hideki. Tōjō, an Army General, preferred to rely on military personnel and had difficulty dealing with civil officials. Ōtani Keijirō, a high-ranking military police officer, states that Tōjō wanted to use the military police for everything. Murata Gorō, a senior civil police official, recalled that Home Ministry officials viewed Tōjō's appointment of himself as Home Minister at the beginning of his tenure as Prime Minister as a jurisdictional infringement. Ministry officials, from top to bottom, believed that one of their own high-ranking members should head the Ministry, and they openly expressed their resentment of Tōjō's appointment. Murata noted that it was impossible to conceal this state of affairs because news of the bad relations between the Ministry and the Prime Minister was spread throughout the country by means of the Home Ministry's daily practice of sending ten messagers from the capital to its regional offices.⁷⁹

Information provided by his private secretary, Akamatsu Sadao, reveals that Tōjō himself did little to conceal his low opinion of non-military personnel.⁸⁰ Tōjō complained that, in comparison with military officials who underwent a long period of rigorous training, civil officials received little schooling after they graduated from university and were far too hesitant and lax in dealing with threats to internal security. During a February 1944 conference

---

77. Gibney, Sensō, The Japanese Remember the Pacific War, 177.
78. Nakanishi, Chūgoku kakumei, 273-74.
79. Ōtani, Shōwa kempeishi, 410; Murata Gorō shi danwa sokkiroku 3, 103-4.
80. Sadao Akamatsu, Tōjō hishokan kimitsu nisshi (Tokyo: Bungei shunjū, 1985), 97-98,
133.

for Justice Ministry officials he demanded that officials attempt to detect crimes even before they occur. Moreover, at a Cabinet council meeting he reportedly discussed at length foreign reports of considerable support for the enemy cause within Japan and then proceeded to chide the Home and Justice Ministry for being slow in dealing with subversives.[81]

Tōjō appears to have been a man who favoured prompt, if not reckless, action. He was the Kwantung Military Police Commander in Manchuria when an attempted coup d'état by radical young military officers broke out in Tokyo on February 26, 1936. By orchestrating rapid mass arrests of suspected supporters of the revolt among the military personnel stationed in Manchuria, he won the admiration of his superiors. However, more than a few individuals believed that Tōjō had been excessive in carrying out these arrests. Tōjō insisted that "all those connected with the Imperial Way Faction be arrested," and according to one civil police official, he even travelled from the Asian mainland to Tokyo to pressure the Home Ministry into doubling its efforts to hunt down individuals connected with the February 26, 1936 Rebellion.[82]

On the very day that the Pacific War began, moreover, the Tōjō Cabinet carried out wholesale preventive arrests of leftists and their suspected sympathizers, and as the war situation worsened, there may have been plans for other precautionary measures. Following the announcement of the Saipan emergency in June 1944 Military Police Central Headquarters Chief Katō Hatsujirō called a meeting to prepare for the mass arrest of suspected anti-war, anti-military elements throughout the country. Katō and others worked throughout the night on the plans. But, in the end, the plans were shelved because it was concluded that they would only temporarily silence dissent and could undermine public morale.[83]

Tōjō did not enjoy dictatorial powers and the extent to which he contributed to the hunt for subversives and ultimately to the wartime "Red Scare" should not be exaggerated and must be measured against various other factors. Still, his perceived patronage of the military police, advocacy of prompt action against threats to security as well as his reportedly lax attitude toward proper procedures could have influenced the conduct of peace preservation personnel. According to his wartime personal secretary, for example, Tōjō openly declared that problems had to be dealt with in an

---

81. Akamatsu, *Tōjō hishokan*, 107. The date of this conference is unclear; it was held possibly in September 1943.
82. Ōtani, *Shōwa kempeishi*, 410; Hoshino, *Jidai to jibun*, 256-57; *Abe Genki shi danwa dai nikkai sokkiroku*, 78.
83. Tōyama, *Shōwashi*, 210; Ōtani, *Shōwa kempeishi*, 449.

unhesitating manner and that legal niceties were useless if they meant that the country perished.[84] Such views could only encourage a reckless campaign to stamp out potential dissidence and thus facilitate the occurrence of cases such as the Yokohama Incident which, in the words of one noted specialist on the history of thought control, was "the fruit of Home Ministry superiors consistently allowing *Tokkō* to operate outside legal norms."[85]

THE IMPACT OF POLICE INVESTIGATIONS ON THE RULING ELITE

It is clear that wartime arguments about a growing communist threat were not concocted out of thin air. They were more than often interpretations of certain changes in society and were substantiated by what was accepted at the time as expert opinion.

According to members of his wartime coterie, Prince Konoe Fumimaro was acquainted with individuals from all walks of life who could provide him with news of recent domestic and foreign developments. Informants among high-ranking civil police officers included Murata Gōrō who in his reminiscence of Konoe has revealed something of the wealth of contacts the Prince had among the police. Murata had wished to act as a liaison between Konoe and former prime minister Hiranuma Kiichirō who shared many of the former's ideas about the wartime Communist threat. In order to fulfil his self-appointed role of maintaining a line of communication between the two men, Murata turned down a request to become a prefectural governor. Murata had no intention of informing Konoe of his decision, but his colleagues among the civil police appear to have quickly passed along the news to the Prince. Soon after his rejection of the governorship, Murata met with Konoe who nonchalantly explained that, given his contacts among officials, it was inevitable that he would have learnt about such matters.[86]

Years after the Pacific War Murata would continue to insist that Communists had been behind a government campaign against hoarding, which was crowned by the slogan, "Shortages are not regrettable. Inequality is regrettable." Measures to enforce "equal living standards," Murata argued, suggested Communist thinking.[87] Such opinions as well as corroborating

---

84. Akamatsu, *Tōjō hishokan*, 107.
85. Mitchell, *Janus-Faced Justice*, 153.
86. Tomita Kenji, *Haisen Nihon no uchigawa: Konoe kō no omoide* (Tokyo: Konjyaku shoin, 1962), 212; *Murata Gorō shi danwa sokkiroku 5*, 79-81, 82-88.
87. *Murata Gorō shi danwa sokkiroku 3*, 40-41.

assessments about the state of public peace made by other police officials would have no doubt bolstered concerns about wartime trends and Communist conspiracies. In his diary, for example, Hosokawa Morisada recorded a meeting between Konoe and another high-ranking police official who described conditions in Japan as being potentially "explosive":

> In June [1944], Konoe invited Hata Shigenori, chief of the first section of the Special Police division of the Metropolitan Police Board to Tekigaisō, with Hosokawa and Takamura Sakahiko, where Hata spoke at length about recent communist movements in Japan. His comments heightened Konoe's growing anxiety about a communist revolution. Hata explained that since no communist party existed in Japan, communist movements were unorganized, but the communists were active at their places of work, carrying on as they considered appropriate under the particular circumstances. The deteriorating of the national economy during the War had provided a seedbed for communist movements. The activists did not openly reveal their ideology, but most of them were trying to cultivate and train new communists in anticipation of defeat. In short, the situation was a "pile of dry hay" that would flare up as soon as anyone set a match to it. The Metropolitan Police Board classified those who rejected the national polity (*kokutai*) as leftists and those who supported it as rightists, but it was clear that the so-called rightists included many leftists. In the right-wing cry to "restore industry to the throne," for example, could be heard the voice of the Left, and, moreover, most of the so-called converts from the Left were not true converts.[88]

It was probably more than a coincidence that Hata's description of communist activity closely conformed with assessments contained in some of the documents on the Yokohama Incident. The January 1944 "Explanation on the State of Public Peace," which was delivered at a Conference of Police Chiefs and which used the Incident to analyze the future actions and direction of the Japanese communist movement, came to the following conclusion:

> In the course of the present year, with the deteriorating war and domestic situation, the communist movement has

---

88. Yoshitake Oka, *Konoe Fumimaro: A Political Biography*, trans. Shumpei Okamoto and Patricia Murray (Tokyo: University of Tokyo Press, 1983), 167-68.

progressed and gone from a preparatory stage to a stage of active resistance. That is, the communists are trying to organize their scattered forces into an illegal, radical vanguard organization. In the meantime, they have put forth a plan to encourage popular discontent by addressing those problems which, under the strained domestic situation, are directly affecting the living conditions of the people. And they are attempting to prompt outbursts of this discontent in every sector of society.[89]

A high-ranking thought control official like Hata Shigenori would have known been privy to such reports about the Yokohama Incident. The Incident thus contributed to his nightmarish description of how the communists were a widespread force within the country, were benefitting from the deteriorating war situation and were becoming more active in making preparations for a revolution. In the final analysis, the determined hunt for leftists by the police forces did not contribute to a greater sense of internal security. Rather, it heightened insecurities by substantiating the impression that communists numbered in the thousands and were a force to be considered. The Yokohama Incident and other wartime incidents, the products of anxieties about communism, only served to intensify fears about leftists and, in this fashion, may have contributed to desires to end the Pacific War. That is, those who advocated peace and an end to military rule pointed to the supposedly large number of communists and argued that the War was encouraging leftist sympathies among the people and thereby pushing the nation toward collapse and revolution.

At the end of the Pacific War Japan was indeed a physically shattered nation with a shocked and bewildered people. Since the start of the undeclared war with China, about 3.1 million Japanese had died (800,000 of whom were civilians) and over 30 percent had lost their homes.[90] Industry had been reduced to one quarter of its previous capacity, and inflation had reduced the *yen* to barely a hundredth of its prewar value. Severe food shortages resulted in near starvation for most of the population. Those who had enjoyed social, political, administrative, and economic influence were demoralized and fearful that the people would soon turn against them and join the Occupation authorities in demanding their removal.

---

89. "Chian jōkyō ni tsuite," 310.
90. John Whitney Hall, *Japan: From Prehistory to Modern Times* (Ann Arbor: University of Michigan Press, 1991), 349-50.

The Occupation authorities' October 4, 1945 Civil Liberties Directive proclaimed guarantees for freedom of expression and resulted in the rescindment of the Peace Preservation Law and the abolition of the thought control police. Popular support for change and a drive to address past and present injustices did become manifest, at least, at the beginning of the Occupation. These feelings found expression in tremendous labour agitation, political activity and even one independent legal initiative meant to be a citizens' repudiation of the wartime state: the Trial of the Yokohama Incident Police Officers.

However, the prewar order and its elites could not be so easily eradicated, and the Occupation fell short of being a veritable "heyday" for the former victims of state oppression. The purge of wartime elites was poorly administered and eventually reversed. Censorship was maintained, and those who had been unjustly sentenced under the Peace Preservation Law did not have their names cleared. Leftist parties and groups whose members included many former victims of thought control, moreover, remained divided during the Occupation, unable or unwilling to unite behind campaigns denouncing the abuses committed by wartime officials.

5
The Postwar Trial of the Yokohama Incident Police Officers

The Campaign Against the Wartime State

Scholars have noted the continuing need for the historiography of the Occupation to focus more on independent Japanese activities during the period.[1] That is, more studies of the Occupied as well as the Occupiers is still required to construct a clearer picture of the Occupation and the hopes that it seemed to present. "Future students," one writer has observed, "must take seriously Japanese ideas and proposals for change-initiatives which were often ignored by SCAP [Supreme Commander for the Allied Powers]."[2]

The prosecution of the police officers responsible for investigating the Yokohama Incident was one of those independent Japanese initiatives which has received little attention, but which provides a means of examining developments from the point of view of the Occupied. It was in November 1945 that those arrested in the Yokohama Incident lodged a complaint against the officers who had tortured them.[3] Circumstances initially favoured such a legal endeavour, which seemed to reflect the popular antipathy toward the old establishment that emerged with Japan's surrender. Even before official promises regarding freedom of expression had been made, the Japanese people

---

1. Carol Gluck, "Entangling Illusions—Japanese and American Views of the Occupation," *New Frontiers in American-East Asian Relations: Essays Presented to Dorothy Borg*, ed. Dorothy Borg (New York: Columbia University Press, 1987), 190; Ray A. Moore, "Reflections on the Occupation of Japan," *Journal of Asian Studies*, Vol. 38, No. 4, August 1979: 723; Masanori Nakamura, "Sengo kaikaku to gendai," 2-6.
2. Ray A. Moore, "The Occupation of Japan as History: Some Recent Research," *Monumenta Nipponica*, Vol. 36, No. 3: 325.
3. *The Yokohama Case and Tortures in Japan*, 8.

had begun to express their resentment of the political and economic elite. Polls taken at the time revealed that many considered it "natural" and "essential" that the *zaibatsu* be dissolved and the militarists and ultranationalists be removed in order to reconstruct the nation.[4]

This anti-establishment and reformist drive unfortunately proved to be short-lived. As one scholar has observed, the "revolutionary ferment" which erupted during the first nine months of the Occupation and which resulted in vigorous labour movements could not be easily sustained: "Too much was against it-the early surrender, the retention in power of the old guard, the divisions of the left, the presence of SCAP."[5] Strikes, demonstrations and other more radical manifestations were soon suppressed and much of the ebullience of the early reformist drive subsided. The court case against the Yokohama Incident Police Officers, which took over six years before finally being resolved in April 1952, was one wholly independent initiative that survived the waning of this early anti-establishment mood. Those who initiated this legal action nevertheless were forced to carry out a lonely battle, unable to attract support even from groups that could have been expected to have favoured their cause.

Because the Trial of the Yokohama Incident Police Officers was never widely publicized, the Occupation authorities may have never learned of the affair or the court case. The same cannot be said for the leftist parties and the Japanese publishing industry. Those arrested in the Incident had connections with both groups. The early Occupation authorities had freed both the Japan Communist Party (JCP) and the publishing industry from many of the past restrictions on their activities, and they appeared to face no official obstacles in assisting members involved in a legal battle against wartime officials. Yet, neither group rallied behind the campaign of those arrested in the Yokohama Incident.

Even among one-time critics of the Japanese state there individuals during the Occupation who were uneasy about their relationship to the old regime. Whereas those arrested in the Yokohama Incident may have felt confident in their identity as innocent victims of the thought control system and thus could freely launch attacks against the former state, others may have feared being criticized for having cooperated in some fashion with the prewar authorities. Concerns about being accused of collaboration, if not war crimes, were said to have been aroused in a variety of individuals as the military

---

4. Gluck, "Entangling Illusions," 194.
5. Joe Moore, *Japanese Workers and the Struggle for Power 1945-1947* (Madison: The University of Wisconsin Press, 1983), 243.

execution of low-ranking soldiers as Class B or C War Criminals and the purge of minor officials seemed to indicate that punishment would not be restricted to national leaders and prominent members of society.[6]
As mentioned earlier, the prewar thought control system was not perfect and ended up creating rather than simply preventing internal security problems. It was nevertheless able to complicate the lives of its former targets even during the Occupation. Many who had worked in the publishing industry throughout the War were worried about being denounced as propagandists and, as a result of the 1930s' *Tenkō* policy, even members of the Japan Communist Party may have felt vulnerable to charges of collaboration. Although the JCP possessed better credentials than other political organizations for leading an attack on the prewar order, its calls for pursuing the topic of war responsibility were little more than "lip-service." In accounting for the weakness of the Party's commitment, writers have taken note of the fact that its membership included individuals who had undergone ideological conversion in the prewar period and who had enjoyed some measure of official patronage.[7]

The JCP as well as the publishing industry felt that they had to handle the issue of war crimes and related matters with considerable care. Both Groups had come to the conclusion that independent activities in this area could arouse the displeasure of the Occupation authorities. In addition, both the Party and the publishing industry suffered from problems of factionalism or internal strife, which created further disincentives to deal with matters such as the court case against the Yokohama Incident Police Officers. During the Occupation many of those who had been arrested in the Incident became associated with factions within the JCP or were caught up in efforts on the part of labour unionists to purge the publishing industry of prewar management. Under these circumstances, support for the legal campaign of these individuals could have been criticized as a move to aggrandize some faction or defend the prewar management.

That the Trial of the Yokohama Incident Police Officers never became widely-known and that this legal initiative failed to attract popular support does not make the topic less worthy of examination. As one specialist of Occupation labour history has observed, consideration must be also given to "paths not taken and possibilities unfulfilled."[8] The Trial, in challenging the conduct of the wartime authorities, embodied some of the early ideals expressed by American officials and embraced by a good portion of the Japanese people

---

6. Akazawa Shiro, "Sengo shisō to bunka," *Senryō to sengo kaikaku*, 178-80.
7. Sodei and Takemae, "Nihon senryō to wa nani ka," 352.
8. Moore, *Japanese Workers and the Struggle for Power*, xiv.

soon after the surrender. Some similarities between it and the Tokyo War Crimes Trials have been noted.⁹ However, unlike the Allied Powers' Tokyo Trials which emphasized issues of international conduct and the responsibility of the Japanese leadership for the recent War, the Trial of the Yokohama Incident Police Officers focussed on atrocities committed by Japanese officials against their own citizens and raised the question of the kind of treatment that the people should expect from their state.

The Trial of the Yokohama Incident Police Officers was one of the most, if not completely, successful challenges to government authority initiated by private citizens in Japan, and an examination of it and the conditions within which it took place can reveal both the repercussions of as well as the eventual obstacles to the reformist, anti-establishment impulse that emerged at the beginning of the Occupation. Japan's defeat appeared to have discredited the wartime state, but even at a time when it was most open to attack, a domestic campaign against representatives of the state who had abused their authority was bound to face difficulties. This chapter thus discusses the Trial of the Yokohama Incident Police Officers, its significance and the issues that it covered, and the response or non-response of the Japan Communist Party and the publishing industry to it.

THE POSTWAR TRIAL OF THE POLICE OFFICERS IN CHARGE OF INVESTIGATING THE YOKOHAMA INCIDENT

In his testimony against his former interrogators, one journalist described how the Police Officers placed a large wooden stick between his knees, forced him to sit with his legs folded under him, and stepped on his thighs until the pressure caused by the stick on his knee joints became excruciating. On one occasion he was forced to endure this ordeal for about an hour while being simultaneously beaten with bamboo swords and ropes. Another individual, the only woman among those arrested in the Yokohama Incident, also testified against the Officers and spoke of how they sexually tortured her. At one point, the Officers almost beat her until she was unconscious and had to be hospitalized.¹⁰

---

9. Kimura, *Yokohama jiken no shinsō*, 111. Kimura Tōru, for example, argues that it could be viewed as a scaled-down version of the Tokyo War Crimes Trial.
10. "Kōjutsusho, Kimura Tōru to Katō Seiji," 86; "Kōjutsusho, Kawada Sadako," *Yokohama jiken shiryōshū*, 80.

Torture had been officially abolished in 1879; forced confessions had been declared unacceptable; and the Meiji Constitution, the Penal Code and Criminal Procedural Code had mandated punishment for officials who committed or permitted such illegal acts.[11] In the prewar Japanese courts, judges were expected to render all confessions illegal if there was physical evidence of torture. However, even when a suspect could prove that his confession had been forcibly obtained, a judge could penalize the suspect for having made the confession and thereby misleading the procurator and preliminary trial judge. Consequently, from the beginning, prosecuting the Yokohama Incident Police Officers was not an easy task.

Although guards, doctors, and other prisoners originally agreed to stand as witnesses against the Kanagawa Prefectural Police, they later refused. Those arrested in the affair suspect that someone may have pressured these prospective witnesses into changing their minds. Because of a lack of evidence, most had their cases against the Police dismissed.[12] The exception was Masuda Naohiko, who had been arrested as a member of the Soviet Research Group. While he was in custody Masuda had been able to smuggle out to his wife a large piece of preserved scab and with this as evidence, he was able to take his case to the Tokyo District Higher Court. At the March 28, 1951 Trial the Judges accepted the charge that three of the police officers, "in a conspiracy with other Justice and police officials," tortured Masuda during his cross-examination.[13]

The former Officers immediately lodged an appeal with the Supreme Court of Japan on the advice of their defense attorney, Usami Rokurō. Usami had defended one-time Justice Minister and Premier Hiranuma Kiichirō during the Tokyo War Crimes Trials. Usami argued that it was unfair that only the plaintiff Masuda had been allowed to summon witnesses. He observed that a request had been made to summon witnesses on behalf of his clients and that Tokyo District Higher Court Judges had rendered their final verdict without passing a decision on all of the witnesses. Rendering a decision before passing a decision on witnesses, Usami argued, was a violation of Article 31 of the

---

11. Mitchell, *Janus-Faced Justice*, 34, 113.
12. Nakamura, *Yokohama jiken no hitobito*, 67; Ono and Kiga, *Yokohama jiken: Tsuma to imōto*, 43-44. Ono Sada recalls that, once when she went to the police station to collect her husband's laundry, she discovered an item of clothing that was practically covered in blood. Ono states that she unfortunately disposed of the stained piece of clothing and could not provide it as evidence of torture.
13. "Tōkyō kōkō saiban hanketsu," *Yokohama jiken shiryōshū*, 101.

Constitution which read that "punishment could not be imposed unless the established procedures of law were carried out."[14]

Usami had wished to summon two superiors of the former Police Officers. The Tokyo District Court Judges had rejected one witness, the Chief of the Kanagawa Prefectural Police, but had neither rejected nor approved of the other, the Special Higher Thought Control Police Section Chief of the Kanagawa Police. Usami insisted that both witnesses could have provided information on the character and professional conduct of the defendants, as well as information on the strained internal conditions, state of intellectual crimes, methods of control used by the police.

In concluding his appeal, Usami referred to the statement of the Tokyo District Court Judges that his clients tortured Masuda Naohiko "in a conspiracy with other Justice and police officials." Usami insisted that the Judges levied responsibility for the actions of these "Justice and police officials" on his clients without specifically identifying these other officials. The Judges, thereby, had tried to punish his clients for the misdeeds of others.[15]

In April 1952 the Supreme Court of Japan upheld the decision of the Tokyo District Higher Court.[16] The Supreme Court sentenced Police Inspector Matsushita Eitarō to one and a half years of penal servitude and Assistant Police Inspectors Mori Seizō and Karasawa Rokuji to a year of penal servitude each for their torture of Masuda. In this respect, the Japanese courts appear to have maintained the publicized promise made by Justice Minister Iwata Chuzō on October 5, 1945. In an interview with the *Asahi shimbun* the Justice Minister responded to a question regarding the possible prosecution of wartime officials responsible for torturing political prisoners by declaring that punishment would be meted out if an investigation uncovered proof that such crimes had been committed.[17]

The Trial of the Yokohama Incident Police Officers, however, did not end in complete victory for those who had been arrested and tortured. The attitudes of the Occupation authorities toward former wartime personnel had changed, and by 1947 they were clearly considering releasing many of them from the purge and allowing them to return to government service.[18] The end

---

14. "Bengonin Usami Rokurō no jōkoku shui," *Yokohama jiken shiryōshū*, 109, 104.
15. "Bengonin Usami Rokurō," 110, 112.
16. "Saikō saibansho hanketsu," *Yokohama jiken shiryōshū*," 103-4.
17. Takemae Eiji, *Senryō sengoshi: Tainichi kanri seisaku no zenyō* (Tokyo: Keisō shobo, 1980), 117-19.
18. "General Headquarters Far East Command, Military Intelligence Section, General Staff, General Activities, Memorandum to Mr. Sumino, C.L.O., 13 June 1947, Subject: Reinstatement in Government Service of Former Special Higher Police (TOKKO KA) Personnel," *Documents*

of the Occupation, which coincided with the conclusion of the court case, further freed the Japanese government of its obligation to punish wartime officials.

Four days after the Supreme Court of Japan handed down its decision against the Yokohama Incident Police Officers, the San Francisco Peace Treaty came into effect on April 28, 1952. In celebration of the nation's independence from the Occupation, the Japanese government declared a general amnesty that both freed many convicted war criminals and allowed the Police Officers to escape punishment.[19] Those arrested in the Incident, preoccupied with the pressures of earning a living, were unable to act as watchdogs against such government decisions. It was only decades later that they learned that the Officers who had tortured them had not been obliged to serve out even single day of their prison sentences.

THE SIGNIFICANCE OF THE TRIAL

Individuals have argued that what distinguishes the Yokohama Incident from other peace preservation incidents was the use of torture during the interrogations. Those arrested in the Cabinet Planning Board and Mantetsu Incidents, for example, were not physically abused. In recalling his experiences during the Mantetsu Incident, one individual observed that while guards beat to death a suspected Korean revolutionary in the cell next to him, they provided him with sweets, library books, paper and pencils. The guards, he believes, treated him and his fellow suspects with considerable civility because they respected them as government officials and because they did not view thought offenders as the most nefarious of criminals.[20]

Richard Mitchell observes that "while high social rank did not ensure proper treatment, upper-class criminal suspects, or those with close ties to the directive elite, were insulated from police brutality."[21] Many of those arrested in the Cabinet Planning Board and Mantetsu Incidents were themselves high-ranking government officials and were closely acquainted with influential

---

concerning the Allied Occupation and Control of Japan, Vol. II: Political, Military and Cultural (Tokyo: Division of Special Records, Foreign Office, Japanese Government, 1949), 123-24.
19. Nakamura, *Yokohama jiken no hitobito*, 276.
20. Okudaira Yasuhiro, "Yokohama jiken to chian ijihō," *Yokohama jiken: genron dan'atsu no kōzu*, 49; Ishidō, "Mantetsu chōsabu wa nan de atta ka I," 77; Ishidō Kiyotomo, *Waga itan no Shōwashi* (Tokyo: Keisō shobō, 1987), 242-43; Itō, *Life Along the South Manchurian Railway*, 194, 195, 200.
21. Mitchell, *Janus-Faced Justice*, 133.

persons. The Commanding Officer of the Kwantung Military Police, who was on friendly terms with many of the Mantetsu researchers, reportedly interceded on their behalf to make sure that they received military rations and were never brutalized while in custody.[22] Moreover, the superiors of both the suspects in the Cabinet Planning Board and Mantetsu Incidents made efforts to see that those arrested had the charges against them reduced.

There is thus no consensus on the degree to which the prewar police resorted to physical coercion in dealing with suspects. But it is impossible to deny police brutality, and prewar government officials themselves acknowledged the incidence of torture. High-ranking ex-thought control police official Miyashita Hiroshi said, "there were cases of torture, but things could be quite different depending on the individual officer, the geographical location and the period."[23]

The prewar thought control system was never uniform in its treatment of offenders. Around 1937, the Home Ministry verified police torture cases in Aomori, Okinawa, and Kanagawa Prefecture. Police in certain jurisdictions were notorious for their frequent use of physical coercion, and those in Kanagawa Prefecture, who were responsible for investigating the Yokohama Incident, had a reputation for brutality. In 1937 one House of Peers member noted that "many cases of the use of torture by the police had were reported. Such cases occurred in Kanagawa, Kagoshima, Yamaguchi, Iwate, and Okayama prefectures, and the forms of torture resorted to by the Kanagawa Police are the most shocking."[24]

The torture suffered by those arrested in the Yokohama Incident is its most conspicuous and tragic feature. But the Trial of the Yokohama Incident Police Officers did more than provide proof of prewar police brutality. The Trial was meant to be a people's repudiation of the wartime state and marked the first time in Japanese history that the courts ruled in favour of private citizens in a case against state officials. Moreover, it was clear from the statements made by the Judges during the Trial that what was at issue was whether the state and its representatives could be absolved of misdeeds committed during the recent War.

The Tokyo District Higher Court Judges had observed that the investigations were conducted in a period when the war situation was quite grave and rigorous efforts to suppress thought crimes were being undertaken. But they argued that in a constitutional state, whether it be democratic or

---

22. Ishidō, "Mantetsu chōsabu wa nan de atta ka I," 77.
23. Miyashita, *Tokkō no kaisō*, 313.
24. Mitchell, *Janus-Faced Justice*, 125.

monarchical, violent and unbecoming actions by procurators, judicial and police officials could not be tolerated.[25] During an appeal to the Supreme Court of Japan Defense Attorney Usami Rokurō, who had experience defending accused war criminals, unsuccessfully tried to counter this argument by suggesting that the Tokyo District Higher Court Judges had been under the mistaken idea that they were presiding at some endeavour such as the Tokyo War Crimes Trials. These District Higher Court Judges, Usami declared, were not supposed to render a decision on the future of democracy in Japan but were simply expected to help determine the innocence and guilt of his clients. Usami furthermore insisted that adequate consideration had to be given to the strained conditions under which his clients had been forced to carry out their duties, and he described the recent War as a life-and-death struggle for the nation during which the violation of human rights had become a non-issue.[26]

Although caution should be maintained against exaggerating any comparison, one could argue that the Trial of the Yokohama Incident Police Officers was similar to the Tokyo War Crimes Trials insofar as it was an investigation of the conduct of wartime government officials. In fact, the offenses committed by the Police Officers fell under one of the official definitions of "war crimes":

> Murder, extermination, enslavement, deportation and other inhumane acts committed against *any* civilian population, before or during the war or prosecutions on political, racial or religious grounds in execution of or in connection with any crime defined herein *whether or not in violation of the domestic law of the country where perpetrated* [italics mine].[27]

Still, the Trial of the Police Officers had a different emphasis and dealt with issues not explored by the War Crimes Trials.

The Tokyo War Crimes Trials began in 1946, and at the onset, there was support among American officials in both Washington and Tokyo for a thorough investigation of suspected war criminals. Officials in the U.S. capital even complained that the number of Japanese set to be tried as war criminals was too small. Tokyo War Crimes Trials Chief Prosecutor Joseph B. Keenan would later concur and told members of the Far Eastern Commission that the Trials of all individuals in Japan suspected of war crimes could not be

---

25. "Tokyo kōtō saiban," *Yokohama jiken shiryōshō*, 102.
26. "Bengonin Usami Rokurō," 105-7.
27. "Apprehension, Trial and Punishment of War Criminals in the Far East, FEC Policy Decision, April 3, 1946," *Documents concerning the Allied Occupation and Control of Japan*, 257.

concluded in a single lifetime. However, by 1948, those in the State Department expressed regret that the Trials had even taken place.[28]

Both contemporary observers and subsequent writers have criticized the War Crimes Trial for various reasons, including the failure to allow for Japanese involvement in the prosecution, the narrowness of the topics investigated, and the arbitrary selection of defendants. Critics have observed that, while some individuals were tried and sentenced for crimes committed by their subordinates or superiors, important suspects were simply released due to political considerations and even those who had committed the most heinous crimes were never brought before the Tribunal. U.S. authorities, for example, extended their protection in exchange for information on bacteriological warfare to Lieutenant General Ishii Shirō whose gruesome experiments on prisoners-of-war were known to both American officials and journalists residing in Occupied Japan.[29]

These opportunistic decisions regarding war criminals as well as the failure to involve the Japanese in judging their former officials have resulted in a widespread perception of the War Crimes Trial as "victor's justice." Chief Prosecutor Keenan had proposed in 1946 that Japanese judges be included in the proceedings. However, this was essentially a precautionary move to counter the demands of other Allied Powers to have Emperor Hirohito placed on the list of war criminals. Keenan, it is argued, assumed that Japanese judges could be expected to vigorously fight for the legal immunity of the Emperor.[30]

The main reason for the exclusion of Japanese judges was no doubt concern that their involvement would result in reduced sentences. Scholars have revealed that Japanese officials had attempted to carry out their own trials in which defendants were given relatively light sentences for serious crimes involving murder. These autonomous trials took place from September 1945

---

28. Richard B. Finn, *Winners in Peace: MacArthur, Yoshida, and Postwar Japan* (Berkeley: University of California Press, 1992), 85; Kentarō Awaya, "In the Shadows of the Tokyo Trial," *The Tokyo War Crimes Trial: An International Symposium*, ed., C. Hosoya, N. Andō, Y. Onuma, and R. Minear (Tokyo: Kodansha International Ltd., 1986), 82-83.

29. Awaya Kentaro, *Tokyo saibanron* (Tokyo: Otsuki shoten, 1989), 170-71; Sheldon H. Harris, *Factories of Death: Japanese Biological Warfare, 1932-45, and the American Cover-Up* (London: Routledge, 1994), 114. Harris observes that on "6 January 1946, the American Armed Forces newspaper *The Pacific Stars and Stripes* had carried a story attributed to Japanese communist sources that Americans were among Ishii's BW [bacteriological warfare] victims.... [and] The *New York Times*, citing the same sources, indicated that POWs were inoculated with bubonic plague bacterium."

30. Awaya Kentarō and Aiko Utsumi, "Tokyo saiban: Nihon no sensō sekinin," *Sengo Nihon no genten: Senryōshi no genzai*, Vol. 1, ed. Sodei Rinjiro and Takemae Eiji (Tokyo: Yūshisha, 1992), 231-32.

until March 1946 when the Occupation authorities forbade the Japanese government from investigating war crimes. It is evident that Japanese government officials were trying to find ways to turn the issue of war crimes to their own advantage and perhaps absolve and protect the prewar structure. Awaya Kentarō, for example, has discovered a remarkable document, the "Emergency Imperial Decree for the Purpose of Independently Establishing the National Ethic Necessary for the Stabilization of Public Sentiments and the Maintenance of the National Order (Draft)" [*Minshin o antei shi kokka chitsujo iji ni hitsuyō naru kokumin dōgi o jishuteki ni kakuritsu suru koto o mokuteki to suru kinkyū chokureian*], which presented the idea of prosecuting war crimes under the imperial system. This document, in other words, called for the punishment of those who committed treason by undertaking aggressive actions in defiance of the emperor's "spirit of peace."[31]

Occupation authorities simply assumed that Japanese participation in the War Crimes Trials meant the involvement of judicial officials who would unquestionably have tried to blunt attacks against the wartime state. Little, if any, consideration was given to the idea of selecting Japanese participants from outside of official circles because the Japanese people were perceived as lacking the abilities to effectively judge their government. American publications around the time of Japan's surrender had argued that the prosecution of war criminals would be an effective means of discrediting the nation's leaders in the eyes of the people and encouraging popular regret for all that had occurred during the Pacific War.[32] As polls taken near the start of the Occupation indicate, the Japanese people were quite disillusioned with the old order. Many might have welcomed involvement in the Allies' prosecution of their former leaders. Moreover, if the War Crimes Trials had, like the Trial of the Yokohama Incident Police Officers, also addressed the abuses committed by state officials against their own people, they might have helped develop among the public a more profound sense of identification with the other peoples victimized by the Japanese state.

Yet, as it was, the Tokyo War Crimes Trials focussed more on "crimes against peace" rather than "crimes against humanity." Scholars, in comparing the Nuremberg and Tokyo Tribunals, have noted that the former placed greater importance on "crimes against humanity" and that the obvious need to

---

31. Awaya, *Tokyo saibanron*, 153-54; Awaya, "In the Shadows of the Tokyo Trial," 81, 87-88.

32. H. Vere Redman, "Japan's Surrender: What Next?," *Asiatic Review*, October 1945: 407-9; Henry Cutler Wolfe, "Suzuki-san, Our Major Problem in Japan: On the Common Man Depends the Success of Our Occupation," *New York Times Magazine*, August 26, 1945: 5-7.

prosecute the mass murder of German Jews as a war crime meant that the acts of German leaders against their own citizens became objects of judgment. The Tokyo Tribunal, on the other hand, lacked this emphasis and thus "failed not only to prosecute criminal acts committed by Japanese leaders against Japanese nationals, but also to try acts committed against the peoples of Japanese colonies, such as the forced mobilization of Koreans."[33]

In spite of the War Crimes trials and some of the early reforms of the Occupation, it was clearly those who had served the prewar state rather than its victims who enjoyed more social benefits in the long run. The Occupation had done away with Japanese military pensions and veterans' benefits. However, with the end of the Occupation in 1952, the Japanese government reinstated these pensions with the result that even convicted war criminals began to receive these benefits. Many war criminals were released from prison immediately after the Occupation ended, and, as an added bonus, they were granted government pensions that counted their prison terms as a period of service. In contrast, soon after the nation's surrender, the Japanese government stripped its Korean residents who had been forced to serve in the war effort of their Japanese citizenship. Without the rights of citizenship, these individuals had no claim to most social welfare benefits, such as medical treatment or therapy for disabilities suffered while performing military service. Moreover, unlike the German authorities who have as of 1992 voluntarily paid 70 billion U.S. dollars to foreign individuals victimized in the war, the Japanese authorities have adamantly refused to make such reparations. Consequently, even as foreign casualties of Japan's war, mobilized Koreans have never received any form of compensation.[34]

The acts of officials against the citizens of the former Japanese empire, both those who remained Japanese nationals and those who lost their citizenship after the Pacific War, never became an object of judgment during the Tokyo War Crimes Trials. In this respect, the Trial of the Yokohama Incident Police Officers was a little-known endeavour that confronted an important issue ignored by the Allied Powers.

---

33. Awaya, "In the Shadows of the Tokyo Trial," 85.
34. B.T. Wakabayashi, "'Imperial Japanese' Opium Operations and Postwar Historiography," paper presented at the Conference on Opium in East Asian History: 1830-1945, Toronto, Canada, 9-10 May 1997: 7, 10-11. Wakabayashi cites as the sources of this information, Tanaka Hiroshi, "Kokka wa izoku ni dō hoshō shita ka," *Izoku to sengo*, ed. Tanaka Nobumasa (Tokyo: Iwanami shoten, 1995), 95, and *Aera*, No. 19, May 1992: 31-43.

THE EARLY OCCUPATION: THE LIMITS OF THE "GOLDEN AGE"

Although they realize that the Occupation never succeeded in being a panacea for all of Japan's prewar problems, some of the individuals involved in the recent Yokohama Incident retrial movement do believe that a real chance for justice and reform had been lost at that time. Mrs. Ono Sada, the wife of one of the journalists arrested in the affair and a major participant in the retrial movement, has remarked that the present legal campaign was long overdue and that it should have taken place fifty years earlier.[35]

Many continue to view the Occupation period as some "golden age of postwar democracy," and it has been noted that present-day commentators on the period often speak not of "the hardships that predominate in the popular memories of those years, but of the political potential that they feel was lost as the conservative structures of authority were reestablished." An examination of the circumstances surrounding the Trial of the Yokohama Incident Police Officers reveals nevertheless that reformist initiatives such as the court case were conducted in a circumscribed age of democracy with limits on its political potential. Arai Naoyuki, for example, states that the period during which the Occupation authorities sought to dismantle the prewar order and promote democracy and freedom of speech was very short, lasting a brief seven months from the arrival of the American forces to the spring of 1946.

Understanding the qualified nature or limits on the American commitment to certain policies in Japan as well as the actual or self-imposed restraints placed on certain Japanese groups can reveal more clearly some of the obstacles faced by domestic campaigns against the wartime state. SCAP's encouragement of individuals who could be classified as enemies of the wartime state was tied to American attitudes toward Japanese communists, who were undeniably the main target of prewar official persecution. As will be discussed below, tolerance of leftists and active efforts against the old order were transitory.[36]

At the beginning of the Occupation there was a number of calls for an overhaul of the Japanese state. Supreme Commander for the Allied Powers (SCAP), General Douglas MacArthur even became the target of criticism for being too tolerant of the Japanese elite. Writers for the *Canadian Forum* observed in October 1945 that it seemed that social and economic patterns in Japan were to be left intact and remarked about MacArthur, "what else could

---

35. Ono and Okawa, *Yokohama jiken mitsu no saiban*, 9.
36. Gluck, "Entangling Illusions," 195; Arai Naoyuki, "Senryō seisaku to jyaanarizumu," *Kyōdō kenkyū/Nihon senryō*, ed. Shisō no kagaku kenkyūkai (Tokyo: Tokuma shoten, 1972), 180.

be expected from the hero of the Republican Party?" In addition, *The New Republic* had insisted that this hero of the Republican Party would have to be replaced with a civilian administrator if he did not act more decisively to mete out punishment to militarists and industrialists who had promoted Japan's wars of aggression.[37]

SCAP's initial response to such demands seemed quite dramatic. On January 4, 1946 a SCAP memoranda was sent to the Japanese Government demanding the removal from office of individuals who were unsuitable for public duties. The action appeared to herald a new age, and the *Asahi shimbun*, in reference to the January 4 purge directive, declared in its headlines that a "bloodless revolution" was underway. The purge directive surprised not only the Japanese public. It also perturbed more than a few Americans, and it has been observed that MacArthur himself had from the start some reservations about the purge and the loss of capable Japanese administrators.[38]

U.S. strategic planning for Japan was initially grounded in the two goals of demilitarization and democratization. However, Japanese scholars of the period have observed that the Occupation Army never provided a clear definition of what it meant by democracy. In addition, it may not be correct to assume that equal emphasis or value was placed on these goals. It is quite possible that a number of American policy-makers, despite their declarations about the democratizing purpose behind their actions, saw democratization more as a secondary goal or means of achieving the main objective of demilitarization. It has been observed that "nothing in the Potsdam Proclamation even hinted that an Allied occupation would require a social democratic government; it implied an anti-military government, but not an anti-conservative regime." Dismantling the prewar order by actions such as the purge was designed to eliminate what Assistant Secretary of State Dean Acheson described as Japan's "will to war." Disarmament or demilitarization was the real target; the promotion of democracy was just a welcome by-product.[39]

Historians of the purge, moreover, have observed that the removal of wartime officials was from the start hampered by difficulties in formulating a criteria that could satisfy both the objectives of demilitarization and

---

37. "Fate of Japan," *Canadian Forum*, October 1945: 152; "Getting Tough with Japan," *The New Republic*, September 24, 1945: 363-64.
38. Matsuura Sozo, "Hanminshushugi no tenkan katei: Senpan tsuihō kara reddo paaji made," *Kyōdō kenkyū/Nihon senryō*, 148-50.
39. Sodei and Takemae, "Nihon senryō to wa nani ka," 336; Moore, "Reflections on the Occupation of Japan," 728; John W. Dower, "Occupied Japan and the Cold War in Asia," *Japan in War & Peace: Selected Essays*, by John Dower (New York: New Press, 1993), 165.

democratization. Opposition to military policies did not necessarily translate into support for democracy. Among the opponents of the prewar Army were those who upheld the primacy of the state over the individual. Problems with establishing a criteria delayed the purge for eighteen months. According to Hans Baerwald, those removed were thus able to exercise their authority and train subordinates to continue their policies during the delay in carrying out the purge.[40]

Difficulties in executing the purge of officials most probably owed something to the fact that Japanese officials themselves were given a lot of responsibility for selecting those who would be removed and for judging appeals.[41] Prior to the arrival of the American Occupiers the Japanese government had taken precautionary steps to protect its members. Incriminating records were destroyed, and administrative personnel were shifted about in order to complicate any efforts to collect compromising information from local people. The authorities were particularly conscientious in trying to protect the police, their old instruments of control. "The government," it has been noted, "internally reshuffled officials like prefectural governors and school officials on a large scale, but gave the police special attention, transferring over two-third of them."[42]

The purge had in fact a negligible impact on the police. Among the Special Higher Thought Control Police, only those who had occupied the position of inspector and above during the War or for more than eight years were in danger of being purged. As few prewar officials served in the same capacity for such a period of time due to the practice of frequent bureaucratic transfers, the number of officers who were purged was quite small. Former police officers were barred from reappointment in the Home and Justice Ministries, but were free to apply for positions in other ministries.[43]

American reporter Mark Gayn wished to know what had happened to high-ranking thought control police and had an opportunity to meet one such individual, Hata Shigenori. Hata, it should be remembered, was the police official who, near the end of the Pacific War, described the domestic situation to Prince Konoe as being potentially explosive. Mark Gayn met with Hata on November 27, 1946, and in his diary recorded both Hata's statements and his own reaction to them:

---

40. Hans H. Baerwald, *The Purge of Japanese Leaders Under the Occupation* (Berkeley: University of California Press, 1959), 1-2, 105, 9-10, 41.
41. Hata Ikuhiko and Sodei Rinjiro, *Nihon senryō hisshi* (Tokyo: Asahi shimbunsha, 1977), 210.
42. Moore, *Japanese Workers and the Struggle for Power*, 15.
43. Baerwald, *The Purge of Japanese Leaders*, 46-47.

> "We [Hata explained] served through the years of the China Incident, the Great Far Eastern War, and the early days of the Occupation. We knew the purge directive was coming out in October 1945, and we resigned beforehand.
> Today most of us are back in important posts. Some are in the Ministry of Education. Others are in the Ministry of Welfare. These include the chief of the Labour Division. Still others are in the Ministry of Commerce. Several, including the chief of the Wood and Charcoal Section, are in the Ministry of Forestry and Agriculture."
> The list grew. It was not amusing that the man in charge of charcoal rationing was a *Tokkō* man: charcoal is a Japanese housewife's only fuel for warmth or cooking, and it is a potent instrument of political pressure. It was even less funny that the man who watches over the growth of democratic labour unions is a man who once helped to destroy them.
> "Two prefectural governors," said Hata, "are *Tokkō* alumni. Two or three *Tokkō* men who served in Korea through the war have now come back to key positions in the Home Ministry. Minor *Tokkō* officials, who had served in the provinces, have now pulled back to Tokyo, to fill subordinate government jobs."[44]

Even before the Americans had arrived in Japan and before those arrested in the Yokohama Incident had launched their court case, effective steps had been taken to protect law enforcement officials and other representatives of the prewar state.

The criteria, in the final analysis, for being purged or patronized depended on the individual's usefulness and/or support for whatever goals the Occupation authorities held at the time. The January 4, 1946 instruction, "SCAPIN 550: The Removal and Exclusion of Undesirable Personnel from Public Office," allowed for the removal of those "who manifest hostility to the objectives of the military occupation."[45] As these objectives moved from making Japan a peaceful, non-threatening nation to making it an economical, political and possibly military ally of the United States, the Occupation authorities began to turn against individuals who had formerly looked upon the American forces as an army of liberation.

---

44. Mark Gayn, *Japan Diary* (Tokyo: Charles E. Tuttle Company, 1984), 458.
45. Finn, *Winners in Peace*, 82-83.

Many victims and critics of the prewar Japanese state once again found themselves under attack. Just as the prewar Japanese officials had tried to utilize the skills of Marxist and former leftist researchers and then later reversed their policy of patronage as concerns about wartime internal security increased, American Occupation authorities would consider it necessary to abandon the early policy of tolerance toward Japanese communists. Both prewar Japanese and American Occupation officials had hoped to use leftists as weapons to oppose an "enemy"-each other. That is, the former used them to try to prepare the state for possible conflict with the Anglo-American powers; the latter thought they provided a means of combatting the residual forces of the prewar state. Yet, eventually, many Japanese and American officials came to view the forces of the Left as the greater threat to the future of the country.

Japanese communists had benefitted from early Occupation policies. Many owed their freedom to SCAP's October 4, 1945 directive for the release of all political prisoners jailed by the prewar governments. Even before the Pacific War had ended, in the summer of 1944, the U.S. State-War-Navy Coordinating Committee had decided to release these prisoners. Influential American officials such as John K. Emmerson who had been in contact with Japanese communists in China had a major influence on U.S. policy toward leftists in Japan. Of the opinion that the proposals for creating a new Japan put forth by China-based communists were akin to "the American Bill of Rights," Emmerson argued that Japanese communists could be content with just legal recognition by the Occupation forces.

Emmerson later became one of General MacArthur's first political advisers and was directly involved in the release of the jailed communist leadership.[46] He justified a positive policy toward such individuals as the best way to undermine the potential influence of the Soviet Union and "prevent

---

46. Takemae, "Early Postwar Reformist Parties," 347-8. In this article, Takemae describes the circumstances and events leading to the release,

Three foreign reporters—R. Guillain, J. Marquise, and H. Isaacs—visited Fuchū Prison on October 1; correspondents for United Press, Associated Press, Dōmei, and other wire services visited Fuchū Prison and Toyotama Detention Center on October 2; and the UP Japan Bureau Chief and people from theAcme Film Company visited these two facilities on October 3, with the result that news of these political prisoners was cabled world-wide, thus sensitizing GHQ to the possibility of negative public opinion in the United States, the Soviet Union, Britain, China, and elsewhere. Emmerson obtained the Isaac report and other reports of these visits to Fuchū and Toyotama and concluded that GHQ should release the political prisoners as soon as possible.

Japan's political system from again becoming a danger to us."⁴⁷ Consequently, writers have argued that the October 5, 1945 directive for the release of political prisoners was not planned with any intention of democratizing Japan. It instead simply reflected the persistent "war mentality" of certain Occupation officials who still thought in terms of the need to mobilize all possible forces to eliminate the influence of Japan's military and its allies.⁴⁸

Americans saw the Japanese communists as weapons, but it should be noted that qualms about utilizing them were evident from the start. Emmerson had drawn up plans during the last months of the Pacific War to use the Yenan-based communist Nosaka Sanzō and other influential Japanese living abroad in forming a pro-peace alliance against the Japanese government. These plans encountered consideration opposition. According to Emmerson, "cautious bureaucrats in the State Department, shying at communism, rejected any connection with the Japanese in China and restricted membership in the organization to Japanese nationals in the United States and in American-controlled territory."⁴⁹

American officials in Japan who were willing to look upon leftists as makeshift allies in eradicating militarism and those aspects of the prewar system that seemed to promote it did not maintain influence for long. They experienced a rather rapid decline in authority, and scholars have noticed that the movement of American support from the Japan Communist Party to more mainstream or even prewar elite groups followed in step with the shift in influence from Emmerson's Office of the Political Adviser to the Government Section (GS) to the Intelligence Section (G-2). "People left for home, or were driven out for political reasons," and Carol Gluck has written that these changes in personnel or the balance of authority within GHQ can help to explain "how 'the same' Occupation both promoted unions and halted the general strike." "It was not," she points out, "in the course of years, 'the same' Occupation at all."⁵⁰

The Occupation bureaucracy, like the prewar Japanese government, suffered from internal rivalries, and competition in setting policy and personal antagonisms had a considerable impact on its operation. The most famous of the SCAP bureaucratic struggles was between General Courtney Whitney, the

---

47. Takemae, *Senryō sengoshi: Tainichi kanri seisaku no zenyō*, 101; Eiji Takemae, "Early Postwar Reformist Parties," *Democratizing Japan: The Allied Occupation*, ed., Robert E. Ward and Yoshikazu Sakamoto (Honolulu: University of Hawaii Press, 1987), 343; Emmerson, *The Japanese Thread*, 200, 201.
48. Hata and Sodei, *Nihon senryō hisshi*, 216.
49. Emmerson, *The Japanese Thread*, 225.
50. Takemae, "Early Postwar Reformist Parties," 360; Gluck, "Entangling Illusions," 186.

head of GS, and Major-General Charles Willoughby, the head of G-2 and an open admirer of fascist Spanish leader Francisco Franco. Whereas Willoughby relied on military intelligence agents, Whitney, whose section was in charge of personnel, tended to hire specialists of Asia and New Deal lawyers.[51] Even before the Pacific War had ended, with the Democrats losing the U.S. Congress to the Republicans in 1944, the balance of power within the Occupation bureaucracy was turning against the "New Dealers" around Whitney. They found themselves gradually eclipsed by pro-business specialists with increasingly active and influential allies in Japan and the United States. Members of the so-called "Japan Lobby" of financial, diplomatic and government figures, using the magazine *Newsweek* as their mouthpiece, harshly berated GS personnel as "immature, untrained, and impractical officers" who were "responsible for a program that would undermine American capitalist principles in Japan." Outside interference from such groups simply aggravated the conflict between GHQ sections which was rapidly deteriorating into a campaign against suspected leftists among Occupation officials.[52]

Howard Schonberger has observed that the Occupation authorities' ability to act as a watchdog against the Japanese government's efforts to subvert or tamper with reform legislation was probably hampered by the fact that Willoughby, who was in charge of GHQ's surveillance system, was "more concerned about left-wing infiltration of the Occupation by people like [GS New Dealer T.A.] Bisson than in eliminating the reactionaries of Japan."[53] The intra-bureau rancour bred by competition and suspicions about ideological sympathies eventually resulted in Willoughby conducting investigations on GS officers. Like wartime Japanese officials who drove out former leftists and thought control offenders from government institutions, Willoughby tried to initiate a purge of so-called leftist Americans from GHQ and from Japan.

In 1946 and 1947 he submitted to MacArthur secret memoranda on "Leftist Infiltration into SCAP." In his G-2 reports on leftist infiltration Willoughby named nine Occupation employees whom he accused of "having seriously misdirected the policies of the United States by attempting to discredit the Yoshida Cabinet and thereby promote the interests of the Japan Communist Party." These men, he argued, were known communist

---

51. Roger Bowen, *Innocence is Not Enough: The Life and Death of Herbert Norman* (New York: M.E. Sharpe, Inc., 1986), 116-17.

52. Herbert Passin, "The Occupation—Some Reflections," *Showa: The Japan of Hirohito*, 109; Howard Schonberger, "The Japan Lobby in American Diplomacy, 1947-1952," *Pacific Historical Review*, Vol. XLVI, 1977: 330.

53. Howard Schonberger, "T.A. Bisson and the Limits of Reform in Occupied Japan," *Bulletin of Concerned Asian Scholars*, Vol. 12, No 4 (Oct-Dec) 1980: 30.

sympathizers and associated closely with "leftist" journalists such as Mark Gayn and Andrew Roth. Willoughby succeeded in getting Roth and Gayn expelled from Japan and hounding Bisson from his position. However, he could not get General Whitney or MacArthur to act on his allegations. In a later correspondence he mentioned that he was even ordered to impound his study and stop it from being circulated.[54]

In response to their criticism and scepticism, Willoughby insisted that Whitney and MacArthur wake up to the fact that "The national trend is anti-communistic" and avoid "the mistake of being soft on communism." This advice in 1947, however, was not necessary as it was apparent since 1946 that GHQ was drifting toward a more anti-communist stand. Reaction against early Occupation policy and reforms occurred sooner than the dates given in conventional assessments. Joe Moore states that, in terms of labour reform, the so-called "reverse course" began in May 1946 and not in 1947 or 1948. Eiji Takemae supports this view and provides the same date as marking a turning-point in GHQ's attitude toward communists.[55]

Takemae notes that it was on May 15, 1946 that State Department Political Adviser to SCAP George Atcheson, Jr. delivered at the Fourth Meeting of the Allied Council for Japan a very thinly-veiled attack against the Soviet Union and the Japanese communists. May Day demonstrators had sent a message to SCAP and to Allied Council members, which declared that the "Execution of purge directive issues by the Allied Forces have [sic] been perverted" by the "enemies of the democratic revolution" within the Japanese government. When the Council's Russian delegate raised the issue of the message at the Fourth Meeting and requested that SCAP look into the matter, Political Adviser Atcheson, who was also Council Chairman, dismissed the message as nothing more than communist propaganda. He disputed the authorship of the message, stating that SCAP translators noticed that it was not written in idiomatic Japanese and claimed that it had been originally composed in a foreign language. It has been argued that Atcheson was not being truthful and that he knew that the Allied Translator and Interpreter Section had concluded that the document was written in standard Japanese and was not a translation from Russian or any other language. His speech was nevertheless an emotional and clear reflection of the suspicions that SCAP and Washington

---

54. Bowen, *Innocence is Not Enough*, 182; 388; Schonberger, "T.A. Bisson," 32.
55. Bowen, *Innocence is Not Enough*, 182, 191; Moore, *Japanese Workers and the Struggle for Power*, xviii; Takemae Eiji, "Reddo paaji," *Kyōdō kenkyū Nihon senryō: Sono hikari to kage*, ed. Shisō no kagaku kenkyūkai (Tokyo: Gendaishi shuppankai, 1977), 280.

in 1946 were beginning to harbour against both the Soviets and the Japanese communist movement.[56] Takemae provides the following chronology of the drift from GHQ support of the JCP to an anti-communist policy: the Atcheson speech in 1946; SCAP's prevention of the February 1st Strike in 1947; the so-called March Conflict of 1948; the establishment of the Dodge Line in 1949; the "Red Purge" of the Japanese civil service and union leaders in 1949-50.[57] He also directs attention to the establishment in the United States of the Taft-Hartley Labour Act of 1947 as marking the way toward the Red Purge in Japan. He believes that this Act which obliged union officers to sign affidavits that they were not communists encouraged American officials in Japan to assume a hardline attitude toward labour unions. One notable episode of extreme bullying and persecution of unions, which Takemae describes as a precursor to the Red Purge in Japan, was the Yokosuka Case of 1949.

At an April 1949 meeting Occupation officials ordered labour union representatives in the Yokosuka area to have their members fill out forms providing information about their family, employment history, the political orientation of their union and its personnel. Officials warned the representatives against communism and declared that anyone found giving false information in the forms would be punished. When some of the union leaders decided to oppose this order by issuing a petition to MacArthur on behalf of their members, the Yokosuka Base Commanding Officer unilaterally ordered their arrest on charges of trying to mislead the Supreme Commander. Although the union leaders enjoyed the support of a sympathetic GHQ Labour Section officer who was willing to testify that they were not communists, an official investigation found them guilty and sentenced them to six months in custody and a fine of one hundred dollars. Few Japanese learned about the Yokosuka Case as GHQ forbade newspapers in the country to discuss it.[58]

SCAP was never a reliable ally of individuals who had opposed or been victimized by the prewar state and its thought control system. Japan Communist Party leaders upon their release from prison had proclaimed the Occupation forces to be an army of liberation. However, they were aware that American patronage could be withdrawn and soon came to understand that the Occupation authorities did not necessarily appreciate their involvement in the

---

56. Moore, *Japanese Workers and the Struggle for Power*, 177-79; "Speech by Mr. George Atcheson, Jr., Chairman, at the Fourth Meeting of the Allied Council for Japan," *Documents concerning the Allied Occupation and Control of Japan*, Vol. II, 2.
57. Takemae, *Senryō sengoshi: Tainichi kanri seisaku no zenyō*, 157-58.
58. Takemae, *Senryō sengoshi: Tainichi kanri seisaku no zenyō*, 159-60, 170-72, 175-76.

prosecution of war crimes. Fears about alarming SCAP, but also concerns about preserving the status quo within the Japan Communist Party probably stymied any impulse to participate in matters involving wartime Japanese personnel, such as the court case against the Yokohama Incident Police Officers.

THE JAPAN COMMUNIST PARTY AND THE PROBLEM OF THE WARTIME RULING ELITE

Former *Chūōkōron* journalist Kimura Tōru, the only surviving member of the so-called Hosokawa Group which was accused of leading the conspiracy, has been the main source of information on the postwar legal activities of those arrested. He and the others who brought charges against the Police Officers who had tortured them had aspired to carry out a completely autonomous Japanese endeavour. Kimura stated that they had never considered trying to gain the support of the American authorities because they believed that, like the Japanese people in general, they had to exercise their own initiative in dealing with the abuses committed by their officials.[59] They instead had looked to domestic support for their endeavour. Unfortunately, influential groups whose membership included many casualties of the prewar thought control system remained divided and reluctant to rally behind the causes of fellow victims. Neither the Japanese publishing industry nor the Japan Communist Party, the two most likely allies of those who had been arrested in the Yokohama Incident, paid much attention to the court case.

In view of the JCP's avowed stand on war crimes and popular involvement in Occupation reforms, one could have expected the Party membership to have loudly applauded the activities of those arrested in the Incident. Support for the Trial of the Police Officers would have been in keeping with the JCP's demands for a popular rejection of the prewar state, the punishment of prewar officials, and the greater involvement of the people in the creation of a new society. Support would also have been an act of Party solidarity. Although the vast majority later left or were expelled from the Party, a number of those arrested in the Yokohama Incident joined the JCP soon after their release from custody. Kimura Tōru states that he and many others simply followed their mentor Hosokawa Karoku into the Party, or

---

59. Personal interview with Kimura Tōru, October 12, 1992.

became members because they naively believed that the JCP would be above the corruption of conventional parties.[60]

On October 20, 1945, in its first postwar edition, the Party's newspaper *Akahata* [*Red Flag*] carried an article that observed that "Japan's democratization under the Potsdam terms would provide a 'shield' protecting JCP activists from attack by the right, but [that] the party must not lean on SCAP or forget that the people must be the ones to realize the democratic revolution."[61] Party leaders agreed that they had to encourage the people to become more politically active. Nosaka Sanzō felt that the Japanese people were inexperienced in exercising and protecting their rights and that they had to become more fully involved in establishing a new Japanese society and government. He came into conflict with SCAP for the first time during the Diet debates on the New Constitution of 1946. The Japanese people, he insisted, should have participated more in its creation.[62] He observed that it was the people's participation in the creation of the constitution rather than the document itself that would safeguard their rights. Unless the people could create their own constitution, he pointed out, the time was not right for a new constitution.

Although the JCP leadership declared that the people must be the ones to realize a democratic revolution, the Party often revealed itself to be unprepared to deal with popular initiatives. It did not participate in the first *Yomiuri* newspaper dispute of 1945, became only marginally involved in the "People's Court" Incident initiated independently by the Mitsubishi miners against management of 1946, and hesitated to capitalize on the mass demonstrations against the Shidehara Cabinet of the same year. "They did not gamble on another mass mobilization in the streets," Joe Moore writes, "no doubt believing SCAP to be opposed to another street demonstration that might develop into violent direct action. In short, the leaders of the left showed a certain distrust of the mass movement."[63]

Party leadership was no doubt restrained by their awareness that American support was conditional. GHQ was very concerned about JCP policies, and the Office of the Political Adviser was ordered to study the backgrounds and characteristics of Party members and make weekly reports on

---

60. Personal interview with Kimura Tōru, October 12, 1992.
61. *Fifty Years of the Japanese Communist Party*, revised and enlarged edition (Tokyo: Central Committee, Japanese Communist Party, 1980), 116.
62. Antonia Judith Levi, "Peaceful Revolution in Japan: The Development of the Nosaka Theory and its Implementation under the American Occupation," Ph.D diss., Stanford University, 1991: 130-31.
63. Moore, *Japanese Workers and the Struggle for Power*, 50, 126-32, 177.

their activities. Occupation officials had interviewed and questioned in detail JCP members and other political prisoners about their ideas of Japan's future before releasing them on October 10. Shiga Yoshio, a leading Party member, recalled that when the first Occupation Army representative came to see him and told him that "MacArthur hates communists," he replied, "I know it."[64] Party leadership realized that American support could not be taken for granted, but had to cultivated. They, according to SCAP political adviser John Emmerson, frequently visited Occupation personnel and were careful to provide them with copies of Party plans and programs. Occupation reports also indicate that some Japanese communists went so far as to suggest that GHQ "use" the Party as a "mouthpiece" to transmit its objectives to the people.[65]

Besides calling for greater political activism on the part of the Japanese people, the JCP leaders had also demanded an extensive investigation of war criminals. Tokuda Kyūichi considered the Emperor a war criminal and on the very day he was released from prison, October 10, 1945, he attacked the Imperial Family and argued for the abolition of the emperor system. Party members even provided SCAP with information on individuals in order to help the Occupation authorities investigate potential war criminals and carry out a purge of prewar officials. However, they may have come away from this experience believing that SCAP did not necessarily appreciate their help and involvement in such issues. U.S. officials, for instance, had no desire to draw too much attention to former Japanese military personnel who were guilty of conducting bacteriological experiments on Chinese and American prisoners-of-war. JCP members nevertheless had been so active in spreading information about some of these individuals that word soon leaked out to the press. JCP leader Shiga Yoshio had informed American reporters of his own efforts to track down the notorious Ishii Shirō with the result that in early January 1946 both the *Pacific Stars and Stripes* and the *New York Times* ran stories about these Japanese experiments. Occupation authorities acted swiftly, making its disapproval known by sending Counter-Intelligence agents to talk to the United Press Association's Tokyo Bureau Chief to request that the media refrain from covering these topics in the future.[66]

---

64. Takemae, "Early Postwar Reformist Parties," 348-49; Shiga Yoshio, "Shutsugoku zengo no koto-Watakushi no shōgen," *Kyōdō kenkyū Nihon senryō:Sono hikari to kage*, ed. Shisō no kagaku kenkyūkai (Tokyo: Gendaishi shuppankai, 1977), 425.

65. Kumei Shigeru, "Tokuda Kyūichi ron," *Kyōdō kenkyū/Nihon senryō*, ed. Shisō no kagaku kenkyūkai (Tokyo: Tokuma shoten, 1972), 449; Takemae, "Early Postwar Reformist Parties," 358; Emmerson, *The Japanese Thread*, 261.

66. Levi, "Peaceful Revolution in Japan," 114-6; Harris, *Factories of Death*, 176-77.

The JCP may have interpreted such actions as a warning to keep their hands off the issue of war crimes, and this may account for Shiga Yoshio's rejection of the idea of a people's trial of war criminals. Immediately after the end of the Pacific War, Hosokawa Karoku had told Kimura that the trial and punishment of those responsible for the Pacific War by the Japanese people themselves was necessary for the creation of a new society. Through such a trial, the Japanese people would begin to appreciate their political rights; that is, they hopefully would come to understand that the leaders of a country are accountable not only to the rulers of victorious nations, but to their own people for their misconduct and irresponsibility.

Kimura shared Hosokawa's view and after he was released, he attempted to get the editors of the *Akahata* to support a movement for a "People's Trial of War Criminals."[67] In January 1946, the very same month that the Occupation authorities seemed to suggest that they did not appreciate outside involvement in their investigation of Japanese wartime bacteriological experiments, *Akahata* staff held an editorial meeting during which Kimura made the following the statement:

> Shouldn't we attempt to establish a people's tribunal for the prosecution of war crimes? Shouldn't we expose the crimes of war criminals before all the people and judge them openly through our own people's tribunal?

Shiga Yoshio, who himself had helped spread information about potential war criminal Ishii Shirō much to the displeasure of American officials, was at the time the Chief Editor of *Akahata* and responded angrily to Kimura's suggestion. Shiga argued that

> We cannot forget that we are under the rule of the Occupation forces. They consider it their job to tackle the problem of war crimes, and we have no right to interfere. It's fine to debate the issue of responsibility. But war crimes are to be left to the Occupation forces. We must, by all means, keep quiet.[68]

About thirty people attended the meeting, but they were so intimidated by the Chief Editor's angry outburst that not one person came forward to support the proposal for an independent trial of war criminals.

---

67. In his book on the Yokohama Incident, Kimura did not give the name of the newspaper and referred to the chief editor only as "S." He later revealed that "S" was Shiga Yoshio and that the newspaper in question was *Akahata* during a personal interview on June 12, 1992.

68. Kimura, *Yokohama jiken no shinsō*, 112-13.

Gratitude to or, more likely, fear of SCAP resulted in the adoption of a hands-off attitude toward issues related to the punishment of wartime officials. Such issues appeared to invite only SCAP displeasure and had the potential to aggravate splits within the membership. Soon after the re-establishment of the JCP, the leadership had to work out a compromise between those (e.g., Shiga and Tokuda) who felt that Hirohito should be tried as a war criminal and those (e.g., Nosaka and Nakanishi Kō) who argued that attacks against the Emperor only alienated the Party from the majority of the people. The Party initially adopted Nosaka's more moderate position, which was openly declared in January 1946 under the slogan of a "lovable" (*aisaseru*) JCP.[69] But there may have been a tendency to avoid matters involving war criminals or the misdeeds committed by former officials because they could reopen or aggravate splits within the Party.

Indifference to the Trial of the Yokohama Incident Police Officers may also have been linked to divisions within the Party. In the early postwar years, the Party had two major factions: the Fuchū and the Kuramae Factions. The Kuramae Faction took its name from the Kuramae Industrial Hall where members had tried to establish a communist organization after Japan's surrender. Hosokawa Karoku, the most prominent individual arrested in the Yokohama Incident, was associated with the Kuramae Faction. The others arrested in the Yokohama Incident who entered the JCP, whether they liked it or not, were probably linked to the Kuramae Faction through Hosokawa.[70]

The Kuramae Faction's membership was largely made up of intellectuals, and such Party intellectuals sometimes found themselves slighted or even openly attacked. Leading Fuchū members Tokuda and Shiga were known to look down on the Kuramae intellectuals for allegedly compromising their convictions in order to retain their freedom. In 1950, moreover, the JCP split over the Cominform's rebuke of its policy of moderation, and one of the results was an attack on "communist men of culture and cultural organizations." According to one Party history, "this meant the loss from the cultural front of a wide-range of the intelligentsia and men of culture, who had aligned themselves with the Party and around the Party before the split took place."[71]

The Fuchū Faction, on the other hand, took its name from the Fuchū Penitentiary, and the majority of its members had spent more than a decade in prison. One's standing in the Party depended on the number of years spent in

---

69. Levi, "Peaceful Revolution in Japan," 117, 121.
70. Levi, "Peaceful Revolution in Japan," 147; Robert A. Scalapino, *The Japanese Communist Movement, 1920-1966* (Berkeley: University of California Press, 1967), 90.
71. *Fifty Years of the Japanese Communist Party*, 155.

prison and the degree to which one had openly defied the prewar authorities and suffered official persecution. Consequently, the Fuchū Faction enjoyed more prestige and influence.

It is not likely that influential Fuchū members would have pushed for Party support of the Trial against the Yokohama Incident Police Officers since it would have benefitted the rival faction. Party support of the Trial invariably meant recognition of the official persecution suffered by certain Kuramae members and a consequent rise in that Faction's prestige. It would not have been in the interest of certain elements in the JCP and in the publishing industry to allow too much attention to be focussed on the Yokohama Incident and the subsequent legal activities. Like the Party, the publishing industry was plagued by internal divisions that prevented it from coming to the assistance of fellow victims of wartime state and the thought control system.

THE PUBLISHING INDUSTRY AND THE PROBLEM OF THE WARTIME RULING ELITE

Members of the Japanese press, at least, initially gave their support to those arrested, and the *Asahi shimbun* ran a detailed article on the Yokohama Incident in October 1945. During the first years of the Occupation, newspapers and journals faced shortages in paper and material which, no doubt, restricted the number of events that they could cover. However, the Yokohama Incident was a topic of interest for many individuals in the publishing industry. It had involved major publications and had resulted in the arrest of many colleagues and friends.

The publishing industry had been subjected to government pressure to conform to censorship laws and official propaganda demands throughout the prewar period. Individuals in the industry included many casualties of the thought control system, those who had suffered state persecution because they openly opposed, or simply were suspected of opposing government policies. Yet, the industry also included individuals who had been unable to withstand government pressure to participate in propaganda campaigns as well as those who had enthusiastically supported such campaigns. Accusations of wartime collaboration provided labour and union leaders with a convenient means of countering any management opposition to their demands. Consequently, attacks against wartime collaborators or suspected collaborators became part and parcel of labour-management disputes in the publishing industry during the Occupation.

These internal struggles played a major role in the industry's growing aversion to anything dealing with the Yokohama Incident. Journalists shied away from the topic of the Incident and the Trial of the Police Officers because it was too strongly connected with partisan interests. The Incident could be used by those who had held management positions during the recent War to defend themselves against the accusations of collaboration put forth by postwar union activists.

In October 1945 SCAP's Civil Information and Education Section (CIE) came into being, and its main duties included informing the Japanese people of the reasons and purposes behind Occupation policies such as the punishment of war criminals and collaborators. Even before the establishment of the CIE, however, the newly created unions of Japan's three largest newspapers accused top management personnel of having been militarist collaborators and demanded their resignation. The president of the *Asahi shimbun* agreed to the demands and dismissed the newspaper's editor-in-chief, two chief editorial writers, as well as the managing editors of the Tokyo, Osaka, and Western Japan regions. In contrast, *Yomiuri* President and owner Shōriki Matsutarō responded by firing five of the union leaders. Shoriki claimed that the five men were communist conspirators who sought to undermine the industry and, ultimately, destroy the nation.[72]

In terms of his views as well as his career experience, Shoriki seemed to embody the old, authoritarian state. After a thirteen-year career with the Metropolitan Police Board, during which time he rose to the position of Chief of the Criminal Affairs Bureau, he took over the *Yomiuri* in 1924. In the immediate postwar period, it was openly known that Shōriki gave strict orders against any references in the paper to the war responsibilities of the Imperial Family, the government, and financial elites. On the occasion of an interview of the Emperor by two American correspondents, Shōriki ordered his news editors not to carry any word of the interview since it seemed to raise doubts about the Emperor's divinity. The Occupation authorities eventually heard about Shōriki, and on December 3, 1945, SCAP ordered him and fifty-eight others to turn themselves in as suspected war criminals. A noted liberal then took the place of Shōriki as the new president of the *Yomiuri*.[73]

During their struggle with Shoriki the *Yomiuri* Union members succeeded in staging what has been called Japan's first "production control"

---

72. Fukushima Juro, "Senryō shoki ni okeru shimbun ken'etsu," *Kyōdō kenkyū Nihon senryō: Sono hikari to kage*, 121-22; Moore, *Japanese Workers and the Struggle for Power*, 50.
73. Theodore Cohen, *Remaking Japan: The American Occupation As New Deal*, ed. Herbert Passin (New York: The Free Press, 1987), 241-2; Gayn, *Japan Diary*, 21-22.

strike. They ignored any announcement of dismissals and instructed workers to refuse all orders coming from management. Outsiders initially greeted these efforts with considerable praise and support. Writing on December 11, 1945, American journalist Mark Gayn observed that "the conflict on the *Yomiuri* had become a symbol. This was the old order fighting the new one, a struggle between entrenched nationalism and democracy." Japanese labour organizers looked upon the actions of the *Yomiuri* unionists as a model for other workers and many throughout the country flocked to Tokyo to learn first-hand how to mobilize themselves in a similar fashion. In addition, public approval showed itself in a sharp rise in the newspaper's circulation.[74]

However, the *Yomiuri* Unionists soon discovered that there were limits to the Occupation authorities' tolerance. American officials in Japan insisted that newspapers continue operations because they were an essential instrument in popularizing Allied policy. Although these officials were pleased that the recent strike had not interfered with the publication of the *Yomiuri*, many in SCAP had misgivings about the specific tactics adopted by the unionists. The production control strike was a fundamentally anti-capitalist act in that it ignored the rights of private property, opposing the demands of owners and managers to control the production process, and it has been observed that, as such, toleration of such activities could only have been temporary. As stated earlier, by the summer of 1946 Occupation labour reform was undergoing a reverse course. Moreover, there were changes in CIE personnel that would have a profound effect on the publishing industry. As Joe Moore points out, the replacement of the relatively liberal Brigadier General Kermit R. Dyke as Press Section Chief by notably ultra-conservative officers signalled a campaign against left-leaning or simply recalcitrant publications. The main target of this campaign quickly became the *Yomiuri shimbun*.[75]

Following the removal of Shōriki, the *Yomiuri* displayed considerable independence in its reportage. Unlike other publications which tried to conform to what was believed to be SCAP's stand on the Emperor, it continued to call for the abolition of the emperor system. With headlines blaring, "Dance Hall at the Legal Village," the paper also ran on May 3, 1946, a critical account of the living accommodations enjoyed by the Allied judges and attorneys of the Tokyo War Crimes Trials. The CIE responded by levelling a suspension order against the *Yomiuri*. But, more important, in a move that passed authority back to individuals such as *Yomiuri* owner Shōriki Matsutarō, the CIE Press Section Chief declared that responsibility for the editorial policy and content of a

---

74. Gayn, *Japan Diary*, 23; Moore, *Japanese Workers and the Struggle for Power*, 52, 55.
75. Moore, *Japanese Workers and the Struggle for Power*, 102-3, 190.

newspaper would rest with the owner and his appointed management. In effect, when Union-supported editors displayed too much independence, criticizing what they believed was a tardy approach to reform and maintaining a more hard-line stand on war crimes issues, Occupation authorities decided to allow the old management to reinstate itself in power. Intimidated by what they saw as SCAP's open support of management, workers at the *Yomiuri* began to lose faith in their earlier tactics. As a result, a strike in the summer of 1946 ended in failure due to a lack of employee participation.[76]

In an effort to prevent further disobedience the CIE then embarked on a mass media union-busting campaign. The *Jinmin shimbun*, a socialist paper with a circulation of 250,000, was ordered to abandon its "pro-Communist policy" or risk suppression, and the *Hokkaidō shimbun*, a well-known provincial daily, was forced to dismiss fifty-nine union members who were accused of being "communist racketeers." More than one writer has commented on the ramifications of CIE's treatment of the publishing industry's unions. In his study of the purge of wartime personnel, Hans Baerwald has suggested that the Occupation authorities did not need to attack the unionists and instead, could have encouraged and guided them. "Had the Occupation," he writes, "taken advantage of these early spontaneous developments by immediately drawing up a program which would aid this new leadership a tremendous stimulus to unfettered thought would have been provided." As it was, the Occupation authorities' involvement only heightened the bitterness and discord of management-union conflicts, which were also being played out in the offices of *Kaizō* and *Chūō kōron* and which eventually would have an impact on attitudes toward the Yokohama Incident and the court case against the Police Officers.[77]

Although GHQ had applauded the re-establishment of both *Kaizō* and *Chūō kōron* after the Pacific War, Occupation authorities soon called for the removal of the Presidents of these publications as part of a purge of wartime collaborators from important private industries. Carrying out a purge of individuals outside of the government was a difficult task because of the problem of determining what constituted collaboration. With regard to the publishing industry, committees were organized to determine which companies had contributed to ultranationistic and chauvinistic thinking, and they based their selection on two factors: the number of times a company had involved itself in propaganda activities and its influence as determined by circulation figures. When reviewing the careers of individuals in the publishing industry,

---

76. Cohen, *Remaking Japan*, 244, 246-7; Gayn, *Japan Diary*, 253.
77. Gayn, *Japan Diary*, 264-65; Baerwald, *The Purge of Japanese Leaders*, 37-39.

these committees were called upon to see if the person had "persecuted or denounced liberals or persons espousing anti-militaristic ideologies," or "in any other way advocated or championed militarism or ultranationalism."[78] An individual such as Shōriki Matsutarō fell within the purge guidelines. The *Yomiuri* was a major newspaper and, under Shōriki, had been one of the most jingoistic publications in Japan. However, others in the industry did not present such clear-cut cases of collaboration. In the end, even the Presidents of *Kaizō* and *Chūō kōron*, two publications with notably progressive and liberal reputations, eventually found themselves accused of supporting the wartime government.

Justification for the purge of *Kaizō* President Yamamoto Sanehiko rested mainly on the fact that on July 1945, after the shut down of publication, he had accepted a position as counsellor in the East Asia Ministry. His critics claimed he was self-serving and had not done enough to resist the wartime regime or help those arrested in the Yokohama Incident. *Kaizō* employees, moreover, accused him of interfering in their efforts to form a company union. In January 1947, Occupation officials ordered the removal of Yamamoto. However, Yamamoto's departure did not eliminate the internal strife plaguing the publication. Despite SCAP intervention in December 1948 to settle a labour dispute, conflict continued and eventually resulted in the dismissal of all employees who opposed company policy. Finally, around 1955, the so-called Society to Protect *Kaizō* was formed to protest Management's high-handedness and succeeded in enlisting the cooperation of hundreds of writers in boycotting the journal. Given these circumstances, the journal could not continue publishing.[79]

The purge orders against their Presidents caused the same problems or controversy within both *Kaizō* and *Chūō kōron*. The only exception was that, in contrast to *Kaizō* President Yamamoto Sanehiko, *Chūō kōron* President Shimanaka Hōji was able to retain his position.[80] In June 1947 Shimanaka was slated to be removed under the G-Section Mass Media purges for having cooperated with the wartime military. Shimanaka's involvement in the Yokohama Incident, specifically his defense of those arrested, presented the greatest argument against removing him. Management at *Chūō kōron* were prepared to oppose the purge order and requested that the publication's Union

---

78. Baerwald, *The Purge of Japanese Leaders*, 39.
79. *Kaizō mokuji sōran*, Vol. II, ed. Yokoyama Haruichi (Tokyo: Shinyaku shobō, 1968), 23, 28-29.
80. Nakamura Tomoko, *Fūryū mutan jiken igo: Henshūsha no jibunshi* (Tokyo: Tabata shoten, 1976), 102-3; *Kaizō mokuji sōran*, 22-23.

cooperate in providing evidence to the contrary; that is, support Management's claims that Shimanaka had tried to assist those employees who had been apprehended by the Kanagawa Police. However, at a meeting attended by most of their 48 members, the Unionists agreed that "following the Yokohama Incident, the magazine gave in to the military" and voted against helping to defend Shimanaka. The decision not to cooperate with Management in contesting the purge order may have been, at first, simply an act to display or reinforce the Union's new independent status within the Company. The *Chūō kōron* Union had been established and initially functioned as simply a part of the Company. But in September 1946 it had merged with and become a branch of the All-Japan Printing and Publication Union.

Shimanaka, in the end, escaped being purged because media purge officials reversed their original decision on his removal in December 1947. They had come to the conclusion that Japanese publications had little recourse but to obey the orders of the government after the start of the Pacific War; they therefore decided to make essays written before December 8, 1941 the focus of examination. The Union's refusal to cooperate nevertheless poisoned relations within the Company and marked the beginning of the so-called First *Chūō kōron* Company Incident, a bitter labour conflict that resulted in CIE's intervention on the side of management.

The Management and Union of *Chūō kōron* initially attempted to settle their differences privately. Both sides agreed that news of the crisis over the possible purge of President Shimanaka and other issues of contention between labour and management should not be leaked outside of the Company. However, two Union members on the editorial board made the mistake of divulging information to outside sources. Consequently, the company conflict was discussed by two major newspapers, the *Asahi* and the *Jiji tsūshin*, and came to the attention of the anti-communist CIE Press Section Chief, Major Daniel Imboden. Imboden apparently called in some of the *Chūō kōron* Union leaders and made it clear that he would not tolerate any actions he believed were too radical. Believing that it had the support of Imboden and SCAP, Management became more bold, began ordering personnel transfers and even threatened to dismiss those considered trouble-makers.

The First *Chūō kōron* Company Incident blemished the publication's progressive reputation. Supporters of the Union denounced the Company for calling on Occupation officials to suppress the Union. Moreover, employees accused President Shimanaka Hōji, who had been so much admired for his liberalism and progressive views during the prewar and wartime periods, of acting like a despot. Conflict between labour and management eventually resulted in the resignation of eleven persons.[81]

Among those who resigned from *Chūō kōron* were two individuals who had been arrested during the Yokohama Incident. One of them had joined the journal after the Pacific War and became its publication chief, and he explained that he left because relations within the Company had become unbearably tense and strained. The other individual, who had been working at *Chūō kōron* when he was arrested in the Yokohama Incident, had returned to the publication after his release from custody and became its Editorial Section Chief. In his memoirs, he suggested that blame could be levelled equally against the Management and the Union, both of which were only interested in controlling the publication. Unable to accept the conduct of both sides, he felt compelled to resign.[82]

It is against this background of labour-management conflict that one can perceive some of the reasons why the publishing industry kept its distance from the topic of the Yokohama Incident and the court case. Unionists and those eager to carry out a change in editorial policy perceived the old Management as a potential obstacle to their aims and used charges of wartime collaboration to oust opponents. The Unionists and their allies were probably sympathetic to the plight of those arrested in the Yokohama Incident. However, the Incident could weaken their arguments of Management's wartime collaboration. Consequently, the Unionists and their supporters could ill afford to draw attention to an affair that could be used to prove that those who worked in the industry during the War, including the old management, were the victims of the prewar state and not its willing supporters.

The Incident thus became a taboo subject among *Chūō kōron* employees and within the publishing industry in general. Journalist Nakamura Tomoko, who would later conduct extensive interviews with those arrested in the Yokohama Incident, was a staff member at *Chūō kōron* in the 1950s. She recalled that, despite the fact that the issue of purging Shimanaka had been resolved, it was apparent that the Incident had become a controversial subject because of its association with the conflict between the Union and Management. Nakamura observed that, as a consequence, both managers and co-workers appeared to shun the subject and anyone directly involved with it.[83] Instead of being commended and supported, those arrested in the affair found themselves in an awkward position in the publishing industry, and their efforts

---

81. Nakamura, *Fūryū mutan jiken igo*, 104, 112, 107-11, 112-13.
82. Hatanaka, *Nihon faashizumu*, 148, 142.
83. Nakamura, *Yokohama jiken no hitobito*, 207-8.

to bring charges against the Police Officers who had tortured them were ignored by fellow journalists.

Even during the Occupation, which is often reminisced about as some "golden age of democracy," individuals who sought to mount an attack against the wartime state faced considerable obstacles. It could be easily argued that those wartime officials and notables, who feared that a continuation of the Pacific War could lead to a devastating communist revolution, were at least right in assuming that surrender and occupation by foreign powers posed a lesser threat to the existing order in Japan. SCAP's active attack of the existing order and promotion of the opponents of the wartime state was quite short-lived.

There is little reason to believe that Occupation authorities were immune to some of the problems, such as internal conflict, security concerns and anti-leftist attitudes, that plagued the prewar Japanese governments. The former's attitude toward leftists in Japan, for example, seemed to evolve in a manner not so different from Japanese official policy from the 1930s to about 1941-drifting from almost patronage to suppression. Around 1942 Japanese wartime officials had abandoned the relatively tolerant *Tenkō* policy and began to purge suspected leftists and former thought control offenders from all positions of influence; around 1946 American Occupation policy was moving in a similar fashion.

Politically or socially influential groups, those which could be expected to rally to a cause such as the court case against the Yokohama Incident Police Officers, had reason to believe that SCAP did not necessarily support independent initiatives to address the abuses committed by Japanese officials. The ebullient reformist impulse which erupted at the end of the Pacific War and which manifested itself in demands both in Japan and abroad for the purge of wartime officials, the abolition of thought control organs and laws, and the release of political prisoners was soon tempered.

All this being said, however, it would be incorrect to say that this reformist impulse had no impact or was completely extinguished. In the words of one distinguished historian,

> Postwar Japan is undeniably a more democratic country than before the war, and many of the reforms and ideals of the early Occupation period survive to the present. They survive for many reasons, but the most important is that from the onset they have had the support of the Japanese people. In many critical areas, the "democratization and demilitarization" ideals of the immediate postwar years have been upheld despite policies and

pressures to the contrary from both the United States and its most conservative Japanese allies.[84]

The more recent legal activities of those arrested in the Yokohama Incident, their efforts to win a retrial and clear their names, exemplifies an adherence to these early ideals as well as a dogged will to try to confront the legacy of the Japanese wartime state.

---

84. John W. Dower, "A Rejoinder," *Pacific Historical Review*, Vol. 57, No. 2: 208-9.

Conclusion

The Yokohama Incident was more than a mass-media suppression case and conventional explanations of it must be reconsidered. There is little to support arguments that the Incident was linked to a conspiracy against Prince Konoe or was devised for the sole purpose of shutting down intellectual publications such as *Kaizō* and *Chūō kōron*. In fact, the closing of these publications may very well have been an unexpected consequence of the police investigation of the affair. Consequently, rather than being a triumph of government control over the publishing industry, these shut downs could have been an instance of matters developing beyond the control or expectations of the authorities. It is apparent that during the prewar period controlling thought was not easy and that difficulties in administering thought control heightened insecurities about the state's hold over the people. It was also apparent that the state had little control over their own instruments of control.

Those in the lower ranks of the state administration, eager to please their superiors, tried to use every means to root out dissent. Individuals higher up in the ruling establishment had limited means of determining if communist incidents were fabricated or not, and used police reports to assess the state of leftist activity. Konoe Fumimaro and those who shared his concerns constructed their vision of a leftist threat from observations of foreign and domestic developments as well as official assessments of communist activities.

During the Pacific War many members of the social, economic and administrative elite believed that the country was faced with two foes-external enemies in the guise of the Allied powers and internal enemies in the guise of thought control offenders. They observed the presence of former leftist thought control offenders in important sectors of society and spread word that communists had infiltrated the highest levels of government and industry. Increased efforts on the part of wartime governments to apprehend hidden communists did nothing to ease these fears. The discovery by the police forces of large numbers of alleged communist conspirators in noteworthy positions only strengthened the image of a substantial leftist presence and seemed to vindicate arguments that the War had to be terminated in order to avert a revolution.

The Yokohama Incident reveals much about the wartime ruling elite's views of communist activities, the difficulties in maintaining and administering thought control, and the changes in the official treatment of thought control offenders. The experiences of the researchers arrested in the affair show that the thought control system was neither consistently brutal nor mild in its treatment of offenders. Former offenders were allowed to reassume a place in society and even find employment in the government during the 1930s, but fell under suspicion once again and became the target of a wartime purge.

Japan's surrender nevertheless did not signal an end to all issues and events related to the Yokohama Incident and wartime Japan. Almost immediately after their release from custody, those arrested in the affair lodged a court case against the Police Officers who had tortured them. This court case was one of the most enduring and perhaps successful of the Japanese initiatives that were stimulated by the reformist, anti-establishment impulse that emerged at the start of the American Occupation. The Trial of the Police Officers, which represented one notable challenge of the wartime state by its former victims, marked the first time that the Japanese courts had ruled in favour of private citizens in a case against government representatives.

Yet, the Trial of the Yokohama Incident Police Officers was not a complete victory for those arrested and reveals that even during the Occupation, when the wartime state seemed most open to attack, domestic campaigns against the old regime faced considerable obstacles. Groups such as the Japanese publishing industry and the Japan Communist Party were keenly aware that SCAP's patronage could be easily withdrawn, and they had come to the conclusion that Occupation authorities did not necessarily welcome Japanese initiatives in issues related to war crimes and the conduct of wartime personnel. In addition, there may not have been a great number of individuals who were absolutely confident of their reputation as enemies or victims of the old order and who could denounce the wartime state with no fear of being accused of hypocrisy. If resistance to the state can be defined as only open or active opposition to official polices, an opinion that more and more Japanese began to express in comparing their wartime conduct with that of individuals in other countries, then almost anyone in Japan could have been charged with collaborating with the prewar authorities in some fashion. Even groups with reputations of having opposed or been persecuted by prewar authorities included members whose actions at some time in their lives could be interpreted as assisting the prewar order. Among those who joined or rejoined the Japan Communist Party after the Pacific War were individuals who had renounced leftist ideologies in the 1930s and who had been employed in government or government-affiliated organizations. Publications that supported the works of progressive and liberal writers had continued their operations during the War, and the concessions they made to censors left them open to charges that they had contributed to propaganda efforts.

Those who had launched the court case against the Police Officers in charge of investigating the Yokohama Incident had entertained hopes that it would lead to a popular movement against the wartime state. Their legal action, however, failed to attract public attention or even the participation of groups which would have been the most likely sources of support. In addition, the Trial failed to completely satisfy the litigants' demand for justice. Not only did they later discover that the Police Officers who had tormented them for years during the Pacific War had never served out a single day of their prison sentences. They also learned that all those arrested in the Yokohama Incident retained their criminal records. The rescindment of the Peace Preservation Law did not mean that individuals convicted under the Law were retroactively declared innocent of the charges against them. Consequently, in order to conclusively establish their innocence and draw public attention to what they insist are unresolved wartime issues, survivors among those arrested in the Incident and their families have resumed their legal activities more than three decades after the Trial of the Police Officers.

These recent legal activities present yet another little-known aspect of the Yokohama Incident. It has been observed that since the 1980s more and more groups and individuals have come forward to demand redress for Japanese wartime atrocities and abuses. The retrial movement of the Incident's survivors and their families reveals some of the problems which such redress campaigns can encounter. The prewar state was not completely effective in dealing with its perceived enemies. But in the years after 1945, factors such as legal obstacles and public indifference have frustrated the efforts of its present-day opponents.

In November 1985 Kimura Tōru and others sought the advice of Lawyer Morikawa Kinju about appealing for a retrial of their case. Lawyer Morikawa observed that the Japanese courts could try to reject the appeal on the grounds that the records of their original 1945 trials were unavailable. Still, he noted that there were precedents for reexamining prewar criminal cases. There was, for example, the Yoshida Iwakutsu and the Katō Shin'ichi Cases. Both were murder cases that had taken place at the beginning of the Taisho period and involved decades-long struggles for a retrial. Yoshida Iwakutsu who was originally sentenced in 1913 was, after 50 years and four appeals, granted a retrial in 1963 and found not guilty. Katō Shin'ichi who was originally sentenced in 1915 was, after 60 years and 6 appeals, granted a retrial in 1977 and also found not guilty. The Japanese courts, Lawyer Morikawa observed, agreed to a retrial of both the Yoshida and Katō Cases despite the fact that many of the records from the original trials had been lost in the intervening years.[1]

In August 1986 nine former suspects and family members of deceased suspects in the Yokohama Incident submitted an appeal to the Yokohama District Court. From the outset, the appellants encountered difficulties in justifying their actions to individuals both inside and outside the courts. Kimura Tōru has claimed that the Japan Communist Party in an April 9, 1988 edition of *Akahata* announced that a retrial was unnecessary because a December 29, 1945 Imperial Decree had pardoned those charged with violating the Peace Preservation Law.[2] In response, supporters of the retrial movement have pointed out that this Decree did not erase the criminal records of those wrongly accused and convicted under the Peace Preservation Law.

In March 1986 the Yokohama District Court rejected the appeal without even questioning the appellants or their witnesses. The District Court Judges explained that a retrial was impossible because the unavailability of the original court records which, they observed, had been lost during the chaos that accompanied the arrival of the American Occupation forces.[3] The appellants quickly brought their case before the Tokyo High Court, and when the Tokyo Court upheld the earlier decision, they turned to the Supreme Court of Japan in December 1988. However, in March 1991, the Supreme Court rejected their appeal on the grounds that the appellants had been tried under the prewar Criminal Code and that a retrial would require a special emergency legal measure. The Supreme Court Judges observed that this measure could be applied only in cases involving constitutional violations and that they did not believe that such violations had been committed during the original 1945 trials of the suspects in the Yokohama Incident.[4]

The appellants for a retrial and their legal advisers, needless to say, disagree with the ruling of the Supreme Court and have insisted that the original trials did indeed involve a constitutional violation. They have argued

---

1. "Nenpyō 'Yokohama jiken,'" *Yokohama jiken o kangaeru kai*, November 24, 1995: 17.
2. Letter dated September 28, 1993 from Kimura Tōru.
3. "Nenpyō 'Yokohama jiken,'" 21.
4. *Nihonjin no ōkina wasuremono no jinken: Yokohama jiken 50 nen no tatakai* (Tokyo: Yokohama jiken o kangaeru kai, 1993), 13; "Nenpyō 'Yokohama jiken,'" 22-23.

that the present Japanese courts have ignored the question of what exactly had happened to the original records. To say that these documents were lost is euphemistic. Wartime officials were aware that the American occupiers would be interested in examining Japanese documents. In October 1945 SCAP ordered the Japanese government to "ensure the security and preservation of all records and any and all other materials" held by certain organizations and commanded that these records "not be destroyed, removed, or tampered with in any way."[5] The directive was issued far too late. Japanese officials had already disposed of many possibly incriminating documents. One former Home Ministry official, for example, admitted years later that he and three others had been ordered to visit ministry offices throughout the country to see that sensitive papers were destroyed before the arrival of the Americans.[6]

The appellants for a retrial believe that their original court documents were also deliberately destroyed by wartime officials and that such actions amount to a constitutional violation. According to Article LXI of the Meiji Constitution, "no suit of law, which relates to the rights alleged to have been infringed by the illegal measures of the administrative authorities . . . shall be taken cognizance of by a Court of Law." In addition, the appellants oppose the present courts' suggestion that the original court documents had been lost during the chaos that accompanied the September 2, 1945 arrival of the American Occupation forces and thus, disappeared only after those arrested in the Incident had been sentenced by the Yokohama District Court. They instead contend that these documents had probably been destroyed prior to their sentencing and insist that there are individuals who can corroborate this argument.

Among those who had been willing to testify on behalf of the appellants was a former guard who had been assigned to those arrested in the Incident. This former guard had offered to come before the present courts to state that he himself had seen judicial officers burning documents on the grounds of the Yokohama Court during the trials of his wards and that he believed that they included materials related to these trials. Consequently, retrial appellants and their supporters have argued that, if the court records had been destroyed prior to or during the original proceedings, then many of the sentences that were

---

5. "Office of the Supreme Commander for the Allied Powers, Memorandum for Imperial Japanese Government, 4 October 1945, Subject: Removal of Restrictions on Political, Civil, and Religious Liberties," *Documents concerning the Allied Occupation and Control of Japan*, Vol. II, 82-86.

6. *Yamazaki naimu daijin jidai o kataru zadankai*, 3-4.

rendered were invalid because the defendants would have been in all probability tried without the benefit of all the documents related to their cases.[7] According to Mrs. Ono Sada, the wartime judges who sentenced her husband and the others arrested in the Yokohama Incident also failed to examine what she believed was an important piece of evidence-the Hosokawa Karoku essay itself. Mrs. Ono had been a major participant in the retrial movement since its start. Confident that the Hosokawa essay constituted new evidence which could establish the innocence of some of those arrested in the affair, she launched in July 1994 what has been called the second movement for a retrial by petitioning the present courts to reexamine her late husband's case.

Mrs. Ono's husband, who had been a journalist for the prominent publication *Kaizō*, was accused and found guilty of promoting communism because he had helped edit Marxist scholar Hosokawa Karoku's essay and had contributed to a 20 yen donation to the Hosokawa family after the scholar had been arrested.

But, as Mrs. Ono has pointed out, if making the donation truly constituted an act of promoting communism, then others who tried to financially help out the Hosokawa family such as former Justice Minister Kazami Akira should also have been arrested. As for the charges involving the editing of the essay, Mrs. Ono has argued that if it can be shown that the Hosokawa essay was not leftist propaganda, then it will be clear that her husband had been innocent of the charges that he had tried to promote communism in assisting in its publication.[8] Many have insisted that the Hosokawa essay, at its core, was simply proposing that Japanese authorities consider tactics, such as those adopted by the Soviet Union, to assist the Asian peoples and cultivate their good will. Consequently, on the grounds that the Judges at the original 1945 trial of her husband had failed to consider the actual contents of the essay and had simply assumed that it was a seditious work, Mrs. Ono and her legal advisers have proposed that respected scholars of Japanese wartime history and specialists of prewar censorship, such as Yokohama City University Professor Emeritus Imai Seiichi and International Christian University Professor Okudaira Yasuhiro, be asked to evaluate the nature of the Hosokawa article.[9]

---

7. Ono and Okawa, *Yokohama jiken mitsu no saiban*, 22, 77-78; "Nenpyō 'Yokohama jiken,'" 9; "Appendix X: Constitution of the Empire of Japan 1889," *The Making of the Meiji Constitution: The Oligarchs and the Constitutional Development of Japan, 1886-1891*, by George M. Beckmann (Lawrence: University of Kansas Press, 1957), 155.
8. *Yokohama jiken: Saishin saiban o shien suru kai*, No. 25, 1994.9.9, 1; Ono and Okawa, *Yokohama jiken mitsu no saiban*, 116-24.
9. *Yokohama jiken: Saishin saiban o shien suru kai*, No. 25, 1994.9.9, 1; No. 28, 1995.9.15, 1.

On September 30, 1995, Mrs. Ono died at the age of eighty-six and after a decade of fighting for a retrial for those arrested in the Yokohama Incident. Her son Shin'ichi assumed responsibility for Mrs. Ono's recent campaign, but made it known that while he would continue to participate in retrial efforts, he would resign from taking the lead in future legal actions if the courts rejected the appeal presented by his mother. In July 1996, the Yokohama District Court rejected the Ono family's appeal for a retrial on the grounds that the Hosokawa essay or "submitted evidence is not new." However, both Mrs. Ono's legal advisers as well as other individuals who had been arrested in the Yokohama Incidents, such as Kimura Tōru, have publicly declared their intention to continue the movement for a retrial.

In the summer of 1996, before the grave of his mentor Hosokawa Karoku, Kimura announced that he would present to the courts yet another retrial appeal and persist in his efforts to make the international community more aware of such activities taking place in Japan.[10] Kimura has stated that he and others have realized that they cannot look just to domestic support in promoting their cause or rely on the Japanese courts to mete out justice. They have in recent years also presented their case to the United Nations Human Rights Committee. "Appealing to the international community," he argued, "may expose some of the perversions of the Japanese legal system." Consequently, every summer since 1991 retrial supporters have travelled to Geneva, Switzerland to outline their activities and discuss both the past and present abuse of prisoners in their country.[11]

At the Asia-Pacific Area Policy Conference in the summer of 1992 retrial supporters declared that unfortunate events such as the Yokohama Incident are not a thing of the past. They have observed that, just as those arrested in the affair were victims of a police frame-up, the lack of safeguards in the present system of interrogating individuals in Japan has continued to result in false arrests and the mistreatment of suspects. In addition, in a pamphlet on the Japanese police detention system, they have noted that the

---

10. "Saishin seikyū mata kikyaku: Yokohama jiken de chisai," *Asahi shimbun*, July 31, 1996: 1; "Yokohama jiken no Kimura san 'Enzai harasu' 5 nichi, Toyama no onshi no hakamae ni chikau, Konshū ni mo saishin seikyū, Daiyō kangoku no futōsei uttaeta 'Kokuren enzetsu' mo hōkoku," *Mainichi shimbun*, July 3, 1996: n.p.; "Senjichū, genron dan'atsu no 'Yokohama jiken,' Ryōtei de no atsumai tokkō ga maaku dōshi Hosokawa shi hakamae no hattan no chi: Asahi de saishin chikau gen hikoku Kimura shi," *Kita Nihon shimbun*, July 6, 1996: n.p.; "'Minshūshugi uranuku tame ni,' 'Yokohama jiken' no Kimura san Saishin seikyū e ketsugi arata, 'enzai' 54 nen seoi, Onshi no hakamae ni 'Kuni no sensō sekinin tsuikyū,'" *Mainichi shimbun* [Chiiki no nyuushu], July 7, 1996: n.p.

11. *Nihonjin no ōkina wasurerumono no jinken*, 15; "Nenpyō 'Yokohama jiken,'" 26-27.

postwar Japanese Constitution's announcement that "the infliction of torture by any public officer and cruel punishments are absolutely forbidden" has not put an end to such abuses. In the decade or so after the Pacific War alone there had been four instances of police suspects being physically coerced into confessing to crimes: the Menda Case (1948), the Saitama Case (1950), the Shimada Case (1954) and the Matsuyama Case (1955). In all four cases it was discovered decades later that the suspects had been innocent of the charges levelled against them.[12]

According to retrial supporters, the police had been able to freely terrorize those arrested in the Yokohama Incident because the detention system, established in 1908, had permitted officers to hold suspects in special inaccessible quarters where they could be interrogated for long periods of time. This system, they noted, had not been abolished after the Pacific War and has become a target of criticism both in Japan and abroad. On September 20, 1988 the *New York Times* ran an article on how suspects in Japan were subjected to lengthy detention in police stations and pressured into making confessions. In the same year, moreover, the system of detention at police stations became an issue of dispute between the U.N. Human Rights Committee and the Japanese government. In a 1988 report on "Police Cell Detention in Japan: the *Daiyo Kangoku* System" members of the International Federation of Human Rights had discussed how in Japan detainees could be subjected to undue pressure and denied legal counsel. In response to such information the U.N. Human Rights Committee in July of the same year requested that the Japanese Government abolish the system of police detention.[13]

In Japan legal organizations such as the three bar associations in Tokyo have also called for the abolition of or limits on the practice of detaining suspects in police stations, and studies of police practices by legal scholars seem to support the concerns of retrial supporters that a potential for cases such as the Yokohama Incident continues to exist in Japan. Miyazawa Setsuo, for example, who was permitted to attend courses for the police and observe detectives during assignments, came to the conclusion that "a system of detention and questioning . . . makes it almost impossible for suspects to maintain their innocence" and "that police detectives are working in an

---

12. *Yokohama jiken: Saishin saiban o shien suru kai*, No. 21, 1992.12.5, 7; *The Yokohama Case and Tortures in Japan*, 2.
13. Setsuo Miyazawa, *Policing in Japan: A Study on Making Crime*, trans. Frank G. Bennett, Jr. with John O. Haley (Albany: State University of New York Press, 1992), 2; *The Yokohama Case and Tortures in Japan*, 5-6.

environment that constantly tempts them into more aggressive and questionable behavior."[14]

A comparison of works on the prewar and contemporary police force reveal considerable continuities in practice and outlook. In her book Elise Tipton revealed the problems of competition among the prewar police, and in his study Miyazawa noted that present-day officers tended to base their professional worth on the number of cases they could investigate and that this desire for cases often fostered what even the police acknowledged as rivalry between detectives and stations.[15] In addition, like their prewar counterparts, Japanese police appeared to rely on obtaining confessions from their suspects rather than other investigative techniques in establishing cases and sometimes tried to uncover other, more serious and unrelated crimes during interrogation sessions. Eliciting confessions was a time-consuming practice; thus detectives preferred to keep suspects in the police station detention cells, where they could more conveniently and frequently interrogate them, rather than at separate holding centres.

Miyazawa never witnessed any acts of violence, but found that police did react particularly forcefully toward certain types of suspects. Police attitudes toward suspected organized crime members, for instance, bore a striking resemblance to prewar attitudes toward leftists. Detectives maintained that "the first principle in dealing with gangs is always use compulsory measures," and Miyazawa deduced that the police felt free to threaten these suspects with harsher sentences and some level of aggression because they believed that the public would support such actions.[16]

Miyazawa's findings indicated that the contemporary police as well as the entire legal system are in many ways slated against suspects. Although Judges could decide where suspects would be held, they usually agreed to the requests of the police and prosecutors to have them placed in police station detention cells. Laws to protect the civil rights of suspects did not necessarily favour those who had been pressured into making false confessions. Article 38 of the present Constitution declares that an individual cannot be compelled to testify against himself; that confessions derived from threats, physical coercion or made after prolonged period of detention are inadmissible as evidence; and that confession alone is not sufficient to convict or punish an individual. However, the courts have been known to rule against cases of involuntary

---

14. Miyazawa, *Policing in Japan*, 236, xi, xiii, 3.
15. Tipton, *The Japanese Police State*, 76-77, 97-98, 52, 65; Miyazawa, *Policing in Japan*, 175-76, 154, 157, 235.
16. Miyazawa, *Policing in Japan*, 152, 157, 235, 20, 161, 89-90.

confession even when conditions have suggested that the defendant had been forced to endure considerable police pressure. In one case, for example, judges concluded that a self-incriminating statement made by the defendant was not coerced despite the fact this individual had been interrogated, without benefit of legal counsel, some fifty times during a period of thirty-nine days.[17]

Just as the Constitution cannot provide a complete safeguard against false confessions, the present Code of Criminal Procedure's declaration on the suspect's right to prepare a defense has been difficult to enforce. Miyazawa found that the majority of suspects could not afford to retain lawyers and that state-appointed legal counsel was often not provided until detectives were in the process of collecting incriminating evidence. Furthermore, legal counsel had no right to be present at the interrogations, and, in accordance with Article 39 of the Code of Criminal Procedure,
defense attorneys had to work out an agreement with the police and prosecutors specifying the time, location, and duration of a meeting before they could even see their clients. Given these circumstances, the limitations on legal counsel and the dependence of detectives on confessions and extended detention, it is easy to understand why those arrested in the Yokohama Incident and their retrial supporters believe that many problems dating back to the wartime period and earlier continue to this day.[18]

Those arrested in the Yokohama Incident were accused of promoting unorthodox ideas. More than fifty years later, they and their supporters are acting in an unorthodox manner through their political activism, their efforts to direct public attention to unaddressed issues dating back to the prewar period. As they are quick to point out, their goal is not just to clear the names of those arrested in the Yokohama Incident, but to remind the Japanese people of their past so that they may better evaluate the present. They believe that the difficulties they encounter in their legal campaigns reflect the degree to which Japan has and has not evolved from its prewar incarnation.

Fujita Chikamasa, a *Chūō kōron* journalist at the time of his arrest, has observed that "many things have occurred in the fifty years since the end of the Pacific War. But has the War truly ended? In light of the problems of the Atomic Bomb victims and the Comfort women, I myself wonder if the War has really ended."[19] There are, no doubt, countless individuals in Japan and abroad

---

17. Miyazawa, *Policing in Japan*, 20, 23-24.
18. Miyazawa, *Policing in Japan*, 19, 22.
19. Fujita Chikamasa, "Jiken o fūkasasenu tame ni," *Yokohama jiken o shien suru kai*, No. 28, 1995.9.15, 2.

who share Fujita's views and who feel the wartime remains more than a momentary nightmare.

Bibliography

COLLECTIONS OF OFFICIAL DOCUMENTS

"Apprehension, Trial and Punishment of War Criminals in the Far East, FEC Policy Decision, April 3, 1946." *Documents concerning the Allied Occupation and Control of Japan.* Vol. II: Political, Military and Cultural. Tokyo: Division of Special Records, Foreign Office, Japanese Government, 1949: 257.

"Chian jōkyō ni tsuite keisatsu buchō kaigi ni okeru hoan kachō setsumei yōshi." Home Ministry, Police Bureau, Security Section, January 14, 1944. *Nihon rikukaigun monjo.* Tokyo: Waseda University Microform Library, MF 1-229, 163 reels, Reel No. 218 F88663: 299-321.

"Chūgoku kyōsantō Tōkyō shibu jiken," "Kominterun no senryaku senjutsu no hensen-shu toshite Nihon no kyōsanshugi undō to no kanren." 1940, Special Research Council on Thought. *Shakai mondai shiryō sōsho.* Vol. 1. Tokyo: Shakai mondai shiryō kenkyūkai, 1975: 566-69.

"General Headquarters Far East Command, Military Intelligence Section, General Staff, General Activities, Memorandum to Mr. Sumino, C.L.O., 13 June 1947, Subject: Reinstatement in Government Service of Former Special Higher Police (TOKKO KA) Personnel." *Documents concerning the Allied Occupation and Control of Japan.* Vol. II: Political, Military and Cultural. Tokyo: Division of Special Records, Foreign Office, Japanese Government, 1949: 123-24.

"Genron, shūkai, kessha nado rinji torishimari hōan." House of Peers Special Committee Record, December 1941. *Gendaishi shiryō 41: Masu media tōsei 2.* Tokyo: Misuzu shobō, 1975: 407-43.

Hosokawa Karoku gokuchū chōsho: Yokohama jiken shōgen. Edited by Morikawa Kinju. Tokyo: Fuji shuppan, 1989.

Japan, Naimushō keihokyoku [Home Ministry, Police Bureau]. *Tokkō geppō.* November 1938: 54-57.

———. *Tokkō geppō*. July 1939: 6-11.
———. *Tokkō geppō*. August 1940: 29-30.
———. *Tokkō geppō*. September 1940: 13.
———. *Tokkō geppō*. March 1941: 4-5.
———. *Tokkō geppō*. January 1942: 4-38, 39-40.
———. *Tokkō geppō*. February 1942: 4-38.
———. *Tokkō geppō*. October 1942: 7-17.
———. *Tokkō geppō*. October 1943: 74-79.
———. *Tokkō geppō*. November 1943: 11-14.
———. *Tokkō geppō*. June 1944: 1.
———. *Tokkō geppō*. August 1944: 3-27.
"Office of the Supreme Commander for the Allied Powers, Memorandum for Imperial Japanese Government, 4 October 1945, Subject: Removal of Restrictions on Political, Civil, and Religious Liberties," *Documents concerning the Allied Occupation and Control of Japan*. Vol. II: Political, Military and Cultural. Tokyo: Division of Special Records, Foreign Office, Japanese Government, 1949: 82-86.
"Saikin no sayoku jiken ni kangami chūi o yōsuru jikō." Home Ministry, Police Bureau, Peace Preservation Section. *Tokkō keisatsu kankei shiryō shūsei*. Vol. 5. Edited by Ogino Fujio. Tokyo: Fuji shuppan, 1991: 371-80.
"Sensō shūketsu ni kansuru byōgi kettei zengo ni okeru chian jōkyō." Home Ministry, Police Bureau, Security Section, September 1, 1945. *Nihon rikukaigun monjo*. Tokyo: Waseda University Microform Library, MF 3, 1-229, 163 reels, Reel No. 221 F92388: 36-77.
"Speech by Mr. George Atcheson, Jr., Chairman, at the Fourth Meeting of the Allied Council for Japan." *Documents concerning the Allied Occupation and Control of Japan*. Vol. II: Political, Military and Cultural. Tokyo: Division of Special Records, Foreign Office, Japanese Government, 1949: 2-3.
"Yokohama jiken hikoku Aikawa Hiroshi shuki." *Zoku gendaishi shiryō 7: Tokkō to shisō kenji*. Edited by Katō Keiji. Tokyo: Misuzu shobō, 1982: 678-722.
Yokohama jiken shiryōshū. Edited by Sasage dōshikai. Tokyo: Tokyo ruliyūlu, 1986.
Zai-Man Nikkei kyōsanshugi undō. Edited by Kwantung kempeitai shireibu. Second printing. Tokyo: Gannandō shoten, 1969.

OTHER PRIMARY MATERIALS

Aoyama Kenzō. *Yokohama jiken: 'Kaizō' henshūsha no shuki*. Tokyo: Kōbundō, 1966.

"'Chūō kōron' 'Kaizō' kaitai no shinsō/Hosokawa shi no ronbun hottan/Henshūjin ni mo mubō na dan'atsu." *Asahi shimbun*, October 9, 1945.

Fujita Chikamasa. "Jiken o fūkasasenu tame ni," *Yokohama jiken o shien suru kai*, No. 28, 1995.9.15: 2-3.

"Habōhō dantai tekiyō no ugoki ni hantai suru seimei ni Yokohama jiken o kangaeru kai mo kuwawarimashita," *Kaihō*, No. 20, September 1995: 3.

Hatanaka Shigeo. *Nihon faashizumu no genron dan'atsu shōshi*. Tokyo: Kōbunken, 1986.

Hiradate Toshio. "Watakushi no Soren kenkyūshi no isshaku." *Senshū daigaku shakaigaku kenkyūjo geppō*, No. 150, March 20, 1976: 2-20.

"Hirogaru habōhō hantai undō: 5 gatsu 24 nichi, Nibenrenga hantai ketsugi," *Kaihō*, No. 23, June 1996: n.p.

Ikejima Shimpei and Mimasaka Tarō. "Genron tōsei ni taeru." *Shōwa shisōshi e no shōgen*. Tokyo: Mainichi shimbunsha, 1968: 272-350.

"'Kaizō' no sanjūnen." *Kaizō*, April 1950: 124-36.

Katsube Gen. "Watakushi no 'Yokohama jiken.'" *Undōshi kenkyū 3*. Tokyo: San'ichi shobō, 1979: 5-17.

Kimura Tōru. *Yokohama jiken no shinsō: Tsukurareta 'Tomari kaigi'*. Tokyo: Chikuma shobō, 1982.

Matsumoto Masao. "Yokohama jiken: Chōōgata detchiage." *Dokyumento Shōwa gojūnenshi*. Vol. 6. Tokyo: Sekibunsha, 1975: 99-120.

Mimasaka Tarō, Fujita Chikamasa, and Watanabe Kiyoshi. *Yokohama jiken*. Tokyo: Nihon editaasukūru shuppansha, 1977.

"'Minshūshugi uranuku tame ni,' 'Yokohama jiken' no Kimura san Saishin seikyū e ketsugi arata, 'enzai' 54 nen seoi, Onshi no hakamae ni 'Kuni no sensō sekinin tsuikyū,'" *Mainichi shimbun [Chiiki no nyuusu]*, July 7, 1996: n.p.

Nakamura Tomoko. "Yokohama jiken: Mitsu no episōdo." *Shisō no kagaku*, June 1992: 104-19.

Nakamura Tomoko. *Yokohama jiken no hitobito*. Tokyo: Tabata shoten, 1979.

"Nenpyō 'Yokohama jiken.'" *Yokohama jiken o kangaeru kai*, November 24, 1995: 1-28.

Nihonjin no ōkina wasurerumono no jinken: Yokohama jiken 50 nen no tatakai. Tokyo: Yokohama jiken o kangaeru kai, 1993.
Nomura Shigeomi, "Sōgō zasshi hihan bunka shikan o tadasu." *Dokusho*, Vol. 4, No. 2, February 1944: 9-12.
Ono Sada and Takashi Okawa. *Yokohama jiken mitsu no saiban: Dainiji saishin saiban saishin seikyūsho.* Tokyo: Kōbunken, 1995.
Ono Sada and Kiga Sumiko. *Yokohama jiken: Tsuma to imōto no shuki.* Tokyo: Kōbunken, 1978.
"Oum e no habōhō ga kakudzi saretara ankoku jidzi ni," *Asahi Shimbun*, January 11, 1996: 3.
"Saishin seikyū mata kikyaku: Yokohama jiken de chisai," *Asahi shimbun*, July 31, 1996: 1.
"Senjichū, genron dan'atsu no 'Yokohama jiken,' Ryōtei de no atsumai tokkō ga maaku dōshi Hosokawa shi hakamae de hattan no chi: Asahi de saishin chikau gen hikaku Kimura shi," *Kita Nihon shimbun*, July 6, 1996: n.p.
Tadokoro Hiroyasu. "Rekishi hitsuzen ron to Soren raisan ron: Hosokawa Karoku shi no 'Sekaishi no dōkō to Nihon' ni tsuite." *Yūkoku no hikari to kage: Tadokoro Hiroyasu ikōshū.* Tokyo: Kokumin bunka kenkyūkai, 1970: 429-36.
Takagi Kenjirō. "Shōwa juku jiken to Unno sensei." *Bengoshi Unno Shinkichi*. Tokyo: Seikōsha, 1972: 535-44.
Takagi Kenjirō. "Yokohama kōchisho no akekure." *Kanagawa ken shi kenkyū.* Vol. 30, December 1975: 53-64.
Unno Shinkichi. "Aru bengoshi no ayumi: IV Yokohama jiken." *Hōritsu jihō*, June 1968: 62-67.
Yahagi Kuniharuō. "Sensō dokusho." *Dokusho shimbun*, September 14, 1942.
The Yokohama Case and Tortures in Japan. n.p.: Association to Concern [sic] the Yokohama Case, n.d.
Yokohama jiken kankeisha tsuitōroku. Edited Sasagekai. Tokyo: Sasagekai, 1977.
"Yokohama jiken no Kimura san 'Enzai harasu' 5 nichi, Toyama no onshi no hakamae ni chikau, Konshū ni mo saishin seikyū, Daiyō kangoku no futōsei uttaeta 'Kokuren enzetsu' mo hōkoku," *Mainichi shimbun*, July 3, 1996: n.p.
Yokohama jiken o kangaeru kai no kaihō, No. 15, 1994, June: 1-6.
Yokohama jiken: Saishin saiban o shien suru kai, No. 20, 1992.6.10: 1-8.
Yokohama jiken: Saishin saiban o shien suru kai, No. 21, 1992.12.5: 1-8.
Yokohama jiken: Saishin saiban o shien suru kai, No. 25, 1994.9.9: 1-8.
Yokohama jiken: Saishin saiban o shien suru kai, No. 28, 1995.9.15: 1-8.

Yokohama jiken: Saishin saiban o shien suru kai, No. 29, 1995.11.10: 1-8.

BOOKS

Abe Genki shi danwa dai ikkai, nikkai, sankai sokkiroku. Edited by Naiseishi kenkyūkai. Tokyo: Naiseishi kenkyūkai, 1967.

Akamatsu Sadao. *Tōjō hishokan kimitsu nisshi*. Tokyo: Bungei shunjū, 1985.

Aritake Shūji. *Karasawa Toshiki*. Tokyo: Karasawa Toshiki denki kankōkai, 1975.

Awaya Kentarō. *Tokyo saibanron*. Tokyo: Otsuki shoten, 1989.

Baerwald, Hans H. *The Purge of Japanese Leaders Under the Occupation*. Berkeley: University of California Press, 1959.

Bowen, Roger. *Innocence is Not Enough: The Life and Death of Herbert Norman*. New York: M.E. Sharpe, Inc., 1986.

Cohen, Bernard. *The Political Process and Foreign Policy: The Making of the Japanese Peace Settlement*. Princeton: Princeton University Press, 1957.

Cohen, Theodore. *Remaking Japan: The American Occupation as New Deal*. Edited by Herbert Passin. New York: The Free Press, 1987.

The Communist International, 1919-1943: Documents. Vol. III. Edited by Jane Degras. London: Frank Cass & Co. Ltd., 1971.

Cook, Haruko Taya & Theodore F. Cook. *Japan at War: An Oral History*. New York: The New Press, 1992.

The Diary of Marquis Kido, 1931-45: Selected Translations into English. Reprinted from translations prepared for the Tokyo War Crimes Trials. Maryland: University Publications of American, 1984.

Dower, J.W. *Empire and Aftermath: Yoshida Shigeru and the Japanese Experience, 1878-1954*. Cambridge: Council on East Asian Studies, Harvard University, 1988.

Eguchi Keiichi and Kisaka Junichirō. *Chian ijihō to sensō no jidai*. Tokyo: Iwanami bukkuletto, No. 64, 1986.

Emmerson, John K. *The Japanese Thread: A Life in the U.S. Foreign Service*. New York: Holt, Rinehart and Winston, 1978.

Fifty Years of the Japanese Communist Party. Revised and enlarged edition. Tokyo: Central Committee, Japanese Communist Party, 1980.

Finn, Richard B. *Winners in Peace: MacArthur, Yoshida, and Postwar Japan*. Berkeley: University of California Press, 1992.

Fletcher III, William Miles. *The Search for a New Order: Intellectuals and Fascism in Prewar Japan*. Chapel Hill: The University of North Carolina Press, 1982.

Furukawa Takahisa. *Shōwa senchūki no sōgō kokusaku kikan*. Tokyo: Kōbunkan, 1992.
Garon, Sheldon. *Molding Japanese Minds: The State in Everyday Life*. Princeton: Princeton University Press, 1997.
Gayn, Mark. *Japan Diary*. Tokyo: Charles E. Tuttle Company, 1984.
Gotō Ryūnosuke shi danwa dai nikkai sokkiroku, dai sankai sokkiroku. Edited by Naiseishi kenkyūkai. Tokyo: Naiseishi kenkyūkai, 1968.
Hall, John Whitney. *Japan: From Prehistory to Modern Times*. Ann Arbor: University of Michigan Press, 1991.
Harris, Sheldon H. *Factories of Death: Japanese Biological Warfare, 1932-45, and the American Cover-Up*. London: Routledge, 1994.
Hata Ikuhiko and Sodei Rinjirō. *Nihon senryō hisshi*. Tokyo: Asahi shimbunsha, 1977.
Hatanaka Shigeo, Okudaira Yasuhiro, Ebihara Kōgi. *Yokohama jiken: Genron dan'atsu no kōzu*. Tokyo: Iwanami bukkuletto, No. 78, 1987.
Havens, Thomas H.R. *The Valley of Darkness: The Japanese People and World War Two*. New York: Norton, 1978.
Higashikuni Naruhiko. *Ichikōzoku no sensō nikki*. Tokyo: Nihon shūhōsha, 1958.
Hirai, Atsuko. *Individualism and Socialism: The Life and Thought of Kawai Eijiro (1891-1944)*. Cambridge: Harvard University Press, 1986.
Hiranuma Kiichirō kaisōroku. Edited by Hiranuma Kiichirō kaisōroku hensan iinkai. Tokyo: Gakuyō shobō, 1955.
Hoshino Naoki. *Jidai to jibun*. Tokyo: Daiyamondosha, 1968.
Hosokawa Karoku chosakushū: Ajia to Nihon. Vol. 3. Tokyo: Rironsha, 1972.
Hosokawa Morisada. *Hosokawa nikki*. Tokyo: Chūō kōronsha, 1991.
Ikeda Sumihisa. *Nihon no magari kado*. Tokyo: Senjō shuppan, 1968.
Inaba Hidezō. *Gekidō 30 nen no Nihon keizai*. Tokyo: Jitsugyō no Nihonsha, 1965.
Ishidō Kiyotomo. *Waga itan no Shōwashi*. Tokyo: Keisō shobō, 1987.
Itō Takashi. *Konoe shintaisei: Taiseiyokusankai e no michi*. Tokyo: Chūkō shinsho, 1983.
Itō, Takeo. *Life Along the South Manchurian Railway: The Memoirs of Itō Takeo*. Translated by Joshua Fogel. New York: M.E. Sharpe, Inc., 1988.
Iwabuchi Tatsuo. *Sengō Nihon seiji e no chokugen*. Tokyo: Seiyūsha, 1967.
Johnson, Chalmers. *An Instance of Treason: Ozaki Hotsumi and the Sorge Spy Ring*. Stanford: Stanford University Press, 1964.

Johnson, Chalmers. *An Instance of Treason: Ozaki Hotsumi and the Sorge Spy Ring.* Revised edition. Stanford: Stanford University Press, 1964.
Johnson, Chalmers. *MITI and the Japanese Miracle: The Growth of Industrial Policy, 1925-1975.* Stanford: Stanford University Press, 1982.
Kaizō mokuji sōran. Vol. II. Edited by Yokoyama Haruichi. Tokyo: Shinyaku shobō, 1968.
Kasza, Gregory J. *The State and the Mass Media in Japan, 1918-1945.* Berkeley: University of California Press, 1988.
Kazami Akira. *Konoe naikaku.* Tokyo: Chūkō bunkō, 1982.
Kido Kōichi kankei monjo. Tokyo: Tokyo daigaku shuppankai, 1966.
Kido nikki. Vol. II. Tokyo: Tokyo daigaku shuppankai, 1966.
Kitagawa Kenzō. *Kokumin sōdōin no jidai.* Tokyo: Iwanami bukkuletto, shiriizu Shōwashi, No. 6, 1989.
Kiyozawa Kiyoshi. *Ankoku nikki.* Tokyo: Tōyō keizai shimpōsha, 1954.
Koizumi Fumiko. *Mō hitotsu no Yokohama jiken.* Tokyo: Tabata shoten, 1992.
Konoe nikki. Edited by Kyōdō tsūshinsha. Tokyo: Kyōdō tsūshinsha kaihatsu kyoka, 1968.
Kuroda Hidetoshi. *Yokohama jiken.* Tokyo: Gakugei shorin, 1975.
Li, Lincoln. *The Japanese Army in North China, 1937-1941: Problems of Political and Economic Control.* Oxford: Oxford University Press, 1975.
Matsumura Shūichi. *Miyakezaka.* Tokyo: Sankō kobō, 1952.
Matsuo Takayoshi. *Hongura.* Tokyo: Misuzu shobō, 1983.
Mitamura Takeo. *Sensō to kyōsanshugi.* Tokyo: Minshū seidō fukyūkai, 1950.
Mitchell, Richard H. *Censorship in Imperial Japan.* Princeton: Princeton University Press, 1983.
Mitchell, Richard H. *Janus-Faced Justice: Political Criminals in Imperial Japan.* Honolulu: University of Hawaii Press, 1992.
Mitchell, Richard H. *Thought Control in Prewar Japan.* Ithaca, N.Y.: Cornell University Press, 1976.
Miyanishi Yoshio. *Mantetsu chōsabu to Ozaki Hotsumi.* Tokyo: Aki shobō, 1983.
Miyashita Hiroshi. *Tokkō no kaisō: Aru jidai no shōgen.* Edited by Itō Takashi and Nakamura Tomoko. Tokyo: Tabata shoten, 1978.
Miyazawa, Setsuo. *Policing in Japan: A Study on Making Crime.* Translated by Frank G. Bennett, Jr. with John O. Haley. Albany: State University of New York Press, 1992.
Moore, Joe. *Japanese Workers and the Struggle for Power 1945-1947.* Madison: The University of Wisconsin Press, 1983.

Murata Gorō shi danwa sokkiroku 2, 3, 4, 5. Edited by Naiseishi kenkyūkai. Tokyo: Naiseishi kenkyūkai, 1973.

Muroga Sadanobu. *Shōwa juku: Dan'atsu no arashi no naka de mo jiyū no tō o mamoritsuzuketa hitotsu no juku ga atta.* Tokyo: Nihon keizai shimbunsha, 1979.

Naimushōshi. Vol. 1, 2, 3. Edited by Taikakai. Tokyo: Hara shobō, 1980.

Nakamura Tomoko. *Fūryū mutan jiken igo: Henshūsha no jibunshi.* Tokyo: Tataba shoten, 1976.

Nakanishi Kō. *Chugoku kakumei no arashi no naka de.* Tokyo: Aoki shoten, 1974.

Nihon no keisatsu. Vol. 8. Edited by Koike Yoshimi. Tokyo: Nihon keisatsu hensankai, 1968.

Ogino Fujio. *Tokkō keisatsu taiseishi: Shakai undō yokuatsu torishimari no kōzō to jittai.* Tokyo: Sekita shobō, 1984.

Oka, Yoshitake. *Konoe Fumimaro: A Political Biography.* Translated by Shumpei Okamoto and Patricia Murray. Tokyo: University of Tokyo Press, 1983.

Okudaira Yasuhiro. *Chian ijihō shōshi.* Tokyo: Chikuma shobō, 1977.

Ōkura Kōmō nikki dai yon maki: Shōwa 17-20 nen. Edited by Naiseishi kenkyūkai. Tokyo: Naiseishi kenkyūkai, 1975.

Ōtani Keijirō. *Shōwa kempeishi.* Tokyo: Misuzu shobō, 1966.

Rubin, Jay. *Injurious to Public Morals: Writers and the Meiji State.* Seattle: University of Washington Press, 1984.

Scalapino, Robert A. *The Japanese Communist Movement, 1920-1966.* Berkeley: University of California Press, 1967.

Schaller, Michael. *The American Occupation of Japan: The Origins of the Cold War in Asia.* New York: Oxford University Press, 1985.

Sensō, The Japanese Remember the Pacific War, Letters to the Editor of the Asahi Shimbun. Edited by Frank Gibney. Translated by Beth Cary. New York: M.E. Sharpe, 1995.

Shillony, Ben-Ami. *Politics and Culture in Wartime Japan.* Oxford: Clarendon Press, 1981.

Shōwa Tokkō dan'atsushi 2. Edited by Akashi Hirotaka and Matsuura Sōzō. Tokyo: Taihei shuppansha, 1975.

Smith II, Henry Dewitt. *Japan's First Student Radicals.* Cambridge: Harvard University Press, 1972.

Suda Teiichi. *Kazami Akira to sono jidai.* Tokyo: Hatsukakai, 1965.

Takemae Eiji. *Senryō sengoshi: Tainichi kanri seisaku no zenyō.* Tokyo: Keisō shobo, 1980.

Tipton, Elise K. *The Japanese Police State: The Tokkō in Interwar Japan.* London: Athlone Press, 1991.
Tokkō keisatsu kokushō. Edited by Tokkō keisatsu kokushō iinkai. Tokyo: Shin Nihon shuppansha, 1977.
Tomita Kenji. *Haisen Nihon no uchigawa: Konoe kō no omoide.* Tokyo: Konjyaku shoin, 1962.
Toyama Shigeki, Imai Seiichi, Fujiwara Akira. *Shōwashi.* Tokyo: Iwanami shoten, new edition, 1992.
Tsurumi, Shunsuke. *An Intellectual History of Wartime Japan 1931-1945.* London: KPI Limited, 1986.
Yamada Gōichi. *Mantetsu chōsabu.* Tokyo: Nihon keizai shimbunsha, 1977.
Yamazaki naimu daijin jidai o kataru zadankai. Edited by Chihō zaimu kyōkai. Tokyo: Chihō zaimu kyōkai, 1960.
Young, John. *The Research Activities of the South Manchurian Railway Company, 1907-1934: A History and Bibiography.* New York: Columbia University Press, 1966.

ARTICLES

Akazawa Shirō. "Sengo shisō to bunka." *Senryō to sengo kaikaku.* Edited by Nakamura Masanori. Tokyo: Yoshikawa kōbunkan, 1994: 174-95.
Amemiya Shōichi. "1940 nendai no shakai to seiji taisei: Han-Tōjō rengō no chūshin toshite." *Rekishi kenkyū,* No. 308, April 1988: 63-76.
Arai Naoyuki. "Senryō seisaku to jyaanarizumu." *Kyōdō kenkyū/Nihon senryō.* Edited by Shisō no kagaku kenkyūkai. Tokyo: Tokuma shoten, 1972: 177-85.
Awaya Kentarō. "Chian ijihō jidai no ichi danmen." *Nihonshi kenkyū,* No. 166, June 1976: 69-72.
Awaya Kentarō. "In the Shadows of the Tokyo Trials." *The Tokyo War Crimes Trial: An International Symposium.* Edited by C. Hosoya, N. Andō, Y. Onuma, and R. Minear. Tokyo: Kodansha International Ltd., 1986: 79-87.
Awaya Kentarō and Aiko Utsumi. "Tokyo saiban: Nihon no sensō sekinin." *Sengo Nihon no genten-senryōshi no genzai.* Vol. 1. Edited by Sodei Rinjirō and Takemae Eiji. Tokyo: Yūshisha, 1992: 217-92.
Dower, John W. "A Rejoinder." *Pacific Historical Review,* Vol. 57, No. 2: 202-09.
Dower, John W. "Occupied Japan and the Cold War in Asia." *Japan in War & Peace: Selected Essays.* By John W. Dower. New York: New Press, 1993: 155-207.

Dower, John. "Reform and Reconsolidation." *Japan Examined: Respectives on Modern Japanese History*. Edited by Harry Wray and Hilary Conroy. Honolulu: University of Hawaii Press: 343-51.
"Fate of Japan." *Canadian Forum*. October 1945: 152.
Fujita Shōzō. "Shōwa hachi nen o chūshin suru tenkō no jōkyō." *Kyōdō kenkyū Tenkō*, Vol. 1. Ed. Shisō kagaku kenkyūkai. Tokyo: Heibonsha, 1978: 31-63.
Fukushima Jūrō. "Senryō shoki ni okeru shimbun ken'etsu." *Kyōdō kenkyū Nihon senryō: Sono hikari to kage*. Edited by Shisō no kagaku kenkyūkai. Tokyo: Gendaishi shuppankai, 1977: 115-36.
Garon, Sheldon M. "State and Religion in Imperial Japan, 1912-1945." *Journal of Japanese Studies*, Vol. 12, No. 2, 1986: 273-302.
"Getting Tough with Japan." *The New Republic*, September 24, 1945: 363-64.
Gluck, Carol. "Entangling Illusions—Japanese and American Views of the Occupation." *New Frontiers in American-East Asian Relations: Essays Presented to Dorothy Borg*. Edited by Dorothy Borg. New York: Columbia University Press, 1987: 169-236.
Hashikawa Bunsō. "Kakushin kanryō." *Gendai Nihon shisō taikei 10: Kenryoku no shisō*. Ed. Kamishima Jirō. Tokyo: Chikuma shobō, 1965: 251-73.
Hatanaka, Shigeo. "Thought Criminal." *Japan at War: An Oral History*. By Haruko Taya Cook & Theodore F. Cook. New York: The New Press, 1992: 222-27.
Hofstadter, Richard. "The Paranoid Style in American Politics." *The Paranoid Style in American Politics and Other Essays*. By Richard Hofstadter. New York: Alfred A. Knopf, 1965: 3-40.
Ishidō Kiyotomo. "Mantetsu chōsabu to 'Marukushugi.'" *Undōshi kenkyū 2*. Tokyo: San'ichi shobō, 1978: 5-18.
Ishidō Kiyotomo. "Mantetsu chōsabu wa nan de atta ka I." *Ajia keizai*, Vol. 28, No. 6 (June), 1987: 67-88.
Itō Takashi. "Kyū sayokujin no 'Shintaisei' undō." *Shōwaki no shakai undō*. Ed. Kindai Nihon kenkyūkai. Tokyo: Yamakawa shuppansha, 1983: 259-96.
Itō Takashi. "Rikugun panfuretto." *Shōwa keizaishi*. Edited by Arisawa Hiromi. Tokyo: Nihon keizai shimbunsha, 1976: 114-17.
Itō Takashi. "Senji taisei." *Kindai Nihon kenkyū nyūmon*. Edited by Nakamura Takafusa and Itō Takashi. Tokyo: Tokyo daigaku shuppankai, 1983, pp. 87-104.
Itō Takashi. "Shōwa 17-20 nen no Konoe-Mazaki Gurūpu." *Shōwaki no seiji*. By Itō Takashi. Tokyo: Yamakawa shuppansha, 1983: 150-216.

"Itsuka kita michi." *Kanagawa shimbun*, January 16, 1996: 3.
Karasawa Toshiki. "Chian to keisatsu." "Chian ijihō wa dō unyōsareta ka." *Juristo*, July 15, 1952: 17.
"Kikakuin jiken." *Shōwashi no tennō 18*. Tokyo: Yomiuri shimbunsha, 1972: 6-196.
Kiga, Sumiko. "'Isn't my brother one of the 'War Dead'?'" *Japan at War: An Oral History*. By Haruko Taya Cook & Theodore F. Cook. New York: The New Press, 1992: 227-31.
Kumei Shigeru. "Tokuda Kyūichi ron." *Kyōdō kenkyū/Nihon senryō*. Edited by Shisō no kagaku kenkyūkai. Tokyo: Tokuma shoten, 1972: 444-81.
Matsuura Sōzō. "Hanminshushugi no tenkan katei: Senpan tsuihō kara reddo paaji made." *Kyōdō kenkyū/Nihon senryō*. Edited by Shisō no kagaku kenkyūkai. Tokyo: Tokuma shoten, 1972: 147-58.
Miwa Yasushi. "Nihon faashizumu kiseiki ni okeru shinkanryō to keisatsu." *Nihonshi kenkyū*, No. 252, August 1983: 1-31.
Miyanishi Yoshio. "Mantetsu chōsabu to Ozaki Hotsumi, Nakanishi Kō, Himori Torao I." *Ajia keizai*, Vol. 28, No. 7 (July), 1987: 51-67.
Moore, Ray A. "The Occupation of Japan as History: Some Recent Research." *Monumenta Nipponica*, Vol. 36, No. 3: 317-28.
Moore, Ray A. "Reflections on the Occupation of Japan." *Journal of Asian Studies*, Vol. 38, No. 4, August 1979: 721-34.
Morley, James William. "The First Seven Weeks." *The Japan Interpreter*, Vol. VI, No. 2, Summer, 1970: 151-64.
Murata Katsumi. "Shōwa kenkyūkai ni taisuru hyōka." *Tōyō kenkyū*, No. 9, October 1964: 59-72.
Nakamura Masanori. "Sengo kaikaku to gendai." *Senryō to sengo kaikaku*. Edited by Nakamura Masanori. Tokyo: Yoshikawa kōbunkan, 1994: 1-27.
Nakamura Takahide and Hara Akira. "Keizai shintaisei." "'Konoe shintaisei' no kenkyū." *Seiji gaku nenpyō*. Tokyo: Iwanami shoten, 1972: 71-133.
"Oum e no habōhō ga kakudai saretara ankoku jidai ni," *Asahi shimbun*, January 11, 1996: 3.
Passin, Herbert. "The Occupation—Some Reflections." *Showa: The Japan of Hirohito*. Edited by Carol Gluck and Stephen R. Graubard. New York: W.W. Norton & Company, 1992: 107-29.
Redman, H. Vere. "Japan's Surrender: What Next?" *Asiatic Review*, October 1945: 407-9.
Rice, Richard. "Economic Mobilization in Wartime Japan: Business, Bureaucracy, and Military in Conflict." *Journal of Asian Studies*, Vol. 38, No. 4, August 1979: 689-706.

Satō Takeo. "Mantetsu no Soren chōsa." *Ajia keizai*, Vol. 28, No. 9 (September), 1987: 80-99.
Schonberger, Howard. "A Rejoinder." *Pacific Historical Review*, Vol. 57, No. 2: 209-18.
Schonberger, Howard. "The Japan Lobby in American Diplomacy, 1947-1952." *Pacific Historical Review*, Vol. XLVI, 1977: 327-59.
Schonberger, Howard. "T.A. Bisson and the Limits of Reform in Occupied Japan." *Bulletin of Concerned Asian Scholars*, Vol. 12, No. 4 (Oct-Dec) 1980: 26-37.
"Seinen kanshi shain wa nani o kangaeteiru ka zadankai." *Bungei shunjū*, No. 14, July 1936: 216-40.
Shiga Yoshio. "Shutsugoku zengo no koto: Watakushi no shōgen." *Kyōdō kenkyū Nihon senryō: Sono hikari to kage*. Edited by Shisō no kagaku kenkyūkai. Tokyo: Gendaishi shuppankai, 1977: 423-38.
Sodei Rinjirō and Takemae Eiji. "Nihon senryō to wa nani ka: Nihonjin ga etamono ushinatta mono." *Sengo Nihon no genten: Senryōshi no genzai*. Vol. 2. Edited by Sodei Rinjirō and Takemae Eiji. Tokyo: Yūshisha, 1992: 299-359.
Spaulding, Jr., Robert M. "Japan's 'New Bureaucrats' 1932-45." *Crisis Politics in Prewar Japan: Institutional and Ideological Problems of the 1930s*. Edited by George M. Wilson. Tokyo: Sophia University, 1970: 51-70.
Takemae, Eiji. "Early Postwar Reformist Parties." *Democratizing Japan: The Allied Occupation*. Edited by Robert E. Ward and Yoshikazu Sakamoto. Honolulu: University of Hawaii Press, 1987: 339-65.
Takemae Eiji. "Reddo paaji." *Kyōdō kenkyū Nihon senryō: Sono hikari to kage*. Edited by Shisō no kagaku kenkyūkai. Tokyo: Gendaishi shuppankai, 1977: 279-95.
Tamiya Hiroshi. "Yokohama jiken: Gōmon o yonda maboroshi no 'kyōsantō saiken.'" *Nihon seiji saiban shiroku*. Edited by Wagatsuma Sakae. Tokyo: Daiichi hōki shuppan, 1970: 495-542.
"Tenkō shisōshi jō no hitobito." *Kyōdō kenkyū Tenkō*. Vol. 2. Ed. Shisō kagaku kenkyūkai. Tokyo: Heibonsha, 1978: 454-512.
Tsurumi, Kazuko. "Six Types of Change in Personality: Case Studies of Ideological Conversion in the 1930's." *Social Change and the Individual: Japan Before and After Defeat in World War II*. By Kazuko Tsurumi. Princeton: Princeton University Press, 1979: 29-79.
Tsurumi Shunsuke. "Dai ippen no yōyaku." *Kyōdō kenkyū Tenkō*. Vol. 1. Ed. Shisō kagaku kenkyūkai. Tokyo: Heibonsha, 1978: 30.

Tsurumi Shunsuke. "Goki shinjinkaiin: Hayashi Fusao/Ōya Sōichi." *Kyōdō kenkyū Tenkō.* Vol. 1. Ed. Shisō kagaku kenkyūkai. Tokyo: Heibonsha, 1978: 110-44.
Ueda Shunkichi. "Shōwa demokurashii no zasetsu." *Jiyū,* October and November 1960: 81-94, 89-99.
Wolfe, Henry Cutler. "Suzuki-san, Our Major Problem in Japan: On the Common Man Depends the Success of Our Occupation." *New York Times Magazine,* August 26, 1945: 5-7.
Yamaguchi Hiroichi. "Mantetsu chōsabu jiken (1942-45 nen)." *Ajia keizai,* Vol. 29, No. 11 (November), 1988: 62-88.
Yamazaki, Masakazu. "The Intellectual Community of the Showa Era." *Showa: The Japan of Hirohito.* Edited by Carol Gluck and Stephen R. Graubard. New York: W.W. Norton & Company, 1992: 245-64.

APPENDICES/INTRODUCTIONS/EXPLANATORY SECTIONS

"Appendix X: Constitution of the Empire of Japan 1889." *The Making of the Meiji Constitution: The Oligarchs and the Constitutional Development of Japan, 1868-1891.* By George M. Beckmann. Lawrence: University of Kansas Press, 1957: 151-6.
Fogel, Joshua. "Introduction: Itō Takeo and the Research Work of the South Manchurian Railway Company." *Life Along the South Manchurian Railway: The Memoirs of Itō Takeo.* By Itō Takeo. Translated by Joshua Fogel. New York: M.E. Sharpe, Inc., 1988: vii-xxxi.
Katō Keiji. "Kaisetsu." *Zoku gendaishi shiryō 7: Tokkō to shisō kenji.* Edited by Katō Keiji. Tokyo: Misuzu shobō, 1982: v-xxxix.
Ogino Fujio. "[Note on Document], 'Saikin no sayoku jiken ni kangami chūi o yōsuru jikō." *Tokkō keisatsu kankei shiryō shūsei.* Vol. 5. Edited by Ogino Fujio. Tokyo: Fuji shuppan, 1991: 18.

INTERVIEWS/PERSONAL CORRESPONDENCE

Kimura Tōru. Letter to author. September 28, 1993
Kimura Tōru. Personal interview. June 12, 1992.
Kimura Tōru. Personal interview. October 12, 1992.
Kobayashi Eizaburō. Letter to author. February 1, 1994.
Nakamura Tomoko. Personal interview. March 26, 1993.
Ono Sada. Personal interview. March 30, 1993.
Takagi Kenjirō. Personal interview. July 20, 1992.

UNPUBLISHED MATERIAL

Levi, Antonia Judith. "Peaceful Revolution in Japan: The Development of the Nosaka Theory and its Implementation under the American Occupation." Ph.D. diss., Stanford University 1991.
Tipton, Elise Kurashige. "The Civil Police in the Suppression of the Prewar Japanese Left." Ph.D. diss., Indiana University 1977.
Steinhoff, Patricia Golden. "Tenkō: Ideology and Societal Integration in Prewar Japan." Ph.D. diss., Harvard University 1969.
Wakabayashi, B.T. "'Imperial Japanese' Opium Operations and Postwar Historiography." Paper presented at the Conference on Opium in East Asian History: 1830-1945. Toronto, Canada, 9-10 May 1997: 1-12.

DICTIONARIES

Nihon shakai undō jinmei jiten. Edited by Shioda Shōbee. Tokyo: Aoki shoten, 1979.
Uyoku jiten. Edited by Hori Yukio. Tokyo: Sanrei shobō, 1991.

CORNELL EAST ASIA SERIES

No. 4 *Provincial Leadership in China: The Cultural Revolution and Its Aftermath*, by Fredrick Teiwes
No. 8 *Vocabulary and Notes to Ba Jin's Jia: An Aid for Reading the Novel*, by Cornelius C. Kubler
No. 15 *Song, Dance, Storytelling: Aspects of the Performing Arts in Japan*, by Frank Hoff
No. 16 *Nō as Performance: An Analysis of the Kuse Scene of Yamamba*, by Monica Bethe & Karen Brazell
No. 17 *Pining Wind: A Cycle of Nō Plays*, translated by Royall Tyler
No. 18 *Granny Mountains: A Second Cycle of Nō Plays*, translated by Royall Tyler
No. 28 *The Griffis Collection of Japanese Books: An Annotated Bibliography*, edited by Diane E. Perushek
No. 29 *Dance in the Nō Theater*, by Monica Bethe & Karen Brazell Volume 1: Dance Analysis, Volume 2: Plays and Scores, Volume 3: Dance Patterns
No. 32 *Tone, Segment, and Syllable in Chinese: A Polydimensional Approach to Surface Phonetic Structure*, by A. Ronald Walton
No. 35 *From Politics to Lifestyles: Japan in Print*, edited by Frank Baldwin
No. 36 *The Diary of a Japanese Innkeeper's Daughter*, translated by Miwa Kai, edited & annotated by Robert J. Smith & Kazuko Smith
No. 37 *International Perspectives on Yanagita Kunio and Japanese Folklore Studies*, edited by J. Victor Koschmann, Ōiwa Keibō & Yamashita Shinji
No. 38 *Murō Saisei: Three Works*, translated by James O'Brien
No. 40 *Land of Volcanic Ash: A Play in Two Parts* by Kubo Sakae, revised edition, translated by David G. Goodman
No. 41 *The Dreams of Our Generation and Selections from Beijing's People*, by Zhang Xinxin, edited & translated by Edward Gunn, Donna Jung & Patricia Farr
No. 44 *Family Change and the Life Course in Japan*, by Susan Orpett Long

No. 46 *Planning and Finance in China's Economic Reforms*, by Thomas P. Lyons & WANG Yan
No. 48 *Bungo Manual: Selected Reference Materials for Students of Classical Japanese*, by Helen Craig McCullough
No. 49 *Ankoku Butō: The Premodern and Postmodern Influences on the Dance of Utter Darkness*, by Susan Blakeley Klein
No. 50 *Twelve Plays of the Noh and Kyōgen Theaters*, edited by Karen Brazell
No. 51 *Five Plays by Kishida Kunio*, edited by David G. Goodman
No. 52 *Ode to Stone*, by Shirō Hara, translated by James Morita
No. 53 *Defending the Japanese State: Structures, Norms and the Political Responses to Terrorism and Violent Social Protest in the 1970s and 1980s*, by Peter J. Katzenstein & Yutaka Tsujinaka
No. 54 *Deathsong of the River: A Reader's Guide to the Chinese TV Series Heshang*, by Su Xiaokang & Wang Luxiang, translated by Richard Bodman & Pin P. Wan
No. 55 *Psychoanalysis in China: Literary Transformations, 1919-1949*, by Jingyuan Zhang
No. 56 *To Achieve Security and Wealth: The Qing Imperial State and the Economy, 1644-1911*, edited by Jane Kate Leonard & John R. Watt
No. 57 *Like a Knife: Ideology and Genre in Contemporary Chinese Popular Music*, by Andrew F. Jones
No. 58 *Japan's National Security: Structures, Norms and Policy Responses in a Changing World*, by Peter J. Katzenstein & Nobuo Okawara
No. 59 *The Role of Central Banking in China's Economic Reforms*, by Carsten Holz
No. 60 *Warrior Ghost Plays from the Japanese Noh Theater: Parallel Translations with Running Commentary*, by Chifumi Shimazaki
No. 61 *Women and Millenarian Protest in Meiji Japan: Deguchi Nao and Ōmotokyō*, by Emily Groszos Ooms
No. 62 *Transformation, Miracles, and Mischief: The Mountain Priest Plays of Kyōgen*, by Carolyn Anne Morley
No. 63 *Selected Poems of Kim Namjo*, translated by David R. McCann & Hyunjae Yee Sallee, with an afterword by Kim Yunsik
No. 64 *From Yalta to Panmunjom: Truman's Diplomacy and the Four Powers, 1945-1953*, by HUA Qingzhao
No. 65 *Kitahara Hakushū: His Life and Poetry*, by Margaret Benton Fukasawa
No. 66 *Strange Tales from Strange Lands: Stories by Zheng Wanlong*, edited & with an introduction by Kam Louie

No. 67 *Backed Against the Sea*, by Wang Wen-hsing, translated by Edward Gunn
No. 68 *The Sound of My Waves: Selected Poems by Ko Un*, translated by Brother Anthony of Taizé & Young-Moo Kim
No. 69 *Han Sŏrya and North Korean Literature: The Failure of Socialist Realism in the DPRK*, by Brian Myers
No. 70 *The Economic Transformation of South China: Reform and Development in the Post-Mao Era*, edited by Thomas P. Lyons & Victor Nee
No. 71 *After Apocalypse: Four Japanese Plays of Hiroshima and Nagasaki*, translated & introduced by David G. Goodman
No. 72 *Poverty and Growth in a South China County: Anxi, Fujian, 1949-1992*, by Thomas P. Lyons
No. 73 *The Shadow of Arms*, by Hwang Suk-Young, translated by Chun Kyung-Ja, with a foreword by Paik Nak-chung
No. 74 *Informal Empire in Crisis: British Diplomacy and the Chinese Customs Succession, 1927-1929*, by Martyn Atkins
No. 75 *Barbed Wire and Rice: Poems and Songs from Japanese Prisoner-of-War Camps*, collected by Bishop D. McKendree
No. 76 *Restless Spirits from Japanese Noh Plays of the Fourth Group: Parallel Translations with Running Commentary*, by Chifumi Shimazaki
No. 77 *Back to Heaven: Selected Poems of Ch'ŏn Sang Pyŏng*, translated by Brother Anthony of Taizé & Young-Moo Kim
No. 78 *Singing Like a Cricket, Hooting Like an Owl: Selected Poems by Yi Kyu-bo*, translated by Kevin O'Rourke
No. 79 *The Gods Come Dancing: A Study of the Japanese Ritual Dance of Yamabushi Kagura*, by Irit Averbuch
No. 80 *Korean Adoption and Inheritance: Case Studies in the Creation of a Classic Confucian Society*, by Mark Peterson
No. 81 *The Lioness Roars: Shrew Stories from Late Imperial China*, translated by Yenna Wu
No. 82 *The Economic Geography of Fujian: A Sourcebook*, Volume 1, by Thomas Lyons
No. 83 *The Naked Tree*, by Pak Wan-so, translated by Yu Young-nan
No. 84 *The Classic Chinese Novel: A Critical Introduction*, by C.T. Hsia
No. 85 *Playing With Fire*, by Cho Chong-Rae, translated by Chun Kyung-Ja
No. 86 *I Saw a Pale Horse and Selections from Diary of a Vagabond*, by Hayashi Fumiko, translated by Janice Brown
No. 87 *Kojiki-den, Book 1*, by Motoori Norinaga, translated by Ann Wehmeyer

No. 88   *Sending the Ship Out to the Stars: Poems of Park Je-chun,*
         translated by Chang Soo Ko
No. 89   *The Economic Geography of Fujian: A Sourcebook,* Volume 2, by
         Thomas Lyons
No. 90   *Midang: Early Lyrics of So Chong-Ju,* translated by Brother
         Anthony of Taizé
No. 91   *Battle Noh: Parallel Translations with Running Commentary,* by
         Chifumi Shimazaki
No. 92   *More Than a Momentary Nightmare: The Yokohama Incident and
         Wartime Japan,* by Janice Matsumura
No. 93   *The Snow Falling on Chagall's Village: Selected Poems of Kim
         Ch'un-Su,* translated by Kim Jong-Gil
No. 94   *Day-Shine: Poetry by Hyonjong Chong,* translated by Wolhee
         Choe and Peter Fusco
No. 95   *Troubled Souls from Japanese Noh Plays of the Fourth Group,* by
         Chifumi Shimazaki
No. 96   *Principles of Poetry* (Shi no genri), by Hagiwara Sakutarō,
         translated by Chester Wang
No. 97   *Dramatic Representations of Filial Piety: Five Noh in Translation,*
         by Mae Smethurst
No. 98   *Description and Explanation in Korean Linguistics,* by Ross King
No. 99   *Japan's First Bureaucracy: A Study of Eighth-Century Government,* by Richard J. Miller, revised edition edited by Joan Piggott

FORTHCOMING

The Prophet and Other Stories, by Yi Ch'ŏng-jun, translated by Julie
    Pickering
Total War and 'Modernization', edited by Yamanouchi Yasushi, J. Victor
    Koschmann and Narita Ryûichi
*Ben no Naishi Nikki: A Poetic Record of Female Courtiers' Sacred Duties
    at the Kamakura-Period Court,* by S. Yumiko Hulvey
Inventing Nanjing Road: Commercial Culture in Shanghai, 1900-1945,
    edited by Sherman Cochran
*Charisma and Community Formation in Medieval Japan: The Case of the
    Yugyō-ha (1300-1700),* by S.A. Thornton

To order, please contact the Cornell East Asia Series, East Asia Program, Cornell University, 140 Uris Hall, Ithaca, NY 14853-7601, USA; phone (607) 255-6222, fax (607) 255-1388, internet: er26@cornell.edu, http://www.einaudi.cornell.edu/eastasia/EastAsiaSeries.html.

www.ingramcontent.com/pod-product-compliance
Lightning Source LLC
Chambersburg PA
CBHW031629160426
43196CB00006B/346